The Lost World

of Thomas

Jefferson

Daniel J. Boorstin

Beacon Press   **Beacon Hill**   **Boston**

THE LOST WORLD
OF THOMAS JEFFERSON

☆

Daniel Boorstin began his career as a lawyer and legal historian. After graduating from Harvard (where he was an editor of The Crimson), he was a Rhodes scholar at Oxford University and studied at the Inner Temple in London. He has taught legal history at Harvard and has been visiting professor of American history, both at the University of Rome and at Kyoto University in Japan. He is now a professor of American history at the University of Chicago.

Mr. Boorstin's other books include The Mysterious Science of the Law (1941; issued as a Beacon Press paperback in 1958), The Genius of American Politics (1953) and The Americans: The Colonial Experience (published in 1958 and awarded the Bancroft Prize by Columbia University). He is also the editor of the Chicago History of American Civilization series.

☆

To Ruth

'Can the liberties of a nation be thought secure when we have removed their only firm basis, a conviction in the minds of the people that these liberties are of the gift of God?'

THOMAS JEFFERSON, Notes on Virginia.

Contents

CONTENTS

Chapter Four:

THE NATURAL HISTORY OF A NEW SOCIETY 167

CONCLUSION
235

Preface

NOWADAYS—and especially since the Second World War —it has become fashionable to demand that the American past talk to us in our own language, and reinforce our own unconsidered beliefs. Every week we find on the bookshelves another volume to prove that George Washington, Thomas Jefferson, Andrew Jackson or Abraham Lincoln, was an authentic liberal in the contemporary sense. Surely the search for the values of our civilization is a healthful tendency which every historian ought to encourage. But the values which we distill will be enduring and our tradition will be authentic and fruitful only if we face the hard fact that each generation must confront the perennial problems of man in its unique way. If we demand from the past crude slogans and facile answers, we shall get little more than we ask. To try to teach the moral of history without teaching history itself, as a distinguished living historian has remarked, is like trying to plant cut flowers. Our past must serve us not as an anthology from which to cull apt phrases for current needs, but as a stage for observing in all their tantalizing complexity the actual ways in which men in America have faced the ancient problems of the human race.

I have tried in this volume to discover the dominant spirit of the Jeffersonian view of the world. I have not sought to elaborate in detail the applications of those large ideas to the political and social programs of that day; Henry Adams' magnificent volumes would make almost any attempt to recount the political history of Jefferson's day presumptuous. My pur-

pose has been to get inside the Jeffersonian world of ideas—
to see the relation among their conceptions of God, nature,
equality, toleration, education and government—rather than
to describe 'influences' or 'sources.' Those who have been mainly
interested in distinguishing the 'new' from the 'old,' the 'original'
from the 'borrowed,' the 'native' from the 'foreign,' have often
become so preoccupied with separating the threads which made
up the Jeffersonian mind that they have failed to see its texture.
I have also given scant attention to the innumerable analogies
between particular Jeffersonian ideas and those held by men
in other times and places. The author shares with the reader
an interest in such comparisons; but they would have made
another book. From the Jeffersonian's point of view his world
of ideas was vivid and personal; its significance did not depend
on the sources or analogies which later scholars might discover.

In a word, I have been more concerned to recapture the
Jeffersonian world of ideas than to perform an autopsy on it.
And the very nature of Jeffersonian thought increases the difficulty of reconstructing the Jeffersonian cosmos. No one is
more aware than I am of these difficulties and of the imper-
fections of the present volume. The temperament and the
circumstances of the members of the Jeffersonian circle did not
favor the writing of systematic treatises. My task has therefore
involved not merely the interpretation of past documents, but
in a sense the actual reconstruction of the documents. I have
tried to find among the myriad records of Jeffersonian thought
on superficially unrelated projects the connections which the
authors themselves were often reluctant to speak out. I have
made relatively little use of manuscripts, because the Jeffersonian circle have left ample volumes of published materials.
Since it is their leading and pervasive ideas which have concerned me, the ideas which did not find expression in the
hundred-odd volumes of their printed works have seemed unlikely to deserve a place in a study such as the present. I have
thought, for example, that the fifty-odd volumes of printed
writings of Jefferson could provide access to his leading ideas,

even though there still remain unpublished (in the Library of Congress and elsewhere) thousands of other items.

In the matter of annotation it has been my purpose not to distract the general reader but at the same time to provide the scholar some means of verifying my observations. Wherever feasible, several references have been collected in a single footnote; references for quotations not directly footnoted may be found in the next following footnote. For nearly every quotation used in the volume I have had in my possession a dozen or more to the same purpose. Since I have been concerned with the large outlines of Jeffersonian thought, I have given only a subsidiary place to the development of the thought of each individual; however, where that development has seemed necessary to qualify or elucidate my thesis, I have made reference to it. In the notes I have been careful to give dates for the statements quoted so that the critical reader might take account of such development. I have omitted notes in some cases where the specialist might desire them; in defense of this procedure I can simply say that I would gladly have him question my generalizations if he cannot find for himself in the writings of the Jeffersonians numerous other passages to the same effect. Parallel passages to those quoted can in nearly every case be found in the six volumes of the first series of *Transactions of the American Philosophical Society* (available in many libraries), in the published writings of Jefferson, or in the more accessible of the works of the other Jeffersonians.

Just as America will never again be the same kind of wilderness that it was in Jefferson's day, it is surely not in our power to live any more within the Jeffersonian world of ideas. The spirit of Jeffersonian philosophy can be only imperfectly recaptured, at best. Yet the Jeffersonian tradition has played and should continue to play a vital and valuable role in American history: it has provided our principal check on the demands of irresponsible power. If we can improve our definition of the original Jeffersonian world of ideas, we will have gone a long way toward achieving a self-consciousness in American culture, toward discovering the perils of the way of thought which we have inherited from the Jeffersonians, and hence toward strengthening the philosophical foundations of a moral society in our day.

The principal research for this volume was done in the libraries of the American Philosophical Society and of the Library Company of Philadelphia. The staffs of these institutions have been both friendly and helpful. For a generous grant to aid in the preparation of the final manuscript I wish to thank the Social Science Research Committee of the University of Chicago. Many friends and colleagues have helped by their suggestions.

To the Committee on Social Thought at the University of Chicago I am deeply indebted: for the leisure to write this volume, for the example, advice and criticism of its members, and for the symbol it provides of the vitality of scholarship.

My wife, Ruth Frankel Boorstin, has made this volume possible by her encouragement and good cheer; at every stage from the first notes to the final proofs she has provided fresh and perceptive critical eyes.

D. J. B.

Committee on Social Thought
University of Chicago
January, 1948

Introduction

'Landing on this great continent is like going
to sea, they must have a compass, some friendly
directing needle; or else they will uselessly err
and wander for a long time, even with a fair
wind.' CRÈVECOEUR, Letters from an American
Farmer (1782)

1. 'The Influence of America on the Mind'

IN 1823, just three years before the death of Jefferson, Charles Jared Ingersoll, an ardent republican, delivered to the American Philosophical Society in Philadelphia an address entitled, 'The Influence of America on the Mind.' He found the achievements of the past decades to be of a practical, economic, scientific, and mechanical, rather than of a literary or contemplative nature. 'France and England,' Ingersoll explained, 'were enjoying Augustan ages, when the place where we are met to discourse of literature and science, was a wilderness. But one hundred and forty years have elapsed, since the patriarch of Pennsylvania first landed on these shores, and sowed them with the germs of peace, toleration, and self-government. Since then, a main employment has been to reclaim the forests for habitation.' This struggle with nature in which American civilization was born had surely shaped the Jeffersonian mind; through the Jeffersonian tradition and in many other ways it was to affect the whole future character of American thought.

When the intellectually and spiritually mature man of Europe first settled in America, he was forced to relive the childhood of the race, to confront once again the primitive and intractable wilderness of his cave-dwelling ancestors. In America he became an anachronism. This quaint juxtaposition of culture and barbarism—the Bible in the wilderness—which characterized the earliest settlement of the continent, has left a heritage of conflict and paradox for our own time. From the beginning, American conditions sharpened the discord between the active and the contemplative sides of man's nature. The contemplative tradition of European man has not easily har-

3

monized with the active enterprises of the American. The conflict here between man's need to master the earth and his desire to give an inward order to his mind has therefore been most discomforting. Because the demands for action have seemed louder and its rewards richer on this continent, the task of reconciliation has been all the greater.

This discord between man as maker and man as thinker has accounted for much of the restlessness in American political and intellectual life. 'The worst feature of this double consciousness,' Emerson wrote, 'is, that the two lives, of the understanding and of the soul, which we lead, really show very little relation to each other; never meet and measure each other: one prevails now, all buzz and din; and the other prevails then, all infinitude and paradise; and, with the progress of life, the two discover no greater disposition to reconcile themselves.' Even in America, where the challenge of a continent might have seemed to dwarf all other human adventures, man has not pursued his practical conquest without some inner scruple. Puritanism, Jeffersonianism, Transcendentalism, and Pragmatism have all testified to man's inability to turn his back on philosophy. Yet, each in its different fashion, these American movements have ended in a refusal to follow philosophy when it might paralyze the hand of the artisan or the conqueror. Each has found another way of assuaging man's scruples without obstructing the exploitation of the continent; each has found a means to hallow the building of a New World while implying that such building was somehow its own justification. Each has tried to express man's rational nature without denying that activity and physical achievement and novelty were beyond need of ratiocination. Except perhaps for Puritanism (which was after all the least characteristically American), until now American thought has produced philosophies to restrain philosophy. We have allowed the mind enough play to keep it alive and aware of itself and yet seldom have allowed it to doubt the intrinsic virtue of action. Our willingness to begin with the probings of an Emerson is explained by our confidence that we will end with the affirmations of a Whitman.

It would have been surprising indeed if the Jeffersonians confronted by a virgin continent had not undervalued the reflective side of human nature. The stakes to be lost by digression, self-searching and doubt, were colossal and were right before their eyes. In Benjamin Rush's phrase, it seemed absurd 'to turn our backs upon a gold mine, in order to amuse ourselves in catching butterflies.' 'The times in which I have lived,' Jefferson wrote at the age of seventy-six, 'and the scenes in which I have been engaged, have required me to keep the mind too much in action to have leisure to study minutely its laws of action.' He feared that introspection would waste the American's energies on enterprises that could have been undertaken equally well anywhere else on the face of the earth, and that meanwhile the novel and uniquely American opportunities might be lost.

The years of Jefferson's life, from 1743 to 1826, were decisive for the American political, economic and intellectual destiny of the succeeding century and a half. The inward struggle of Jeffersonian thought must be understood in connection with the outward struggle in which the entire generation was engaged—a struggle notable not merely for its magnitude, but for its intensity. In the year of Jefferson's birth, the English-speaking population of North America consisted of about a million settlers huddled along the Atlantic seaboard. They were a fringe of the economy and thought of Europe, and their political, economic and intellectual focus was London. The unsettled portion of the continent was still viewed more as a barrier than as a treasure house. Its climate, animals, plants and mineral resources were hardly known. For knowledge of the stretch of country between the Rio Grande and what is now the Canadian border, in Jefferson's youth one had to rely on the scanty and fragmentary travel books of Catesby and Kalm. The future of North America was still vastly ambiguous. While it seemed not impossible that the settlements might become substantial imperial outposts, it was even uncertain which European empire they might enrich.

By the year of Jefferson's death, the American prospect had been transformed. The lines toward the future had been drawn:

5

an American commonwealth was clearly foreshadowed. The United States had become a nation of ten million. The first-hand information of Lewis and Clark and their fellow explorers had displaced the dark conjectures and third-hand rumors of earlier generations. The continental hinterland had revealed itself as a stock of inexhaustible raw materials. Most important, the road had been irrevocably chosen to some kind of national life. The political bonds with Europe had been broken; a constitutional federal republic had been established, and a national political tradition had begun to emerge. All this within the span of a single lifetime!

What was peculiar to America was not the emergence of an independent national life but the extraordinary speed of the accomplishment, and the prehistoric background in which it occurred. The anachronism which was the keynote of the earliest stages of American settlement has affected American life ever since. The uncovering and mastery of the continent, the building of a constitution and the shaping of a national consciousness had been accomplished in a paroxysm of creative activity. Leon Trotsky has observed that Russian history was decisively affected by the fact that Russia skipped over the 'stages' of Protestantism and capitalist democracy, and was still a feudal economy when in the nineteenth century she tried suddenly to immerse herself in a world of industrial capitalism. But America was the scene of a still more remarkable abbreviation: settlers on this continent transplanted the institutions and techniques of modern Europe to a landscape that had never even experienced the Middle Ages. The American land, outdoing Russian precocity, skipped at least two thousand years of the calendar of western social geography, and in the two hundred years from the early seventeenth to the early nineteenth century hastened from an untamed savage wilderness—the scene of European man in 1000 B.C.—to a developed national capitalist economy, his European scene in A.D. 1800. This is, of course, of the greatest significance not merely for the geographer and anthropologist, but for the student of recent American culture. The institutional scene in which American man has developed has

6

lacked that accumulation from intervening stages which has been so dominant a feature of the European landscape.

This paroxysm of creative activity which enabled the American nation to pass in a hundred years from the provincial thought and character of the young Franklin to the self-conscious nationalism of Noah Webster and Emerson, was necessarily accompanied by a paroxysm of rebellion against the past. Within these years the American people crammed an extraordinary intensity of negation. But the past against which they were rebelling was foreign, distant and vague. The French Revolutionaries were forced into the arena of speculative thought because they were fighting an enemy who possessed an articulate and systematic philosophy: clerical and royalist theorists forced them to devise their own theories and gave them a clue—if only by antithesis—to the dogmas which they should assert in reply. Whatever may have been the legalistic issues of the American Revolution, the larger revolt was against values and traditions which were not indigenous to the American landscape; the Americans had before their eyes the emissaries but not the structure of an *ancien régime*. On this continent there was no Bastille and no Versailles Palace to symbolize the enemy; nor was there a mature and outspoken conservative philosophy to require an outspoken answer.

The Jeffersonian therefore found the keynote of his thought in the American task itself. His community, unlike the Hebrew's or the Puritan's, was not to be the fulfillment of a sacred scripture. And, in contrast to the French or the Russian Revolutionaries, he did not wish to shape his society to fit a theory. The natural landscape and the material problems which he shared with his neighbors seemed themselves to make a kind of community which did not need the fiat of Scripture or the support of doctrine. He expected not thought but action, not ideas but things to hold his society together.

This conception was itself of course a kind of philosophy, in which the desire to get things done predominated over the need to be at peace with God and oneself. To succeed in building and material conquest seemed automatically to do something for one's neighbors. Conversely, to enrich one's neighbor was to improve America and to enhance a corporation in which every settler was a shareholder. The large alternative posed by the Jeffersonian was either to seek power for oneself alone, which was evil; or to increase the power and material advantage of the community, which was good. The great significance of this formulation was of course what it left out: self-scrutiny, self-definition and self-comprehension.

The form as well as the content of the Jeffersonian philosophy has had a subtle influence on the American 'liberal' mind. The urgencies of his age led the Jeffersonian to describe his cosmos, not in spacious treatises, but in discrete and extremely topical letters, speeches, pamphlets and articles. His philosophy was left implicit—in the interstices between observations on particular practical projects. This has made it easy for disciples of Jefferson to mistake his political program for his philosophy, and has fostered a philosophic vagueness which has profoundly affected American political thought. The Jeffersonian or American 'liberal' tradition has thus remained largely unconscious of the philosophy it has adopted. This in turn has encouraged the dangerous assumption that a plan of action is the same as a philosophy. In consequence the Jeffersonian tradition has acquired both a brittleness and an amorphousness which have made all the more obscure what the Jeffersonians can teach us.

2. The Jeffersonian Circle

JEFFERSON and his circle unwittingly accomplished for American civilization something like what St. Augustine did for medieval Christendom. Of course the fragments of the Jeffersonian literature are not to be compared with St. Augustine's greatest work. But if we consider the writings of the

8

Jeffersonian circle as a whole, we will discover that they had a scope and function quite analogous to that of St. Augustine's *City of God*. Writing in the years just after the fall of Rome in 410, St. Augustine had a vision of an eternal city: his vision provided much of the theology and the political theory on which medieval Europe built its alternative to the earthly city. It was such a compelling vision that it remained vivid for centuries after the decay of Rome. The Jeffersonians, in the late eighteenth and early nineteenth centuries, were actually writing before their Rome had been built—before the American continent had been exploited or even explored. And their vision was of that *earthly* city which could and should be built here.

In the years between the founding of the republic and the death of Jefferson, there centered about Jefferson himself a few intellectuals who were sufficiently agreed on their task to give their philosophic adventure the character of a common expedition. These men, whom we are about to describe, were not so much a school of philosophy as a community of philosophers. While 'my country' still meant something different to men in each state of the Union, even before the artificial bonds of political union were well forged, these Americans already felt united by the common challenge of their natural environment. Astronomer, botanist, anthropologist, physician, theologian and political scientist spoke the same language, and thought in the same cosmos. They did not profess an explicit system of philosophy, nor did they publish Articles of Faith; yet their agreement was no less definite than if it had been formally declared.

The intellectual energies of this circle were organized by an institution framed on republican principles—the American Philosophical Society. This Society traced its origin back to the year of Jefferson's birth. 'The first Drudgery of Settling new Colonies, which confines the Attention of People to mere Necessaries, is now pretty well over,' Benjamin Franklin had announced in his circular letter of 1743 which proposed the organization, 'and there are many in every Province in Circum-

9

stances that set them at Ease, and afford Leisure to cultivate the finer Arts, and improve the common Stock of Knowledge.' Franklin accurately sketched the scope of the enlarged intellectual life which he was proposing, and predicted the direction of Jeffersonian interests when he described the proper concerns of such a new society:

All new-discovered Plants, Herbs, Trees, Roots, their Virtues, Uses, &c.; Methods of Propagating them, and making such as are useful, but particular to some Plantations, more general. Improvements of vegetable Juices, as Cyders, Wines, &c.; New Methods of Curing or Preventing Diseases. All new-discovered Fossils in different Countries, as Mines, Minerals, Quarries; &c. New and useful Improvements in any Branch of Mathematicks; New Discoveries in Chemistry, such as Improvements in Distillation, Brewing, Assaying of ores; &c. New Mechanical Inventions for Saving labour; as Mills and Carriages, &c., and for Raising and Conveying of Water, Draining of Meadows, &c.; All new Arts, Trades, Manufactures, &c. that may be proposed or thought of; Surveys, Maps and Charts of particular Parts of the Sea-coasts, or Inland Countries; Course and Junction of Rivers and great Roads, Situation of Lakes and Mountains, Nature of the Soil and Productions; &c. New Methods of Improving the Breed of useful Animals; Introducing other Sorts from foreign Countries. New Improvements in Planting, Gardening, Clearing Land, &c. . . .

The unifying purpose of these miscellaneous activities could not have been better stated than in Franklin's summary phrase: 'all philosophical Experiments that let Light into the Nature of Things, tend to increase the Power of Man over Matter, and multiply the Conveniences or Pleasures of Life.' In 1769, the Junto which grew out of Franklin's earliest effort was merged with a younger American Philosophical Society to form a new and energetic 'American Philosophical Society, held at Philadelphia for promoting useful Knowledge.' Consciously modeled on the Royal Society of London, from which it borrowed its rules, the young organization was nonetheless characteristically American in its interests. Members were classed into one or more of the following committees:

1. Geography, Mathematics, Natural Philosophy and Astronomy.
2. Medicine and Anatomy.
3. Natural History and Chymistry.
4. Trade and Commerce.
5. Mechanics and Architecture.
6. Husbandry and American Improvements.

The Preface of the first volume of the Society's *Transactions*, having explained that merely speculative knowledge might prove of little use, declared that members would 'confine their disquisitions, principally, to such subjects as tend to the improvement of their country, and advancement of its interest and prosperity.'

Including an intellectual élite from every corner of British North America, the American Philosophical Society was truly continental in catholicity and influence. By the time of the Revolution, it had become the main institution through which Americans collaborated to comprehend and master their environment, and the focus, not merely of 'scientific' activity, but of intellectual life on the continent. 'A treasure we ought to glory in,' was Paine's praise in 1775. 'Here the defective knowledge of the individual is supplied by the common stock.' Its meetings were appropriately held at Philadelphia, the political capital until 1800, and for many years the most populous city in the Union. John Adams accurately (if somewhat enviously) described the city as 'the pineal gland' of the continent. In the years between the death of Franklin in 1790 and the end of Jefferson's presidency in 1809, the South showed no comparable intellectual metropolis. New England was on the intellectual periphery; those were dull days for Harvard College and for the theology which she represented. The American Academy of Arts and Sciences (the Boston counterpart of the Philosophical Society) founded by John Adams in 1780 never attained the stature of a rival. It surely was in the Jeffersonian spirit that the center of American action should be the center of thought.

The meaning of 'philosophy' under American conditions had been vividly exemplified in Franklin himself, who was the first president of the Philosophical Society. The model of the American philosopher, he was neither a profound nor a reflective man, but pre-eminently observant and inventive. Serving liberty and philosophy as a single master, he never doubted that a healthy and prosperous America would also be wise and moral. To cast up the national debt, to collect fossils, to experiment with electricity, to measure an eclipse, to shape a constitution or a moral creed—all were part of a single 'philosophic' enterprise. The sheer joy of activity, of physical and social adjustment, and of material achievement seemed to supply some coherence for the miscellaneous practical energies of Franklin's age.

A full generation senior to Jefferson who was not born until 1743, Benjamin Franklin (1706-1790) had grown old in a colonial America. As Franklin's had been perhaps the most energetic and catholic mind of the last age of our colonial existence, Jefferson's was to be the leading mind of the first age of our national life, and therefore in a powerful position for shaping the American intellectual character. When Franklin died in 1790, it was difficult to see who if not Jefferson should rightfully inherit the mantle of the American philosopher.

While it is Jefferson's political thought that has become familiar to us, the sum of Jeffersonian thought was more than a number of political maxims. And the breadth of Jeffersonian interests was not a mere personal idiosyncrasy. It was Jefferson's intellectual comradeship with his contemporaries that provided the incentive and resource for cementing his discrete observations into a whole. We must therefore allow him and a few of his closest and ablest fellow philosophers to collaborate for us, as they did for each other. The Jeffersonian circle with whom we shall be mainly concerned, although of course only a fraction of the Philosophical Society's membership, was the heart of the organization. The investigations of Rittenhouse, Rush, Barton and Priestley—and the popularizations of Paine and Peale—will all be seen focused through Jefferson himself on the central issues of man and society. Before trying to reconstruct the philosophy of this Jeffersonian circle we must examine briefly the characters and careers of these principal collaborators.

12

DAVID RITTENHOUSE (1732-1796), Jefferson's idol, was elected Franklin's successor as president of the American Philosophical Society in 1791. While lacking the flexibility, the culture, and the breadth of others of the Jeffersonian circle, Rittenhouse showed a brilliance and an inventive genius which made him the intellectual prodigy of his day. The son of a Germantown farmer, born eleven years before Jefferson, he had virtually no formal schooling. Yet before he was forty, he had built the famous 'Orrery' or planetarium which came to be considered the first mechanical wonder of the American world. Rittenhouse's work was the subject of the first article in the first volume of *Transactions* of the Philosophical Society. 'When the machine is put in motion, by the turning of a winch, there are three indexes, which point out the hour of the day, the day of the month and the year, (according to the *Julian* account) answering to that situation of the heavenly bodies which it then represented; and so continually, for a period of 5000 years, either forward or backward.' By applying a small telescope to the ball representing the earth, and directing it to any planet, one could register on a dial the longitude and the latitude of that planet (as seen from the earth). The clock mechanism was contrived to produce music while the spheres revolved. Jefferson was so struck by the ingenuity of the machine that he thought it proved Rittenhouse's rightful place in a trio of American genius which included besides him only Washington and Franklin. 'Second to no astronomer living,' was Jefferson's praise. 'In genius he must be the first, because he is self taught. As an artist he has exhibited as great a proof of mechanical genius as the world has ever produced. He has not indeed made a world; but he has by imitation approached nearer its Maker than any man who has lived from the creation to this day.'

Rittenhouse was no secluded genius. He was a successful man of affairs and a consistent fighter for republican causes. By the time the Revolution arrived, he had helped survey the boundaries of half the colonies. After 1775 he was engineer of the Committee of Safety, and it was he who substituted iron for lead clockweights throughout Philadelphia in order to secure lead for Revolutionary bullets; he devised chain protections for American harbors and personally supervised much of the munitions manufacturing for the rebel cause. He served in the General Assembly of Pennsylvania and was a member of the Pennsylvania state constitutional convention of 1776. He was Jefferson's chief adviser on the troublesome problem of defining American units of weights and measures. And after urging by both Jefferson and Hamilton, Rittenhouse accepted appointment in 1792 as the first director of the United States Mint.

DR. BENJAMIN RUSH (1745-1813) was elected to deliver the Society's public eulogy upon the death of Rittenhouse in 1796. Rush himself was one of the most versatile men of the age. His eminence as a physician rivaled Rittenhouse's as an astronomer; and no one excelled him as a promoter of humanitarian projects. Rush's long friendship with Jefferson, amply attested in their correspondence, began in Revolutionary days and continued intimate until death. It was Rush's letter in 1811 that succeeded in reconciling Jefferson with John Adams; the fruit of this reconciliation was the voluminous Adams-Jefferson correspondence which remains among the most revealing intellectual confessions of the age. Born two years after Jefferson, on a farm near Philadelphia, Rush was to acquire the best medical training offered by the English-speaking world in his time. After studying at the College of New Jersey (later called Princeton), he heard the first medical lectures of Dr. William Shippen and Dr. John Morgan at the College of Philadelphia; he then went to Edinburgh, where he imbibed the latest theories of medicine along with an enthusiasm for republicanism. Returning to Philadelphia, he took up the practice of medicine in 1769. His professorship of chemistry at the College of Philadelphia was the first in the colonies, and his *Syllabus of a Course of Lectures on Chemistry*, the first American textbook on the subject. A prosperous medical practice still left him time for active membership in the Philosophical Society and for an energetic part in founding the Pennsylvania Society for Promoting the Abolition of Slavery.

14

After meeting the newly-arrived Thomas Paine in a Philadelphia bookshop in February, 1775, Rush made the fateful proposal that Paine write an appeal for American independence; Rush himself suggested the title 'Common Sense.' It was Rush who heard the early drafts of the famous pamphlet, chapter by chapter as Paine composed them. If he had done nothing more for the rebel cause, this bit of literary promotion would have been an ample service. Actually he attended the Continental Congress, signed the Declaration of Independence, and served as a surgeon-general in the Revolutionary Army. Through a series of articles for Philadelphia newspapers in the years just after the Revolution, Rush, still writing in the revolutionary spirit, persuasively argued for many humanitarian reforms. His essays, collected in a volume in 1798, condemned capital punishment, urged penal reform, called for a temperance movement, proposed a system of education especially suited to American conditions, and demanded the abolition of Negro slavery. Rush's great organizing talents enabled him to establish the first free medical dispensary in the country, to make more humane the treatment of the insane, and to aid James Wilson in securing Pennsylvania's ratification of the Federal constitution.

Rush's original contribution to American thought lay in medical science where he was distinguished as writer, teacher and practitioner. After the death of Dr. John Morgan, he filled the chair of the Theory and Practice of Medicine in the new University of Pennsylvania. If sometimes dogmatic—for example in his uncompromising use of bleeding—Rush often showed courage in opposing the prejudices of the medical profession and the lay public. His theory that the yellow-fever epidemic of 1793 was caused partly by poor sanitation shocked patriotic Philadelphians and caused him to be ostracized by his profession. In that year Rush endangered his life by remaining in the city to help the dying and to learn more about the disease. He pioneered in relating dentistry to physiology and helped found veterinary medicine in America. His remarkable *Medical Inquiries and Observations upon the*

Diseases of the Mind anticipated the approach of modern psychiatry. Perhaps greater than all his particular reforms was his vigorous attack on an antiquated medical terminology. Under his leadership Philadelphia became the center of medical education for the continent. Jefferson remarked at his death in 1813, 'A better man could not have left us, more benevolent, more learned, of finer genius, or more honest.'

BENJAMIN SMITH BARTON (1766-1815), another member, was for some years curator, and then vice-president during Jefferson's leadership of the Philosophical Society. The curiosity which had attracted Rittenhouse to the heavens, and stirred Rush's interest in the human mind and body, had drawn Barton toward the largely unknown botanical products of the continent. He was the greatest American botanist of his age. Barton's *Elements of Botany* (1803), the first important American treatise on the subject, went through several American and English editions and was even translated into Russian. When not yet twenty, he had accompanied his uncle, David Rittenhouse, on the surveying expedition to draw the western boundary of Pennsylvania which then divided it from Virginia. 'I well recollect,' wrote Barton many years later of the influence which his uncle had exerted on him, 'how great were his pleasure and satisfaction, in contemplating the *Flora* of the rich hills of Weeling, and other branches of the Ohio, when I accompanied him into those parts of our Union, in the year 1785. In this wilderness, he first fostered my love and zeal for natural history.' After a trip to Edinburgh, London, and Göttingen, Barton returned to Philadelphia to practice medicine and teach in the College of Philadelphia as professor first of natural history and botany, and later of *materia medica*. On Rush's death in 1813, Barton succeeded him as Professor of the Theory and Practice of Medicine in the University of Pennsylvania.

Barton's interests were in many ways characteristically American. While he devoted most of his life to *materia medica* (especially the uses of American plants for American diseases), his writings on natural history included observations on the

16

pernicious insects of the United States, the Falls of Niagara, the geographical distribution of trees and shrubs, a new species of lizard, the American turkey, the function of absorption in amphibians, the origin of the boundaries of Lake Ontario, the generation of fishes, and the qualities of American honey. He made a beginning in cultural anthropology: his studies of the origin, history and development of the American Indian were summarized in his widely read *New Views of the Origin of the Tribes and Nations of America*, which he dedicated to Jefferson.

JOSEPH PRIESTLEY (1733-1804), the great chemist now remembered for his discovery of oxygen, arrived from England in 1794 to join this circle of American philosophers. Next to Paine, Priestley was the most vivid symbol of the cosmopolitan republican spirit; and while still abroad he had become a close collaborator of the Jeffersonians. At the beginning of trouble between England and her colonies, Priestley had made American friends by his pamphlets favoring the rebel cause. Later his open advocacy of the French Revolution had drawn the wrath of a Birmingham mob, which on Bastille Day, 1791, burned his library and all his personal belongings. In the next year the French people made him a citizen of their republic. Driven from his native England at the age of sixty, Priestley came to Philadelphia as the appropriate asylum for his republican sentiments and philosophic interests.

It was David Rittenhouse who welcomed Priestley on behalf of American philosophy. Barton tells us that in the brief period between Priestley's arrival and the death of Rittenhouse, he often met Priestley at his uncle's house. Priestley's interest in nature went back to his youth in England when he had experimented with spiders; as tutor at an English school he had taken his students on country walks to collect fossils and botanical specimens. In America he was impatient with city life, and after negotiating with Rush (who in addition to all else was a land speculator), Priestley moved into the 'wilderness' of the central part of Pennsylvania at Northumberland. Jefferson was disappointed for he had tried to interest Priestley in settling near Monticello.

Replying to Rittenhouse's welcoming address, Priestley explained that he had left his native land principally 'for the sake of pursuing our common studies without molestation.' A member of the Philosophical Society since 1785, he had long shared the intellectual life of the Jeffersonian circle by correspondence. After settling in this country, he wielded an even greater influence. While Rittenhouse regarded the planets and Rush examined the mind and shape of man, while Barton studied anthropology and explored the world of vegetables and lower animals, Priestley's eye was on another aspect of nature. His principal concern was the composition and behavior of inanimate matter: though best known today for his experiments with gases, his physical researches were numerous and varied. Many years before, when Priestley was in London promoting the American cause, he had formed a friendship with Franklin who stimulated his interest in electricity. At Franklin's suggestion, he had written *The History and Present State of Electricity*. Priestley recorded from Franklin's own mouth the only account which survives of the famous experiment of the electrical kite. Even before Priestley arrived in America, the Philosophical Society had received his manuscript notes of 'Experiments on Phlogiston and the seeming concoction of water into air.' After his arrival he gave them more of his experiments. The Society heard his observations on spontaneous generation, and received his diary of the weather during the sea voyage to America. Like Rush, Priestley had numerous practical interests and a fluent pen from which came essays on history and political science, diatribes against the slave trade, and projects of education. Jefferson relied heavily on his advice for the projected University of Virginia.

Priestley possessed still another qualification for rounding out the American philosopher's view of the world. He had been trained and had long made his living as a nonconformist minister, and throughout his life he remained a preacher. Priestley was perhaps the most influential and articulate exponent of

18

Unitarianism during the first years of the republic. His extensive knowledge of languages, theology and church history enabled him to supply the artillery to defend the Jeffersonian view of religion and metaphysics. A *History of the Corruptions of Christianity,* written before Priestley came to America, was a work which Jefferson read again and again and never ceased to admire. The friendship between Priestley and Jefferson deepened, and their philosophic harmony became closer with the years; with no other theologian did Jefferson feel equally at home. Priestley's extraordinary union of the theologian and the physicist qualified him to expound the materialism on which Jefferson, Rush and others rested their faith. There was surely no hyperbole when Jefferson described him as unexcelled for service 'in religion, in politics, in physics.'

Besides Jefferson himself, Rittenhouse, Rush, Barton and Priestley comprised the major thinkers in that Jeffersonian circle with which we are concerned. Within the circle were two other men—Peale and Paine—who themselves lacked profundity but were admirably equipped for giving popular expression to the ideas which other men understood more profoundly.

CHARLES WILLSON PEALE (1741-1827) served the Jeffersonian circle as its illustrator and showman. Raised in Maryland, where he had received little formal schooling, Peale early agitated against the Stamp Act. When Loyalist merchants cut off his credit, he was forced to abandon his trade of saddle maker, and he turned his amateur hand to painting portraits in order to support his family. Peale soon became one of those itinerant artists who in the days before photography went from village to village, providing town halls with local landscapes and filling commissions for family likenesses. In this way he grew intimately acquainted with the American scene, traveling from Newburyport in Massachusetts south to Virginia. A brief apprenticeship in London under Benjamin West qualified him on his return to America to paint a remarkable series of portraits of the Revolutionary soldiers whom he came to know while serving as a captain of infantry; his numerous paintings of George Washington (including the earliest known) are still considered the most comprehensive and perceptive records of the General and President. The republican enthusiasm which qualified him for membership in the Committee of Public Safety and for active service in the Revolution stayed with him. In the Pennsylvania Assembly he voted for the abolition of slavery; and he himself freed the slaves he had brought from Maryland.

After Peale had settled in Philadelphia in 1776, his association with the leading men of the city gave a philosophic turn to his interests. When Dr. Morgan (Rush's predecessor as Professor of Medicine) gave Peale some mammoth bones from the Ohio, when Franklin presented him with a French Angora cat, and when he received a paddle fish from the Allegheny River, he conceived a plan for a museum of natural history which he founded in 1784. Peale's Museum, of which Jefferson accepted the presidency, was a storehouse and exhibiting place for many curious and interesting objects. Peale was among the first museum makers to reconstruct the natural habitat: sky and landscape were painted behind the animals, and birds' nests were shown as they appeared on the banks of rivers. In 1794, Peale displayed his characteristic showmanship when he made a parade of the removal of the museum from his studio on Lombard Street into the building of the Philosophical Society. At the head of the procession were men carrying an American buffalo, panthers and tiger cats, followed by a long line of boys carrying smaller animals. Until 1802 the Museum remained in the Philosophical Society Hall where it occupied all but the two rooms reserved for meetings, but it prospered and outgrew even these quarters. In 1802, the Legislature offered the free use of Independence Hall. The visitor to the Museum could see a mammoth's tooth from the Ohio, an electrical machine, pieces of asbestos and belts of wampum, stuffed birds, and a large number of Peale's own portraits of heroes of the Revolution.

Peale's talents as artist and artisan qualified him to serve for many years as curator of the Philosophical Society. He arranged and drew the fossil bones presented by Jefferson, he pieced together a skeleton of an Asiatic elephant and won the prize for the best method of warming rooms. The Society's memorial portraits of Franklin and Rittenhouse were done by Peale. His interests, while less deep than those of his fellows, were no less broad, ranging from natural history to dentistry and engineering. Although not a great naturalist, Peale was well known for his lectures on natural history which were accompanied by poetry and music. Jefferson, whose friendship with Peale went back to early Revolutionary days, continually assisted him in his scientific ventures. During Jefferson's presidency, pumps were loaned by the Navy Department to help Peale excavate the mammoth skeletons discovered at Newburgh, New York. It was Peale who engraved the animals discovered by Lewis and Clark. Jefferson frequently suggested objects for the Museum, and when in 1815 Peale finally wished to retire, he sought Jefferson's advice.

THOMAS PAINE (1737-1809), a friend of Rittenhouse, Rush and Jefferson, possessed a rare talent for reducing to simple language and memorable phrase the ideas which other Jeffersonians stated in diffuse and sophisticated fashion. 'No writer,' Jefferson observed, 'has exceeded Paine in ease and familiarity of style, in perspicuity of expression, happiness of elucidation, and in simple and unassuming language.' His career is so familiar that any detailed account here is superfluous. But we should recall that Paine's association with the Jeffersonian circle remained a strong thread throughout his erratic career. An English expatriate like Priestley, Paine did more with his pen than any other man, not excepting Jefferson or Sam Adams, to hasten the Revolution and give heart to the rebels. No works were more effective than *Common Sense* and *The American Crisis* in building Revolutionary morale. While Jefferson was in Paris, he kept in close touch with Paine, exchanging observations on the French National Assembly and the French Declaration of the Rights of Man. Paine's *Rights of Man,* a defense of the world republican revolution, which he wrote after the impending French Revolution had attracted him to Paris, was a

21

work which made Jefferson rejoice; for by it he saw 'the people confirmed in their good old faith.' The storm raised by Jefferson's endorsement of this work, and even the notorious reputation for 'atheism' which Paine had secured by his *Age of Reason*, did not deter Jefferson in 1801 from offering a government ship to bring Paine back to America. In Paine, Jefferson never failed to see the great popular champion of orthodox revolutionary principles: 'In these it will be your glory to have steadily labored, and with as much effect as any man living.'

While Paine was pre-eminently a publicist—and in this he was unexcelled—he also possessed a truly Jeffersonian versatility. His political writings overflowed political science, into economics, theology and natural history. He showed talent as engineer and inventor. Perhaps his best known project was his plan for an iron bridge of a single arch, concerning which he frequently corresponded with Jefferson, and a model of which he actually sent to Peale's Museum. He never was elected to membership in the Philosophical Society but he shared the interests of his friends in it, and corresponded with them on numerous scientific problems. Upon his first arrival in America he urged the fuller exploration of the mineral resources of the country, and proposed 'that were samples of different soils from different parts of America, presented to the [Philosophical] Society for their inspection and examination, it would greatly facilitate our knowledge of the internal earth, and give a new spring both to agriculture and manufactures.' During the Revolution, Paine collaborated with Rittenhouse on a flame-carrying arrow of iron intended to disable the British Army on the other side of the Delaware River. He was full of practical projects, such as the design for a smokeless candle which he communicated to Franklin. Paine's letters to Jefferson include plans for a 'geometrical wheelbarrow,' a new explanation of the cohesion of matter, a method for estimating the amount of cut timber to be had from standing trees, a design for a motor wheel to be revolved by the explosion of gunpowder (said by Paine to excel the steam engine because of its greater simplicity and its cheaper operation), a new design for the roofs of houses, an improved method of constructing carriage wheels, and a scheme for making one gunboat do the work of two. He developed his own theory of the causes and cure of yellow fever, and shared his experiments in this field with his friend Rittenhouse.

It was Paine's extraordinary practical sense and his impatience with metaphysics that qualified him to give a lucid and popular (if sometimes vulgarized) expression to Jeffersonian ideas. He brought the Jeffersonians down to earth when they veered toward the doctrinaire or the esoteric. Paine's humble origins and his association with men of many nations gave his journalistic writings a humanity which still shines through his crude phrases.

The group of philosophers whose thought will concern us we have christened the Jeffersonian Circle, for THOMAS JEFFERSON (1743-1826) stood at the center of this philosophical community. He was the human magnet who drew them together and gave order and meaning to their discrete investigations. As astronomer and mechanic he was surely inferior to Rittenhouse; as physician and psychologist, beneath Rush; as botanist and anthropologist, not the equal of Barton; and as physicist and theologian below Priestley; for he lacked the unbalance of mind required to excel as a specialist. But he possessed a mind more catholic than theirs and better able to see nature as a whole. Being a statesman, he persistently demanded the human implications of their science.

On the death of Rittenhouse in 1796, the American Philosophical Society chose Jefferson for its president. Since he was not a Philadelphian but a Virginian, the choice signified the national character of the Society. Jefferson's re-election for nearly twenty years as president of the body which according to him 'comprehends whatever the American World has of distinction in Philosophy & Science,' was simple recognition of his leadership in American intellectual life. He had become a member of the Society in 1780, a councillor in 1781, and for years had been exchanging observations with fellow philosophers. From Jefferson the Society received an original design for a moldboard plough, observations on weights and measures, and communications on a variety of subjects ranging from meteorology to fossils. Through him were transmitted many interesting communications which he received from correspondents all over the world. After the removal of the capital to Washington, Jefferson no longer lived near the Society's headquarters, but year after year and over his frequent protest, American science honored him as its leader. The Society refused his resignation of the presidency in 1808 when he was about to move from Washington to Monticello; not until 1815 was he permitted to retire.

The most impressive single monument of Jefferson's scientific achievement is his *Notes on Virginia,* which he prepared in response to a request by the French Government in 1781. The little volume collected his observations on every aspect of the Virginia environment: flora, fauna, mountains, rivers, population, laws, manufactures, Indians and Negroes. Even this remarkable work is no full measure of his interests, which we can see only in the wealth of his letters. During his busy political mission to France from 1784 to 1789, he naturally recorded day by day the progress of the Revolution there. But he also found time to note the rivers and the planets, to seek new species of rice, and to find fossil shells.

For Jefferson the Louisiana Purchase was at once a political, an economic and a 'philosophical' event; he congratulated the Society 'on the enlarged field of unexplored country lately opened to free research.' Having initiated the famous Western Expedition (1804-1806) of Lewis and Clark, he took trouble to see that it bore scientific fruit. In his personal instructions to Captain Meriwether Lewis in 1803, Jefferson characteristically listed the kinds of useful information to be collected:

Other objects worthy of notice will be, the soil and face of the country, its growth and vegetable productions, especially those not of the United States, the animals of the country generally, and especially those not known in the United States; the remains and accounts of any which may be deemed rare or extinct; the mineral productions of every kind, but particularly metals, limestone, pit-coal and saltpetre; salines and mineral waters, noting the temperature of the last, and such circumstances as may indicate their character; volcanic appearances; climate, as characterized by the thermometer, by the proportion of rainy, cloudy, and clear days, by lightning, hail, snow, ice, by the access and recess of frost, by the winds prevailing at different seasons, the dates at which particular plants put forth or lose their flower or leaf, times of appearance of particular birds, reptiles or insects.

Among his contemporaries who were qualified to judge, Jefferson had a considerable reputation as a naturalist. When Barton described to the Philosophical Society a new plant, which he christened *Jeffersonia Virginica*, he declared that Jefferson had few peers among natural historians in America. Jefferson exchanged observations on eclipses with Rittenhouse, discussed anatomy and the theory of medicine with Rush, *materia medica* and the habits of plants and animals with Barton, chemistry and theology with Priestley, and engineering and architecture with Paine. He complained that for much of his life public duties interfered with those 'philosophical evenings in the winter, and rural days in the summer' which were always his delight.

Although Jefferson had not the training, the leisure, or the temperament to write out a philosophic system, his social thought nevertheless was not a miscellany of practical maxims. It was actually, as we will see, the minor premise from a world of assumptions in science, metaphysics and theology. Therefore to seize Jefferson's political shibboleths and neglect Jeffersonian ideas is to try to understand the conclusion of an argument without knowing its major premises. In this volume we shall try to make explicit these major premises: to describe the intellectual world in which his political ideas subsisted. To the extent that we succeed we will have helped rescue Jefferson from the vagueness which has enveloped much of liberal thought, and we will see a significance in the Jeffersonian way of thinking, above the special political and practical issues of his or our day. We may hope to find the rightful place of the Jeffersonians in man's continuing quest for the relevance of his knowledge of God and of nature to his conception of

25

society. For this purpose it is convenient that we make our starting point not the particular Jeffersonian conclusions about society but rather their most general assumptions about God and the universe. From here we will proceed to the place of man in that universe and to Jeffersonian theories about the nature of man, human equality, toleration, the quality and scope of human thought, and the proper content of morals. Finally we will be led to the Jeffersonian conclusions concerning government, tradition, education and the future of American society. Having viewed Jeffersonian social philosophy in this large context, we may be better qualified to discover for ourselves the extent to which it remains defensible and applicable in our age.

CHAPTER ONE

The Supreme Workman

'Art lies in limitation.' GOETHE

IN the familiar passage in the Declaration of Independence, the Being who endowed men with their unalienable rights is described as 'their Creator,' and throughout Jeffersonian thought recurs this vision of God as the Supreme Maker. He was a Being of boundless energy and ingenuity who in six days had transformed the universal wilderness into an orderly, replete and self-governing cosmos. The Jeffersonian God was not the Omnipotent Sovereign of the Puritans nor the Omnipresent Essence of the Transcendentalists, but was essentially Architect and Builder. Though this conception was not original either to America or to the Jeffersonians, they surely had reasons of their own for admiring such a deity.

They had cast God in their own image. The talents which they called Godlike were those which men in eighteenth-century America most wanted for themselves. Seeing God not through an ancient revelation or tradition, but through the particular needs of their generation, the Jeffersonians had put God in the service of their earthly American task. In this they shaped a way of thinking, and foreshadowed the persistent tendency of men on this continent to confuse themselves with their deity. While such a view limited their spiritual vision, it did insure that no theological or mystical pretext would seduce men from building a strong New World. If this limitation was to make them and their heirs less eager and less qualified to discover the end toward which they were building, in the Age of Jefferson it did not seem urgent for that end to be made explicit. In that age, the Creator still inspired humility; He was still the symbol of the imperfection of men before their continental task.

In the present chapter we will try to comprehend this Jeffersonian God, in whom were succinctly expressed large beliefs about how the universe had come into being, by what

29

principles it had been shaped, and by what rules its processes were governed. To understand Him is to increase our understanding of the activist temper in which we are the heirs of the Jeffersonians. Moreover, by seeing how God represented the value and the unattainability of Jeffersonian aspirations, we may finally discover that prophetic spirit which decisively distinguishes their pragmatism from ours.

1. Nature as the Work of Art

THE intensity and speed of God's work were an inspiring precedent for eighteenth-century Americans. It seemed axiomatic that the creation of the material universe was not a continuing process, but had been accomplished by a brief series of divine works at the very beginning. The earth and everything in it had been made in a spasm of primordial energy and because of the perfection of that original act, nature could not be improved at any later time. Jefferson on more than one occasion declared 'the eternal pre-existence of God, and His creation of the world' to be the foundation of his philosophy. A correspondent, arguing that the earth's present shape was that which any fluid mass revolving on its axis would gradually assume, once suggested to him that the earth had first been a formless fluid mass, which only in the course of time acquired its oblate spheroid form. But Jefferson emphatically rejected any such hypothesis; the earth must have been a solid from its first creation, and the Creator must, at the outset, have given it its present shape to insure a perfect equilibrium and to prevent a shifting of the poles which might have made life on earth impossible. Jefferson objected to the theory that steam was the agent which threw up mountains and formed valleys.

30

I give one answer to all these theorists. . . . They all suppose the earth a created existence. They must suppose a creator then; and that he possessed power and wisdom to a great degree. As he intended the earth for the habitation of animals and vegetables, is it reasonable to suppose, he made two jobs of his creation, that he first made a chaotic lump and set it into rotatory motion, and then waited the millions of ages necessary to form itself? That when it had done this, he stepped in a second time, to create the animals and plants which were to inhabit it? As the hand of a creator is to be called in, it may as well be called in at one stage of the process as another. We may as well suppose he created the earth at once, nearly in the state in which we see it, fit for the preservation of the beings he placed on it.[1]

By hypothesis, then, the strata of the earth had nothing to tell about the story of the creation. Jefferson was confident that to study 'scratches on the surface of the earth' would not repay the philosopher's effort. It should not surprise us that he lacked our interest in geology—in fact, the word was not used in our sense until nearly 1800. In his curriculum for the University of Virginia, he did allot some time to studying the location of useful minerals. 'But the dreams about the modes of creation, inquiries whether our globe has been formed by the agency of fire or water, how many millions of years it has cost Vulcan or Neptune to produce what the fiat of the Creator would effect by a single act of will, is too idle to be worth a single hour of any man's life.' [2]

If there was a God at all, He must have made it possible for everyone to discover His existence and His character. Those who said that the story of Creation could not be known unless visible facts were supplemented by Christian revelation, were actually giving a handle to atheism; for only one-sixth of mankind had accepted Christianity, and surely the remaining five-sixths could not lack authentic knowledge of a God. The Psalms of Jefferson were no record of inner experience nor affirmations of an overruling power but were precise and circumstantial descriptions of the physical universe. Jeffersonian hymns were to be monographs of natural history. 'It is only in the CREATION,' said Paine, 'that all our ideas and conceptions of a *word of God* can unite. The Creation speaketh an universal language, independently of human speech or human language, multiplied and various as they be. It is an ever existing original, which every man can read. . . . In fine, do we want to know what God is? Search not the book called the scripture, which any human hand might make, but the scripture called the Creation.' [3] Theology thus made the study of natural history a work of religious zeal—even the main avenue to God.

The first quality of the natural universe which struck the Jeffersonian eye was the lavishness of the divine energy. The constructive powers of the Creator seemed without bounds; His variety and ingenuity beyond measure. When the Jeffersonian counted the number of visible objects, he sensed the 'unbounded liberality of nature.' In his writings, we frequently come upon the appropriate verses of the Psalmist, 'O Lord, how manifold are thy works! in wisdom hast thou made them all: the earth is full of thy riches. So is this great and wide sea, wherein are things creeping innumerable, both small and great beasts.'

The Jeffersonian vision of the Creator's works was improved by the microscope which had been made possible by seventeenth- and eighteenth-century advances in lens grinding. Rittenhouse, who himself contributed to these developments in applied optics, urged that use of the microscope go hand-in-hand with that of the telescope, in order that men who regarded the fullness of the heavens should not forget the equal fullness displayed by the Creator on this earth. The microscope had now brought into view minute worlds showing an unimagined profusion of life on this planet, which led Paine to observe:

If we take a survey of our own world . . . our portion in the immense system of creation, we find every part of it, the earth, the waters, and the air that surround it, filled, and as it were crouded with life, down from the largest animals that we know of to the smallest insects the naked eye can behold, and from thence to others still smaller, and totally invisible without the assistance of the microscope. Every tree, every plant, every leaf, serves not only as an habitation, but as a world to some numerous race, till animal existence becomes so exceedingly refined, that the effluvia of a blade of grass would be food for thousands.[4]

The prodigality of nature which the Jeffersonian felt inwardly, was verified not merely by the profusion of objects, but by the artifice revealed in each creature. Priestley, who took special trouble to observe the minute creation, marveled at the intricacy of the smallest plants and animals. A friend of Peale's, who described admiringly to the Philosophical Society the minuscule reproductive apparatus of mosses, adopted a pertinent motto from Pliny, *Nusquam natura major quam in minimis*. The minutely invisible creation was thought surely to hold still more evidence of this pervading quality of the material universe.

The heavens like the earth proclaimed the Creator's prodigality. Shooting stars and the precession of equinoxes, which in different ways produced striking changes in the appearance of the heavens, seemed to Rittenhouse purposely designed to increase 'that endless variety which obtains throughout the works of Nature.' Here, too, the Jeffersonian was not satisfied with what the human eye could see of the Creator's works, and he appealed boldly from the visible to the invisible, from the known to the unknown. He dogmatically insisted that facts which men did not yet know, and could never know, would confirm the quality which already had been proved by astronomic science. As Rittenhouse remarked:

When we consider this great variety so obvious on *our* globe, and ever connected by some degree of uniformity, we shall find sufficient reason to conclude, that the visible creation . . . is but an inconsiderable part of the whole. Many other and very various orders of things unknown to, and inconceiveable by us, may, and probably do exist, in the unlimitted regions of space. And all yonder stars innumerable, with their dependencies, may perhaps compose but the leaf of a flower in the creator's garden, or a single pillar in the immense building of the divine architect.[5]

According to Paine, for example, astronomic space even in its remote and unexplored recesses was not a 'naked void' but must be 'filled with systems of worlds; and . . . no part of space lies at waste, any more than any part of our globe of earth and water is left unoccupied.' Dr. Hugh Williamson, a correspondent of the Philosophical Society, in his 'Essay on the Use of Comets,' disposed of the dangerous suggestion that these bodies possessed extremely high temperatures, which had supported the erroneous belief that they might be uninhabitable. He concluded that there was no reason for doubting that the comets, like our world, had been created to be the residence of intelligent beings and to add to the fullness of life in the cosmos. While Dr. Williamson thus defended the doctrine of the plurality of worlds from the attacks of superficial physicists, Rittenhouse vindicated it against uninformed theologians. Such a doctrine, he insisted, was 'inseparable from the principles of Astronomy.' 'Our ideas, not only of the almightiness of the Creator, but of his wisdom and his beneficence,' observed Paine, 'become enlarged in proportion as we contemplate the extent and the structure of the universe. The solitary idea of a solitary world, rolling or at rest in the immense ocean of space, gives place to the cheerful idea of a society of worlds, so happily contrived as to administer, even by their motion, instruction to man.' [6]

From the Jeffersonian point of view, the order in the created universe did not foreshadow any divine beauty or disembodied truth. What gave design to nature was no overruling ordinance, idea, or essential principle, but the self-evident symmetry of the form and the smooth efficiency of the process. The material order was itself the consummate expression of divinity—all the more real because it was tangible. It was inconceivable that in six days of strenuous labor a God of boundless energy would not have shaped the whole range of possible physical beings. The absolute fullness of nature—by definition, the fullness of the original creation—was described as 'the great chain of beings.' Jeffersonians used this traditional metaphor to state an admirably simple idea. Every kind of natural object was conceived to be a link in an unbroken chain which stretched from the mineral up to man, the highest form of

34

animal life, lower only than the angels. As Peale exclaimed in
lines borrowed from Thomson:

> How wond'rous is this scene! where all
>   is form'd
> With number, weight, and measure! all
>   designed
> For some great end . . . each moss
> Each shell, each crawling insect, holds
>   a rank
> Important in the plan of him who form'd
> This scale of beings; holds a rank,
>   which lost
> Would break the chain and leave behind
>   a gap
> Which nature's self would rue.[7]

Like all Jeffersonian theology, this conception of a chain of
beings was at once an expression of personal faith and a description of the material universe. The Jeffersonian insisted that
the felt qualities of his universe were not the product of his
personal belief; yet his theology had transformed every fact of
natural history into a testimony of faith in the Creator. The
depth of his faith made him all the more resolute not to be
misled by apparent facts which might seem to show qualities
in the creation which he knew to be discordant with the
character of the Maker. 'From the observations made on the
various productions of the natural world, as they present themselves to our view,' Peale explained in the catalogue to his
museum, 'we find that nature gradually, and almost imperceptibly, passes from the most simple beings to the most com-
pound; thus forming that chain or series of being, the parts
of which, with their order and comely proportion, will continue to be the inexhausted subject of the researches of naturalists to the end of time.'

The orderly 'chain of beings' actually became the reality to
be illustrated and confirmed by all particular facts. Long before
Charles Darwin, the enterprising American philosopher had
his own reasons for seeking 'missing links.' In many ways he

35

affirmed his confidence in the fullness and continuity of the chain, in the necessary existence from the beginning of beings of every grade and size. When, for example, an American traveler reported finding what seemed to be gigantic human bones, Benjamin Smith Barton was ready to believe that they belonged to a hitherto undiscovered link. 'There is, certainly, no physical impossibility in the existence of a race of giants,' Barton declared. 'On the contrary, the general scheme of nature, with respect to the creation of the species of animals and vegetables, would lead us to expect a species of giants belonging to the human kind.' [8]

It was axiomatic, of course, that no divine energy had been wasted; no superfluous kind of being had ever been created. Although it might be beyond the philosopher's power to see the whole design, he was nonetheless sure that there had been no errata in the Book of Creation. The whole chain which the Creator had made in the beginning still survived in the eighteenth century. No species of animal ever had, or ever could, become extinct. The 'great-claw,' for example, was an animal of which very little was known: a few fossil bones had been attributed to it, and there were some travelers' tales, but no authentic instance of anyone having actually seen the creature. Yet, Jefferson insisted, the fact that no man had seen the animal did not prove that it had ceased to exist. On the contrary, he assured the Philosophical Society that the great-claw still roamed in some remote and unexplored wilderness.

In fine the bones exist: therefore, the animal has existed. The movements of nature are in a never ending circle. The animal species which has once been put into a train of motion, is still probably moving in that train. For if one link in nature's chain might be lost, another and another might be lost, till this whole system of things should evanish by piece-meal . . . If this animal then has once existed, it is probable on this general view of the movements of nature that he still exists, and rendered still more probable by the relations of honest men applicable to him and to him alone.[9]

36

Observations on the mammoth were based on the same assumptions. In his *Notes on Virginia*, Jefferson included the mammoth in his list of living animals, and he was undisturbed by the lack of evidence of its survival. 'Such is the economy of nature,' he observed, 'that no instance can be produced, of her having permitted any one race of her animals to become extinct; of her having formed any link in her great work so weak as to be broken. To add to this, the traditionary testimony of the Indians, that this animal still exists in the northern and western parts of America, would be adding the light of a taper to that of the meridian sun.' By comparing the range of the mammoth with that of the elephant (the link in the chain of beings closest to it), he showed why each was needed to fill out the gamut of living creatures. The habitat of the mammoth seemed separated from that of the elephant by about 6½ degrees of latitude: the mammoth had been made for the arctic, the elephant for the tropics, according to the universal symmetry. 'When the Creator has therefore separated their nature as far as the extent of the scale of animal life allowed to this planet would permit it, it seems perverse to declare it the same, from a partial resemblance of their tusks and bones.' Just as the jungle would lack an inhabitant without the elephant, the icy tundras would have missed their counterpart, the mammoth. Peale dramatized in his museum the American philosopher's belief in the indestructible chain of the Creation, by placing a skeleton of an American mammoth beside that of an Asiatic elephant.

When the Philosophical Society instructed its permanent committee to procure skeletons of the mammoth and other rare creatures, the information they sought was of 'unknown' and not of extinct animals. By definition there could be no such study as paleontology. Every buried skeleton or any bone which could be unearthed must be a clue to a still-living creature. It was therefore to improve his knowledge of the eighteenth-century fauna that the American philosopher eagerly collected fossil bones. Throughout his life, Jefferson asked remote correspondents to send him such specimens—for him 'the most desirable objects in natural history.' By means of them he hoped to learn of rare animals which still had eluded explorers in the American wilderness.[10]

Just as it was unthinkable that the great-claw, the mammoth or any other original product of divine artifice should become extinct, so it seemed impossible that the primordial release of divine energy and ingenuity should have left any gaps to be filled by the later appearance of novel plants or animals. Such a possibility would have implied a hiatus in the Creation, and would have made it the expression of something less than boundless creativity. The Jeffersonian therefore believed that after the first appearance of life on this earth, no new kind of plant or animal ever had been or ever could be brought into existence. 'Species' was the technical term in which this idea was expressed; and this term suggested to the Jeffersonian both the completeness and the indestructibility of the original set of molds. His conviction that the most reliable, perfect and indestructible order was actually embodied in the physical universe was thus implicit in his very vocabulary. 'We can count as many species,' wrote Linnaeus, the great Swedish naturalist whose system of classification the American philosopher had adopted, 'as there were of different forms created in the beginning.' The laws of reproduction kept species always within the limits of the original number, for God had ordained the fruit tree to yield fruit after his kind, and the winged fowl after his kind. In Linnaeus' words, 'these, each according to its own fixed laws of reproduction, produce more individuals, but always of the same species as the parents.' [11]

If any creature could ever have come into being by spontaneous generation or in any other manner than from a parent of the same species, the whole Jeffersonian vision of nature would have become confused. The American philosopher categorically denied the possibility. Champions of spontaneous generation had made much of the fact that a variety of animals had been found in extraordinary places (for example, in the bodies of other animals), where their origin could not be traced to parents of their own species. In Philadelphia there had appeared 'an horse with a snake in its eye, to be seen in Arch-street, between Sixth and Seventh streets, not only possessed of mere life, but endowed with a very brisk locomotive faculty.' Dr. John Morgan, who reported to the Society in 1782, refused to accept the easy but dangerous hypothesis of spontaneous generation, and concluded his paper in the humble determination 'to reverence the hand that framed not only our bodies, but those of the meanest reptiles, with an exuberance of skill, which proclaims that they are not the effect of chance.' Twenty years later, Joseph Priestley produced his 'Observations and Experiments relating to equivocal, or spontaneous, Generation,' in which he systematically attacked the problem. To admit spontaneous generation, Priestley argued, would be to affirm atheism by denying the unified design of creation:

Completely organized bodies, of specific kinds, are maintained [by the champions of spontaneous generation] to be produced from substances that could not have any natural connexion with them. . . . And this I assert is nothing less than the production of an effect without any adequate cause. If the organic particle, from which an oak is produced be not precisely an acorn, the production of it from any thing else is as much a miracle, and out of the course of nature, as if it had come from a bean, or a pea, or absolutely from nothing at all; and if miracles be denied, (as they are, I believe, by all the advocates for this doctrine of equivocal generation,) these plants and animals, completely organized as they are found to be, as well adopted to their destined places and uses in the general system as the largest plants and animals, have no *intelligent cause* whatever, which is unquestionably atheism. For if one part of the system of nature does not require an intelligent cause, neither does any other part, or the whole.[12]

It was equally perilous to believe that any kind of animal might in the course of time change into another. Such a change would involve the extinction of old and the emergence of new species, and the present material universe would suffer the imputation of incompleteness or imperfection. The special butt of Priestley's ridicule was the suggestion made by the proponents of spontaneous generation (including Erasmus Darwin, grandfather of the great Charles) that lions, horses, and elephants might have arisen from animals of different kinds, and that their remote ancestors might actually have been microscopic animalcules. 'And if they come to be what they now are by successive generations, why does not the change and improvement go on? Do we ever see any small animal become a larger of a different kind? Do any mice become rats, rats become dogs, or wolves, wasps become hornets, &c. and yet this is precisely the analogy that the hypothesis requires.' Priestley steadfastly clung to his belief that even through thousands of years, no species could change so as to become something different from what the Creator had originally made: the plants and animals described in the Book of Job and the dogs, asses and lions of Homer were no different from those of the eighteenth century. Rush, who was always warning his students against a priori theories, nonetheless argued from scant historical facts that the animals and plants of his day were exactly the same in all their properties as those of six thousand years before. And Jefferson himself asserted as an axiom that environment could never change the quality of a species:

Every race of animals seems to have received from their Maker certain laws of extension at the time of their formation. Their elaborate organs were formed to produce this, while proper obstacles were opposed to its further progress. Below these limits they cannot fall, nor rise above them. What intermediate station they shall take may depend on soil, on climate, on food, on a careful choice of breeders. But all the manna of heaven would never raise the mouse to the bulk of the mammoth.[13]

2. The Economy of Nature

AS it was inconceivable that there should have been any transient species, any waste or futility in the original design —so it was unimaginable that the continuing processes of nature should reveal anything but the most frugal expenditure of divine energy. This belief followed directly from the conception of God as the Supreme Workman. For the Jeffersonians it was summarized in 'the economy of nature,' a conception which we will try to grasp in the present section.

Faith in the economy and uniformity of nature had helped convince Jefferson that the mammoth must be among his contemporaries; but it made an insoluble puzzle out of other fossils. Like many of his fellow naturalists, he was baffled by the discovery in the Andes 15,000 feet above sea level, and in other unlikely places, of large numbers of 'shells.' The two least fanciful explanations of the many proposed were, as Jefferson wrote to Rittenhouse (January 25, 1786), that these 'calcareous stones' were actually animal remains; or, on the other hand, that they were nothing more than symmetrical stones 'that grow or shoot as crystals do.' This latter explanation, championed by Voltaire and others, was unacceptable to Jefferson. If in the original scheme of the creation, one of the functions of marine animals had been to produce shells, it was unthinkable that a frugal Creator would have allowed these same shapes to be produced also in the accidental fashion in which crystals grow. 'It is not within the usual economy of nature,' Jefferson observed, 'to use two processes for one species of production.' [14]

We cannot be surprised that a penchant for magic or for miracles was not to be attributed to the Creator; this would have been inconsistent with his workmanlike character. While the Jeffersonian did not flatly deny the Creator's power to per-

41

form miracles, he admired His refusal to do so. To believe in a Creator who worked contrary to natural laws was, according to Paine, 'degrading the Almighty into the character of a show-man, playing tricks to amuse and make the people stare and wonder.' Jefferson remarked that the Almighty Himself could not construct a machine of perpetual motion while the laws existed which He had prescribed for the government of matter. Even to Priestley (whose devout Christian faith would not al-low him to doubt miracles) the undeniable rarity of miracles was admirable. God's desire to preserve the uniformity of nature was shown by the fact that He attained His manifold purposes, not by dissolving physical laws, but simply by creating convenient exceptions, 'which he has done by means of oc-casional and seasonable miraculous interpositions. In fact, the proper use of miracles has been to make more miracles unneces-sary.' [15] The eighteenth-century American must have been im-pressed that his own task of construction would be accom-plished only by acting within the limits of natural rules and within the constraints of environment. That the Creator Him-self had chosen to work within such bounds thus made Him a more precise apotheosis of the Jeffersonian workman.

Doubtless the American philosopher lacked logical consist-ency when he assumed that his God was omnipotent, and yet would not assert that He had the power to change the uniform laws of physical nature. But had the Jeffersonian unrelentingly insisted that there were no rules to restrain Omnipotence, he might have obstructed his demonstration of the salient quality of his universe: it was not the Omnipotence but the Artifice of the Creator which he felt most deeply. Moreover by presup-posing the rigidity of natural laws he actually increased the constructive power of his God. The greatest artist does not effortlessly shape an amorphous medium, but works willingly within rules imposed by a rigid material. By making the uni-formity of the laws of physical nature an axiom of his universe, the Jeffersonian was declaring that his Creator had wrought not in clay but in granite.

42

The more the Jeffersonian emphasized the complexity and power of the artifice, the less need did he feel to seek any end beyond the artifice and the process. The Creation seemed an end in itself. His cosmology thus revealed his pervasive assumption that workmanship, construction and activity were somehow their own justification. Any temptation to confess unsureness about the purpose of life was smothered at the outset by confident affirmation of the aesthetic qualities of nature.

The Jeffersonian seemed to suggest that the harmony of the physical processes of life was the consummation of divinity. His notion of the *economy* of nature implied that the ordering of the universe could be adequately described as the husbanding of divine energy. As Priestley observed:

> The clouds and the rain are designed to moisten the earth, and the sun to warm it; and the texture and juices of the earth are formed so as to receive the genial influences of both, in order to ripen and bring to perfection that infinite variety of plants and fruits, the seeds of which are deposited in it. Again, is not each plant peculiarly adapted to its proper soil and climate, so that every country is furnished with those productions which are peculiarly suited to it? Are not all plants likewise suited to the various kinds of animals which feed upon them? . . . The various kinds of animals are, again, in a thousand ways adapted to, and formed for, the use of one another. Beasts of a fiercer nature prey upon the tamer cattle: fishes of a larger size live almost wholly upon those of a less: and there are some birds which prey upon land animals, others upon fishes, and others upon creatures of their own species.[16]

Priestley was satisfied to enumerate cross-purposes—the creation of plants to be consumed by herbivorous animals, and the creation of the tamer cattle as meat for the carnivores—for by deifying life, activity and intricate construction, he had refused to ask for any meaning beyond nature.

The Jeffersonian cosmology seems vague only if we look for an end outside the physical universe. Its essential quality was not so much its vagueness as its concreteness, its determination

43

to find embodied in the visible universe the uttermost purpose of life. Such a universe was singularly undramatic: in it, as we shall see, there was no ultimate conflict between moral forces. But it was singularly dynamic. Efficient, coherent and intricate motion were the be-all and end-all. Even a casual comparison with other familiar cosmologies will reveal these characteristic qualities of the Jeffersonian view. The ancient Egyptian saw his universe governed toward the realization of a concept of justice. In medieval Europe the final meaning of the material cosmos was to be discovered somewhere outside this earth. For the American Puritan, it was the fulfillment of God's will which was good, which justified the travail of the earthly city. But the Jeffersonian universe was self-justifying. To call it a 'machine' is hardly accurate, for a machine is made toward some end, and the Jeffersonian universe was its own end. 'The "natural laws" which the scientists of that era make so much of,' Veblen has shrewdly observed, 'are no longer decrees of a preternatural legislative authority, but rather details of the workshop specifications handed down by the master-craftsman for the guidance of handicraftsmen working out his designs.' The test of an apparatus was its ability to 'work,' that is to say, to function according to its own rules. Here was the perfect expression in cosmology of the active temperament.

Everywhere appeared the life-giving benevolence of nature. When Rittenhouse looked out of his window, he admired 'that disposition of lands and seas, which affords a communication between distant regions, and a mutual exchange of benefits.' Du Pont de Nemours, Jefferson's French friend and correspondent, expressed the prevailing view when he told the Philosophical Society that the highest mountains must necessarily be found in Africa, since they were needed there to gather rivers large enough to water that most torrid continent. When Paine, in 1801, sent Jefferson the plans for his mechanical wheel to be turned by explosions of gunpowder, he argued that some such constructive use must have been intended. 'When I consider the wisdom of nature,' he remarked, 'I must think that she endowed matter with this extraordinary property for other purposes than that of destruction. Poisons are capable of other uses than that of killing.' [17]

The Jeffersonian found special pleasure in showing how facts which at first glance seemed to obstruct life processes proved on profounder examination actually to serve those processes. Any such fact had the piquancy of a conundrum, since one could be confident that eventually an harmonious, if devious, explanation would appear. 'Nature is silent,' observed Peale, 'only to those who know not how to interrogate her—to the man of inquisitive mind she offers ample instruction.' 'The apparent disorders,' as another philosopher said, 'lessen with our increasing knowledge.'

Prominent among the 'apparent disorders' which piqued the American philosopher's curiosity were those miasmic swamps and marshes which marred the face of the American continent from New England to Georgia. For what purpose had these insalubrious areas been created in the economy of nature? If the Creator loved life, why had He made any of the land unhealthful or uninhabitable? Scientific literature of the period is full of reflections on swamps and marshes. Perhaps the most ingenious and comprehensive explanation was presented to the Society by Adam Seybert, the versatile philosopher from Philadelphia who was pioneer American mineralogist, manufacturer of chemicals, congressman, compiler of statistics, educator of the deaf, patron of discharged prisoners, and analyst of animal blood. Marshes, he said, were:

. . . very necessary to keep the atmosphere in a *proper degree* of purity, for it is not only the impure atmosphere which kills animals, but the too pure also; and . . . animals live too fast in atmospheres overcharged with oxygen gas. They appear to me to have been instituted by the Author of Nature in order to operate against the powers which vegetables and other causes possess of purifying the atmosphere, so that the oxygen may exist in a proper proportion, fit to support animal life and combustion. I am of opinion that ere long marshes will be looked upon by mankind as gifts from Heaven to prolong the life and happiness of the greatest portion of the animal kingdom.[18]

If it was objected that a superabundance of oxygen gas was already prevented (without the aid of marshes) by the ordinary respiration of animals, Seybert not merely answered the objection, but used it to disclose the amazing subtlety of nature. The basic fact was that plant life always 'purified' the atmosphere by producing large quantities of oxygen which had somehow to be counteracted, if animals were to be kept from using up their life energies too rapidly. In tropical lands where there was the greatest number of plants and hence the fastest production of oxygen, the Creator had established the greatest counteracting force by making marshes most abundant. Seybert thought his explanation was supported also by the fact that when vegetable life became paralyzed in winter, the operation of marshes, being unnecessary, was suspended by the freezing of marsh waters.

While the Philadelphian readily saw a providential use for marshes, John Taylor of Caroline County, Virginia, ardent Jeffersonian and the leading Southern agronomist of the day, saw unproductive swamps increasing the problems of the contracting Southern economy. We have further evidence of the character of Jeffersonian science when we see Taylor joining Seybert's quest for a life-saving design—and objecting merely that Seybert had found the wrong one. The Creator, Taylor said, could never have intended that men should leave swamps uncleared in order to prolong human life, and yet, at the same time, have made swamps an obstacle to men's procuring the food needed to live. 'The connexion between draining or drying the earth, and human subsistence, furnishes a kind of argument, neither logical nor demonstrative, and yet of conclusive force to my mind. Can it be believed that the author of creation, has committed the egregious blunder, of exposing man to the alternative of eating bad food, or of breathing bad air? If not, draining whether by the sun, the plough or the spade, being indispensable to avoid the first, cannot wreck him on the second evil.' Taylor actually based his comprehensive theory of manures (which Jefferson shared) on this argument. The main idea, according to Jefferson, was that the atmosphere was the great workshop of nature for producing fertilizing elements and mixing them with the soil. Plants themselves had been destined to 'distil the atmosphere' and draw nourishing ingredients back into the earth. 'The vegetable chymistry by absorption,' Taylor explained, 'is a means provided by providence, for its last filter.' Some plants, like the clover, showed this absorptive power to a remarkable degree, and the symmetry of nature required that all plants have the power if any had. This effectiveness of natural plant fertilizers seemed to prove the futility of seeking mineral or 'fossil' manures. Moreover, on general principles, the Jeffersonian refused to believe that such substances could be of much use to the farmer. 'Indeed,' Taylor remarked, 'it is hardly probable that divine wisdom has lodged in the bowels of the earth, the manure necessary for its surface.' [19]

His conviction of an orderly and coherent process made the American philosopher view nature as if through a kaleidoscope. Fragmentary facts were refracted in the peculiar mirrors of his brain to make an intricate and ever-shifting, but always symmetrical, design: the more intricate and more obscure the facts, the more complicated and shadowy the pattern. The philosopher's justification of swamps, devious though it was, still was relatively simple compared with the operations of his mind in other cases. An example of one of these other cases—interesting too, because it involved relations among living creatures—was his study of the reputed powers of that peculiarly American animal, the rattlesnake.

For several centuries, explorers had nourished a myth that the American rattlesnake had the power of hypnotizing or 'fascinating' its prey. Even the more critical observers, including Linnaeus and William Bartram, had believed the tales which Benjamin Smith Barton in 1794 scrutinized in his 'Memoir concerning the Fascinating Faculty which has been ascribed to the Rattle-Snake, and other American Serpents.' [20] Barton denied the existence of any hypnotizing power, and his whole argument was based on the necessities of an efficiently operating creation. He started by assuming, for the sake of argument, that snakes

47

actually possessed the power to hypnotize, and then he asked for what purpose nature could have endowed them with the supposed power. Credulous observers had all given a uniform answer: so that snakes might obtain their food. If, then, the power did exist, one would expect that the principal food of serpents would be those very birds and squirrels against which the 'evil eye' was said to be used. But, Barton pointed out, this was by no means the case; rattlesnakes lived mainly on frogs.

This incongruity supported Barton's doubts that the power existed at all. When he noticed that the only credible instances of peculiar behavior concerned birds that nested near the ground, and that these had invariably occurred in the spring when such birds would have been nesting, he had his clue. 'Nature has taught different animals what animals are their enemies; and although . . . the principal food of the rattlesnake is the great frog, yet as he occasionally devours birds and squirrels, to these animals he must necessarily be an object of fear. When the reptile, therefore, lies at the foot of a tree, the bird or squirrel will feel itself uneasy.' The parent bird, he explained, would naturally fly about in an apparently demented (or 'fascinated') manner to distract the serpent from the nestlings. Here Barton happily remarked another providential fact: the most vulnerable place in the skull of the rattlesnake (the center of the top, indicated in drawings accompanying the article) was the point most accessible to the sharp bill of the frightened bird. He confidently explained that a marvelous instinct had instructed the parent birds to strike there for the mortal wound which would save the young in the nest. At the same time, the propagation of birds was insured and the number of serpents kept from becoming destructive. Barton felt rewarded for his tortuous interpretation of the scanty facts about the rattlesnake by these 'new instances of the wisdom of providence, and new proofs of the strong affections of animals'—for which natural history would always provide an ample field.

The universal purpose discovered by all these studies was simply an increase in the quantity of creatures and in the efficiency of life processes everywhere. To emphasize the unique role of any creature—even man—would have been discordant with the tone of this cosmos; it would have presupposed some standard outside nature itself against which creatures might be judged. Because the Jeffersonian was so impressed with the unique necessity of *every* animal and vegetable species to the large plan of nature, he could not readily imagine one species to be more necessary than another. He viewed himself as but a link, though the highest, in the great chain of beings, all the parts of which had been closely connected by the hand of the divine Maker. The causes of life were the same in all creatures, and the greater complexity or force of the stimuli which supported human life could be no reason for separating man from the rest of the Creation. 'We must resolve it into that attribute of the Deity, which seems to have delighted in variety in *all* his works.' [21] 'Creature' was one of his commonest words for man, and this the Jeffersonian used in its original sense, to emphasize man's integration by the common Creator into the processes of nature.

To be sure, we do sometimes sense a mild anthropocentrism in Jeffersonian thought. But it is extremely mild. Jefferson, in a well-known passage in his First Inaugural Address, adored 'an overruling Providence, which by all its dispensations proves that it delights in the happiness of man here and his greater happiness hereafter.' Such observations on the fitness of the environment for man were, however, no more confident than remarks on how the lives of *all* animals were prolonged by the use of marshes, or on how the structure of the rattlesnake's skull helped increase the population of birds. Benevolence was universal in nature.

If the fitness of the environment for man seemed more remarkable than its fitness for the marsh plant or for the rattlesnake, it was only because the needs of man were more complex. One correspondent of the Philosophical Society, for example, contributed observations on the chemical composition of the water of the ocean, in which he explained that alkaline substances such as magnesia, lime and soda had been distributed plentifully throughout the ocean in order to keep it from becoming foul, unhealthy and uninhabitable—which would have been the case if the sulphuric, septic and muriatic acids had not been neutralized. When he discovered that the alkalinity of ocean water enabled sailors to keep their clothes clean without using soap, he was inspired to a paean on the economy of Providence.[22]

The Jeffersonian was hardly less impressed by man's service to the lower animals than by their use to human life. 'It is in man alone,' Jefferson observed, 'that nature has been able to find a sufficient barrier against the too great multiplication of other animals . . . an equilibriating power against the fecundity of generation.' Rush noted that the Creator must have made man dependent on other animals (especially domestic animals) in order to give him an interest in protecting and preserving them. The many close analogies of human with veterinary medicine seemed further proof of the integration of all life processes. Whether man fed or slaughtered his cattle, he was always unwittingly serving the increase of life; for even his desire to provide himself with meat was a motive to enlarge the numbers of living cattle. 'By thus multiplying their numbers,' declared Rush, 'we multiply life, sensation, and enjoyment.' [23]

Nowhere is the Jeffersonian sense of design more sharply revealed than in discussions of the seeming evils which afflicted man. What conceivable use could be shown for diseases or the debility of old age? Rush noted cheerfully that the increase of bodily ills with the passing years actually led aged men to look upon death as a welcome relief. 'This indifference to life, and desire for death . . . ,' he explained, 'appear to be a wise law in the animal economy, and worthy of being classed with those laws which accommodate the body and mind of man to all the natural evils, to which, in the common order of things, they are necessarily exposed.' [24] According to Jefferson, nature intended to make death easier by gradually removing man's faculties.

The existence and the distribution of physical debility of all sorts, according to the Jeffersonian, could be explained by nature's needs. Good health was a commodity, like all others, of which the Creator had been frugal. Rush observed in his 'Natural History of Medicine among the Indians' that each society seemed to have just the quantity of health which its activities required: the greater health of the American Indians, like their insensibility to cold and hunger, was proportioned to their need of strength for the rigors of outdoor life; on the other hand, 'the less degrees, or entire want of health, are no interruption to the ordinary business of civilized life.' It could not be surprising then that civilized communities were permitted to be more weakened by disease.

Even those yellow-fever epidemics which decimated American cities in the 1790's seemed not without their use. Jefferson solaced Rush, who had risked his life in the vain search for a remedy, by explaining that the yellow fever would discourage the growth of those large cities which were pestilential to the morals, the health and the liberties of man. But to Rush, the practicing physician, it seemed axiomatic that since every part of the globe was meant to be inhabitable by man, a remedy must have been created for every disease. So sure was Rush that the Creator had universally provided appropriate remedies, that he instructed the inquiring physician always to seek a hint of the remedy in the incidence of the disease. 'From the affinity established by the Creator between evil and its antidotes, in other parts of his works, I am disposed to believe no remedy will ever be effectual in any general disease, that is not cheap, and that cannot easily be made universal.' Even in the familiar fact that most medicines were unpalatable, he found evidence of subtle design; for had the Author of Nature made medicinal substances more agreeable to the taste, 'they would probably have yielded long ago to the unbounded appetite of man, and by becoming articles of diet, or condiments, have lost their efficacy in diseases.' [25]

If, as Rush proposed, every disease had its remedy, the philosopher would expect to find a coincidence between the geographical distribution of diseases and the distribution of those plants which were medicines against them. In the *Transactions* of the Philosophical Society, we meet the confident

51

expectation that a remedy against the snakebite would most likely be found in the very leaves among which the rattlesnake lay hidden.[26] Benjamin Smith Barton, doubly trained in botany and medicine, and familiar with the American countryside, was admirably equipped to trace this part of nature's design.

But Barton leaned more toward Jefferson than toward Rush, and he observed in his *Collections for an Essay towards a Materia Medica*, that man was subject to many diseases, both of body and of mind, for the cure of which Providence had never intended to afford a remedy. The theory which interested Barton most (so widely held that he called it a 'trite observation') was 'that every country possesses remedies that are suited to the cure of its peculiar diseases . . . that the principal portion of indigenous remedies is to be found among the vegetables of the countries in which the diseases prevail.' Barton himself thought that while this generalization was on the whole well founded, it did need some qualification. He noted, for example, that men could and actually did live where hardly a vegetable could be made to grow. If the proposed theory were universally true, then in such countries man would never have suffered disease; yet obviously this was not the case. Barton therefore believed that the Creator had made some diseases necessary to man's nature. But he cautioned against allowing the qualifications required by extreme cases to obscure the large harmony of nature. He ridiculed the objections of reckless critics like Voltaire, who noting that the intermittent fever prevailed in Europe and that its remedy, the Peruvian bark, was not found in Europe but in South America, had challenged the whole providential design. Against such argument, Barton explicitly defended 'the benevolent order of Providence' by underlining two important facts: that the intermittent fever was a disease of almost every climate, and that the Peruvian bark was not its only remedy.

When the weight of the facts forced Rush to admit, in his 'Natural History of Medicine among the Indians,' that remedies for many diseases actually were not to be found in the places where the diseases occurred, he still refused to abandon his belief that the Creator had always provided, somewhere in the world, a remedy for every disease. He discovered in the very geographical separation of some diseases from their natural remedies, a stimulus to human activity, and he concluded that this superficial discord actually aided the Creator's more remote and extensive purpose. 'Societies stand in need of each other as much as individuals; and the goodness of the Deity remains unimpeached, when we suppose that he intended medicines to serve (with other articles) to promote that knowledge, humanity and politeness, among the inhabitants of the earth, which have been so justly attributed to commerce.' [27]

The notion of the prosperity of the human species—or even beyond that, of the functioning of nature as a whole—lay behind Jeffersonian reasoning about the occurrence of good health, the uses of yellow fever in discouraging the growth of cities, and the importance of medicines in stimulating commerce. The man who died of yellow fever in Philadelphia reaped no inward personal reward; but he benefited the human species, which was thereby discouraged from leaving the wholesome farm habitat. The 'economy of nature' thus emphasized a general benevolence and material well-being, rather than the happiness or consciousness of the individual.

The Jeffersonian view of nature was in this sense anthropocentric without being humanistic; 'the species' had virtually pushed man—the unique individual—out of sight. Although the phrase 'pursuit of Happiness' occurs in the Declaration of Independence, in Jeffersonian writing as a whole we find strikingly little discussion of happiness in the humanistic sense of the well-being of the individual, or even in the simple hedonistic sense of the individual's overbalance of pleasure. When the Jeffersonians spoke of 'happiness' it was rather in such phrases as 'the happiness of the species' or 'the happiness of mankind' which signified material prosperity and survival power. The very idea of an economy of nature thus became a way of implying the insignificance of individual man, of his sensations and his consciousness, in comparison with the health and prosperity of the biological group.

53

3. The Apotheosis of Nature

BY admiring the universe as the complete and perfected work of divine artifice, by idealizing process and activity as themselves the end of life, the Jeffersonian was insisting that the values by which the universe was to be assessed were somehow implicit in nature. All facts were endowed with an ambiguous quality: they became normative as well as descriptive. For the best artifice always makes the observer forget the difference between the thing as it is and the thing as it ought to be. By describing a work of art as successful, we mean that it is hard to separate description from judgment, the 'is' from the 'ought,' the facts about the work from the standards against which those facts are to be judged.

The very concept of the Creation, which was the starting point of Jeffersonian thought, was something more than a fact. It symbolized the philosopher's conviction that the processes of nature were universally good—having been conceived by a supernatural power. The original and thorough release of divine energy was evidenced in the plurality of worlds, in the orderly scale of beings, in the indestructibility and fixity of species, in the impossibility of spontaneous generation, in the perfect harmony and efficiency of the processes of nature—all of which seemed authentic visible facts. Thus the Jeffersonian objectified his sense of the primary value of workmanship and energy, and apotheosized the ability to organize a material chaos into a self-governing natural society.

The Creation was the only authentic Scripture, and what could not be found in that book was not likely to be from the Creator's hand. Yet despite the Jeffersonian's disavowals, this

54

book was very much of his own writing. If it was 'fact' against conviction, it was always the fact which had to give way: if astronomical space seemed vacant of life, it was only because human vision was limited; if men had not recently seen a mammoth, it must be the fault of men; if the worm in the horse's eye had no visible parent, it was only because the parent had not yet been discovered; if diseases seemed without remedy or without use in the economy of nature, it was only because man had not yet been clever enough to find the remedy or the use. The Jeffersonian belief in a Creator who required man to learn the nature and purpose of existence solely from the data of sensible experience, itself vividly symbolized the inadequacy of such data for such lessons. The Creator's virtues were surely being illustrated rather than derived from Jeffersonian science. All the while he expectantly gathered his fossils, studied his plants, and peered through his telescope, the main cosmic lessons of these investigations were already in his own breast.

The Jeffersonian's need to elevate craftsmanship into Godhead was at least partly explained by his own objective environment—by the challenge of an unexplored and beckoning wilderness. His workmanlike belief that whatever would function must be good—another way of stating his fusion of 'is' and 'ought'—held profound consequences for his philosophical method. For in the Jeffersonian cosmos, the 'is' and the 'ought' were so thoroughly and universally fused that the very accord of the two hardly seemed remarkable. The Jeffersonian had not only denied himself an opportunity to seek his answers elsewhere than in nature; we have seen that he had given nature itself an uncertain and ambiguous quality which had merged his question and his answer inextricably together.

It was this very ambiguity which admirably suited Jeffersonianism to be the organized forethought of successful men of action—as Pragmatism was to be their organized afterthought. Jeffersonian cosmology provided in advance reasons to believe that a program which would succeed, a philosophy which would facilitate material results, which would propagate life, health and productivity on this continent, must have the sanction of divine design. It thus expressed the prophetic phase of that frame of mind which in its retrospective phase was to produce Pragmatism as a self-conscious and articulate philosophical system. Since the hoped-for physical mastery of the continent was still in the distant future, the Jeffersonian temper was necessarily forward-looking. His pragmatism boasted its theological support; for the Jeffersonian still felt the need of divine assistance in assuring a prosperous America.

The Jeffersonian sense of tension with nature, of the opposition of man to his environment, had been at the root of his need to reverence the Supreme Workman as his God. It explains why the conception of nature as the work of art (expressing all the energy and frugality of the greatest Artist) was for the Jeffersonian even more vivid than any particular scientific fact. It explains why the mere process of nature, the intricacy and smoothness of its operation, seemed to make the search for ends outside of nature superfluous. For the shaping, subduing and organizing of the material environment, in which the Creator had been so impressively successful, seemed itself the overwhelming task of the Jeffersonians. These feelings which we have seen expressed in Jeffersonian theology pervaded their whole view of the universe—and especially of the resources of the New World. The America which gave the Jeffersonians the clue to the character of their God, was also to be the raw material of their conception of man.

CHAPTER TWO

The Equality of the Human Species

'So much is a man worth as he esteems himself.

RABELAIS

THE Jeffersonian science of man which we must now try to understand was something more than anthropology: it was at once an aspect of cosmology and theology and an avenue to ethics and political theory. 'The scene which that country presents to the eye of a spectator,' Paine observed in his *Rights of Man*, 'has something in it which generates and encourages great ideas. Nature appears to him in magnitude. The mighty objects he beholds, act upon his mind by enlarging it, and he partakes of the greatness he contemplates.' The early settlers on this continent were of diverse religions and from many European nations; but since they all sought to escape the persecutions of the Old World, they met in the New World as brothers. The large similarities among men so impressed the Jeffersonians that they actually focused their anthropology on a demonstration of human equality.

The Jeffersonian, unlike the traditional Christian, demonstration of equality did not rest on belief in a soul possessed by all men. It rested ultimately on the similarity of men's bodies. With the Christian the Jeffersonian shared an essentially forward-looking point of view. But while in Christianity the soul is not to receive its proper recognition until some future life, in Jeffersonianism man's destiny was somehow to be realized on this earth and right here in America. The human drama in America had only just begun; there was not yet enough data for retrospective judgment. The opportunity which man had never been given to play his destined role was now offered in the New World—not to fulfill an abstract moral purpose, but to realize the possibilities in the creation. As Paine remarked:

The wants which necessarily accompany the cultivation of a wilderness produced among them a state of society, which countries long harassed by the quarrels and intrigues of governments, had neglected to cherish. In such a situation man becomes what he ought. He sees his species, not with the inhuman idea of a natural enemy, but as kindred; and the example shews to the artificial world, that man must go back to Nature for information.[1]

The Jeffersonians had not yet reached the position of the Social Darwinians a century later for whom the equality of man was the equal right to compete in the market; but they were willing to prove equality by man's peculiar capacity as a species to deal with his environment. The main struggle in America was still not so much against one's fellow men, as among all natural creatures and all natural forces.

The equality of men was to be tested by their equipment for the American tasks of that generation, which would reveal at once human nature and human destiny. Those qualities which especially fitted man for such tasks were considered most characteristically human. As their God was the apotheosis of Jeffersonian aspirations for man, so their conception of mankind universalized what they knew of man in America and what they hoped for him. The Jeffersonians thus tied those beliefs about man for which they claimed eternal validity to the characteristic experience of their generation, and to those particular scientific ideas which were destined in the next century to undergo the most fundamental change. The very origin of mankind and its distinction from the lower animals seemed to them to show simultaneously the equality of men and the essentially pioneering nature of the species. The unity of the human species seemed itself to prove the special fitness of man for the kind of thing tried on this continent. The 'dispersion' of the human species from a single source—the 'fact' which lay at the core of the Jeffersonian history of mankind—seemed to dramatize the cosmopolitan and continent-conquering nature of man. The diversity among individual men and within human culture as a whole, which for the naturalistic heirs of the Jeffersonians was to make human equality seem harder to prove, for the Jeffersonians themselves actually seemed the fulfillment of the similarity of mankind. The present chapter will try to follow the circuitous path by which the Jeffersonians were drawn toward such conclusions.

1. The Adaptability of Man

IT is easy to forget that the assertion of human equality in the Declaration of Independence was not a direct statement of a moral principle, but rather of a scientific and historical fact from which the principle was supposed to follow: 'All men are created equal.' The truth which the authors declared self-evident was not simply that men ought to be treated as equals nor that they were *born* equal: they actually had been *created* equal. This form of the statement plainly declared that the equality of men was derived from the facts of the creation and therefore was to be confirmed by the evidence of natural history. That this way of stating human equality was not a verbal accident is evidenced in the less ambiguous words of Jefferson's earlier draft: 'We hold these truths to be sacred & undeniable; that all men are created equal & independent, *that from that equal creation* they derive rights inherent & inalienable . . .'[2]

The equality of humankind, then, was supposed to have been established by the details of the first creation of the earth's inhabitants, which we must now try to see through Jeffersonian eyes. 'The history of the creation of man,' remarked Rush, 'and of the relation of our species to each other by birth, which is recorded in the Old Testament, is the best refutation that can be given to the divine right of kings, and the strongest argument that can be used in favor of the original and natural equality of all mankind.' 'Mankind being originally equals in the order of creation,' Paine wrote in *Common Sense* in 1776, the equality could not be destroyed by some subsequent circumstance. Paine was confident that the error of those who purported to establish the inequality of man by appealing to history was that the historical events which they considered were not sufficiently ancient.

They stop in some of the intermediate stages of an hundred or a thousand years, and produce what was then done, as a rule for the present day. This is no authority . . . but if we proceed on, we shall at last come out right; we shall come to the time when man came from the hand of his Maker. . . . We are now got at . . . the origin of his rights. . . . It is authority against authority all the way, till we come to the divine origin of the rights of man at the creation.

Most important, as Jefferson said, was knowing the 'rank in the scale of beings' assigned to all men.[3]

Since each species was a single link in the Creator's chain, to show that all men were members of the same species would be the most striking possible confirmation of the indestructible equality of men. This belief that the question of human equality could be answered from the facts of anthropology was underlined by the Jeffersonian idiom. The key word in this connection is 'species.' Next to 'creature,' the commonest Jeffersonian synonym for man was 'the human species.' Where William Bradford and the Puritans had reckoned population in the number of 'souls,' Jefferson and his fellow philosophers counted 'individuals of the human species'—units in the biological creation. As there was an intended precision in the Puritan manner of speaking, so there was in the Jeffersonian. It was 'the human species' that was contrasted to other animals. Primitive man was in 'the infancy of our species.' The oriental suppression of women, in Paine's phrase, was the oppression of 'one half of the human species by the other'; in monarchies, kings were falsely 'distinguished like some new species'; aristocracies generally had 'a tendency to deteriorate the human species.' In European societies, Jefferson discerned a system 'where the dignity of man is lost in arbitrary distinctions, where the human species is classed into several stages of degradation.' So universal was the definition of man by his relation to the biological creation, that by ellipsis 'the species' was understood to mean man. Thus Barton praised physicians as 'benefactors of the species,' and called human history 'the history of the species.'

When the Jeffersonian observed the numerous species of lower animals, he was first struck by the rigid geographical boundaries within which each was confined and by the monotony and uniformity of their life. This suggested that the fullness of nature and the most plentiful population of the earth required that many species of them should have been created. As Barton observed:

Their latitudes are . . . circumscribed, and they have not the capacity of supporting a variety of climates. In the present constitution of those animals, and in the present temperature of the globe, the musk-deer of Thibet could not have travelled to the forests of Mexico or Peru, and the pacos could not have reached the mountains of Caucasus. It seems necessary, then, to have created different species of animals in different parts of the world. This observation applies still more forcibly to many species of vegetables . . . being destitute of loco-motive powers.[4]

But, he noted, man was different; his physical nature, his reason, his industry, and his capacity for communal life equipped him to live in any climate. If one truly believed in a purposeful universe, Barton urged, if the Creator was indeed the frugal artist which no one doubted Him to be, this salient fact about man must be a clue to the number of human species. 'As man is endowed with the capacity of inhabiting every climate; and as he is impelled by many imperious necessities to extend his empire over the whole world, it does not seem to have been at all necessary to have created, as many writers have imagined, a different species of men in every quarter of the world.' There would have been an incongruity, a lack of economy in nature, had there been more than one species of man.

The evidence of human physiology simply confirmed this reasoning. In his essay 'On the Causes of the Variety of Complexion and Figure in the Human Species,' delivered as the annual oration of the Philosophical Society in 1787, Dr. Samuel

63

Stanhope Smith, professor of moral philosophy and later president of Princeton, developed the argument along these lines:

The goodness of the Creator appears in forming the whole world for man, and not confining *him*, like the inferior animals, to a bounded range, beyond which he cannot pass either for the acquisition of science, or, for the enlargement of his habitation. And the divine wisdom is seen in mingling in the human frame such principles as always tend to counteract the hazards of a new situation. Fat protects the vitals from the too piercing influence of cold. But this covering being too warm for southern regions, nature hath enabled the constitution to throw it off by perspiration.

The human constitution is the most delicate of all animal systems: but it is also the most pliant, and capable of accommodating itself to the greatest variety of situations. The lower animals have no defence against the evils of a new climate but the force of nature. The arts of human ingenuity furnish a defence to man against the dangers that surround *him* in every region. Accordingly we see the same nation pass into all the climates of the earth—reside whole winters at the pole—plant colonies beneath the equator—pursue their commerce and establish their factories, in Africa, Asia, and America. They can equally live under a burning, and a frozen sky, and inhabit regions where those hardy animals could not exist.

Man therefore had a future, in a sense which was untrue of any other animal. The ways of living open to the lower species had already been revealed: each lower species had already been dispersed by the Creator over its whole natural habitat. There was no uncertainty about what the figure or the life history of the 'musk-deer of Thibet' would ever be. The lower animals had all been given their chance, had already in a sense exhausted their possibilities. But this was patently not true of man. For him, every uninhabited continent or even every barren waste held the promise of a new and still unrevealed potentiality in his figure and complexion, and in his ways of life.

Man's superior power to overcome the difficulties of any situation was what the eighteenth-century American was understandably eager to emphasize: the special fitness of his species to undertake the founding of new societies in strange continents.

It was no internal or invisible quality, no soul or rational faculty by which he distinguished himself from the lower creation. Even man's power of thought, as we shall see, was considered a mere adaptation of animal matter. 'Varians cultura, loco' was the phrase by which Linnaeus distinguished humankind from its nearest relative, the orang-outang: [5] and the Jeffersonian made much of this idea. The determining role of environment (later important in Darwinian evolutionary thought as a whole) was surely prominent in Jeffersonian thought—but only about man. As man alone was cosmopolitan, so he alone had the capacity to be a pioneer. In the primordial texture of man was discovered a unique and inexhaustible capacity for novelty and change.

Since man was destined to populate the whole globe, it was inconceivable that the Creator would have doomed each generation to start anew adapting itself to its habitat. This would have been an obvious waste of natural energy. The axioms from which he had begun thus induced the Jeffersonian to assume that the effects of the human adaptation which commenced at the first dispersion of mankind must have accumulated from generation to generation, until there had emerged the varieties of mankind found in the eighteenth century—each admirably suited to the continent on which it was found.

Lest we exaggerate the Jeffersonian's readiness to ignore inconvenient facts, we must recall that he had little knowledge which would have made such an explanation seem improbable. The problem of the relative roles of heredity and environment in the emergence of new biologic types, which has seemed so important since Charles Darwin, had not yet arisen for the Jeffersonian. The science of 'genetics' was still unknown; the very word was not to be invented until a century later. His cosmogony, by disposing of the problem of the origin of species, had also forestalled the most puzzling problems of genetics. Since it was only the species-characteristics which were part of the Creator's original design, any other characteristics of a creature might be modified without upsetting His scheme. All this made it easier to extract from anthropology the desired lesson—the descent of all men from parents of a single species.

Jefferson himself, despite his profound interest in human variations, was not much troubled by the question of the precise
scope of environmentally induced variations as factors in heredity. Of course, he insisted that all such variations were confined
within the species-categories of the original creation. But beyond the vague notion that 'moral and physical qualities of
man, whether good or evil, are transmissible in a certain degree
from father to son,' Jefferson had no clear conception of the
operation of heredity.[6]

Even Dr. Samuel Stanhope Smith's essay, probably the most
ambitious American inquiry of the period into physical anthropology, did not linger over the problem. Dr. Smith's description
of how environmentally induced variations were incorporated
into the process of heredity was hardly more than an elaboration
of his assumptions:

Every permanent and characteristical variety in human nature, is
effected by slow and almost imperceptible gradations. Great and
sudden changes are too violent for the delicate constitution of man,
and always tend to destroy the system. But changes that become incorporated, and that form the character of a climate or a nation,
are progressively carried on through several generations, till the
causes that produce them have attained their utmost operation. In
this way, the minutest causes, acting constantly, and long continued,
will necessarily create great and conspicuous differences among
mankind.

The pliant nature of man is susceptible of change from the
minutest causes, and these changes, habitually repeated, create at
length, conspicuous distinctions. The effect proceeds increasing
from one generation to another, till it arrives at that point where
the constitution can yield no farther to the power of the operating
cause. Here it assumes a permanent form and becomes the character
of the climate or the nation.

To those superficial observers who asked why, if there was
only one human species, men were not all born with the same
figure and complexion, Dr. Smith answered that within any
particular *family*, figure, stature, complexion, features, diseases
and even powers of the mind became hereditary; therefore
it could not be surprising that such differences should become

hereditary within the *varieties* of the human species. The Tartars had high shoulders and short necks; this, Dr. Smith said, was because the extreme cold of bitter winters had prompted the early inhabitants to raise their shoulders as if to protect their necks and to preserve the warmth of the blood that flowed to the head; such a posture became habitual and was transmitted to their descendants. The straight hair of the American Indian and the infrequency of curly hair among the Anglo-Americans were both explained by the 'relaxing' influence of the climate and the unusual humidity of uncultivated regions. The peculiar hair, features and expression of the Negro were all the product of a warm climate and a primitive society. According to Dr. Smith, this fact was confirmed by the differences, not only in manners, but in figure and complexion, between the field slaves who still lived like their ancestors, and the domestic slaves who seemed already to be losing their African peculiarities. The coarse features of the Negro were also to be found among those white men who were exposed to the weather during long hours of hard labor; and the faces of the children of workingmen bore the hereditary mark of their parents' condition.

If we suppose several species of man to have been created, Dr. Smith asked, how could anyone determine their number? Were any of them lost? And if not, how were the different species now to be distinguished? He posed the alternative of a single human species or a confusion in the Creator's design:

Or were the species of man made capable of being blended together, contrary to the nature of other animals, so that they should never be discriminated, so rendering the end unnecessary for which they were supposed to be created? If we have reason, from the varieties that exist in the same family, or in the same nation, to conclude that the Danes, the French, the Turks, and people even more remote are of one species, have we not the same reason to conclude that the nations beyond them, and who do not differ from the last by more conspicuous distinctions, than the last differ from the first, are also of the same species. By pursuing this progression we shall find but one species from the equator to the pole.

The very impossibility of enumerating the human species thus became an argument for the unity of mankind: there could not have been indefinitely numerous species of man unless the universe had lacked order.

2. The Dispersion of the Human Species

IF the Jeffersonian was to demonstrate the unity of the human species, it was incumbent on him—by the canons of his own anthropology—to prove somehow that all men were descended from a single pair of original parents. His proof, constructed from the materials of natural history, was surely devious. We cannot understand it, moreover, unless we are willing to follow the Jeffersonian into several curious bypaths of eighteenth-century biology. If we succeed in following him, we will learn much about his whole approach to the study of man and eventually about the context in which he examined the problems of society.

Lacking details of the dispersion of mankind and the adaptation of its branches to different continents, the Jeffersonian had to find other evidence of a single cradle of mankind. The believers in the inequality of man and in its corollary, the multiplicity of the human species, had of course avoided this historical task. They simply assumed that the Creator had in the beginning made several unequal species of man, each with different physical and social characteristics. Captain Bernard Romans, for example, in his *Concise Natural History of East and West Florida*, published in New York in 1775, asserted 'that God created an original man and woman in this part of the globe, of different species from any in the other parts.' It is significant that these opponents of human equality supported their argument by denying the peculiarly cosmopolitan, adaptive and pioneering quality of man. They argued that because among plants and lower animals different species had been created for the different continents, the symmetry of nature required that there should similarly have been created several species of man.

The fact of such a 'separate creation' of plants and lower animals was one the Jeffersonian could not deny. From early times, explorers had found in America many species which seemed to occur nowhere else in the world. Naturalists (except of course proponents of spontaneous generation) were substantially agreed that all species, both those common to several continents and those peculiar to a single continent, could have come into being only at the first creation of the world. They generally assumed that where the same kind of animal was now found both in America and in Europe, the American representative was a descendant of an ancient immigrant from Europe. And they exercised their ingenuity in explaining under what circumstances and subject to what limitations these species had spread. In the mid-eighteenth century, Catesby, the English traveler on whose work Jefferson and his associates freely drew, had portrayed numerous peculiarly American species in the color plates of his magnificent *Natural History of Carolina*. And he explained:

In *America* are very few *European* land birds; but of the water kinds there are many, if not most of those found in *Europe*, besides the great variety of species peculiar to those parts of the World. Admitting the World to have been universally replenished with all animals from *Noah's* ark after the general deluge, and that those *European* Birds which are in *America*, found their way thither at first from the Old World; the cause of disparity in number of the land and water kinds, will evidently appear, by considering their different structure, and manner of feeding, which enables the water fowl to perform a long voyage with more facility than those of the land.[7]

69

Buffon had developed the theory, which according to Jefferson had 'thrown such a blaze of light on the field of natural history,' that only those animals were found on both continents which were able to bear the cold of those regions where Europe and America were thought to be joined. And Jefferson in his *Notes on Virginia* actually employed Buffon's theory to support his own much-disputed assertion that the honeybee (which could not endure the Canadian winter, and hence could not have migrated to this continent in the usual manner across the supposed northern lands) must have been imported by European settlers. Buffon's theory, like Catesby's, presupposed the dispersion from a common original source of all species now found on more than one continent; it too rested on the assumption that all animals of the same species, whether found now in America or in Europe, were descended from the same original parents.

Such theories as these explained why certain species occurred on several continents, but still did not account for the appearance in America of what Catesby called 'species peculiar to those parts of the world.' This was the dangerous fact because it seemed to imply the possibility of a peculiarly American species of man and thereby might imperil the biological foundation of Jeffersonian equality. If all species had been created in the Garden of Eden, how explain the fact that some now seemed peculiar to the American continent? Jefferson himself noted in 1789 that there was not a single species of terrestrial bird, and he doubted that there was a single species of quadruped, common to Europe and America. How account for the presence here of creatures like the wild turkey, the raccoon, the opossum, and others unknown elsewhere in the world? We have already seen that two of the more obvious explanations, because they conflicted with the axioms of Jeffersonian science, were excluded from the very outset. The Jeffersonian would not believe that the American species could have sprung up spontaneously on this continent at some time since the Creation; as Priestley had noted, even a single instance of spontaneous generation would have denied the original perfection of nature.

And it could not be conjectured that these American species might have developed in the course of time through accident and the influence of environment; for the transformation of old species into new was excluded by the fixity of the original units.

Perhaps, the Jeffersonian said, all species which in the eighteenth century were found only in America had come long ago from Europe or Asia, and had now simply ceased to inhabit the other continents. Or, alternatively, in the very beginning when the world and all its inhabitants were made, the Creator might have designed certain plants and animals especially for America. Either of these conjectures was perfectly consistent with the fixity of species and the production of the universe by a primordial creative act. But the Jeffersonian philosophers, without exception, were cautious that facts should not lead them beyond these possibilities. Their controversy over the history of American species became a dispute between those who believed in a 'single creation' in the Biblical cradle (but had difficulty in explaining the dispersion of species), and those who appealed to recent facts as evidence of an original 'separate creation' of certain species for the American habitat. The latter hypothesis, perhaps because it demanded less support from ancient history, was more generally favored.

Probably the most eminent and convincing American exponent of this doctrine of 'separate creation' was Benjamin Smith Barton, who developed the argument in his widely read *New Views of the Origin of the Tribes and Nations of America*. The presence in America of fourteen species of the *Caprimulgus Europaeus* (Night-Hawk) which were not seen in Europe, he found 'an interesting fact, which does not favour the opinion of those writers who have imagined, that all animals and all vegetables were originally created in the old world, from whence they have spread over every portion of the earth: an opinion which ought never to have been advanced by philosophers; and which it is not likely will prevail among those naturalists who observe with attention, and deliver their sentiments without reserve or timidity.' Barton's knowledge of a strange jumping rodent which he found to be peculiarly American, together

71

with a great deal of other information, confirmed his belief 'that with respect to *many* of the living existences, there has been a separate creation in the old and in the new world.' Numerous observers, according to Barton, had made the mistake of identifying American with European animals simply because of superficial resemblances. He admitted, of course, that several species of quadrupeds had come (or had been transported) to America from Asia or from Europe—just as some American species had migrated to those continents. But many animals had never been found outside of America and these he considered exclusively American. Upon any other supposition than that of a separate creation, Barton thought it impossible to explain the presence here of such creatures as the raccoon, the opossum, the woodchuck, the alpaca and the bison.[8]

To round out his demonstration of the separate creation of lower animals, the Jeffersonian had to face one further 'fact' urged by the naturalists of his day. Explorers had long referred to America, with pregnant ambiguity, as 'The New Continent'; in the eighteenth century some European naturalists considered the wildness of the country and the savagery of the natives evidence that the continent itself was in some sense 'newer' than populous and civilized Europe. If conceivably the American continent had not come into being until some time after the early age recorded in the Book of Genesis, the Jeffersonian of course would have had to dismiss his own doctrine of separate creation as absurd. For by hypothesis, all creation of species must have taken place at that remote period. Jefferson himself believed it axiomatic that all the large outlines of the earth, including continents and mountains, had been molded simultaneously in the beginning. Others of his circle revealed both their unwillingness to rest on cosmology alone, and their faith that theology would stand the severest test of natural history, when they adduced facts to confirm the antiquity of the American continent. The vast deposits of silt at the mouth of the Mississippi, one correspondent of the Philosophical Society remarked, must have required thousands of years to accumulate. This seemed conclusive against 'visionary philosophers, who have been pleased to amuse themselves with the pretended infantile state of our continent, compared to their transatlantic world; but, on the contrary, we must grant to it an incalculable antiquity.' Barton himself saw the numerousness of the plant and animal populations, and the great size of some individual plants and animals as irrefutable proof of the same fact. 'In this vast portion of the world, we discover the influence of a hand which moulded matter into forms at periods extremely remote: we have good reasons to believe as remote as in any other parts of the world. The physical infancy of America is one of the many dreams of the slumbering philosophers of our times.' [9]

It may at first seem surprising that the American philosopher should have been willing to admit a separate creation of any animals on this continent. For if unique species of plants and animals had been created for America, then why not of man too? Might not the Indian have been created for this continent, the Negro for Africa—and what then of the unity of the human species? This, of course, was the implication which antiequalitarians like Captain Romans had drawn. But the course of the Jeffersonian argument actually confirmed that concept of the uniqueness of man which we have already described. His belief that man was a peculiarly cosmopolitan species, destined for adaptation, pioneering and conquest on new continents, predisposed the Jeffersonian to consider the existence of endemic species of plants and lower animals irrelevant to the number of *human* species. He could squarely face the fact that the Creator had made some lower species expressly for America, and feel that this in no wise increased the probability of such a separate creation of man. Jefferson himself, who showed great interest in the peculiarly American species of the lower creation, could not conceive the possibility of a 'separate creation' of man on this continent. Such proposals by Captain Romans and others seemed to him patently absurd. 'Romans, indeed, takes a higher stand, and supposes a separate creation,' he wrote to John Adams (May 27, 1813). 'On the same unscriptural ground, he had but to mount one step higher, to suppose no

73

creation at all, but that all things have existed without beginning in time, as they now exist, and may forever exist, producing and reproducing in a circle, without end.'

The Jeffersonian never considered the possibility that the Creator had in the beginning placed representatives of the single human species simultaneously on all the continents. Since a species consisted by definition of the descendants of a single original pair, if men were all of one species, they must of course have originated in the same habitat. Moreover, if the Creator had in the beginning comfortably established each branch of the human family in its respective continental habitat, He would by hypothesis have denied the species the need and the opportunity to advance to new continents, and hence have left unproven man's uniquely adaptive character. To the Jeffersonian, the cosmopolitanism of the human species signalized a quality especially relevant to man's task in America—namely, his ability to migrate successfully to new environments, and to overcome their varied obstacles.

As the Diaspora or Exile—an event of social history—has dominated Jewish thought, so the dispersion of the whole human species from a single source—considered as an event in natural history—set the tone of Jeffersonian anthropology. While Jewish thought has seen dispersion as exile from an ancestral home, the Jeffersonian saw dispersion as immigration—the act by which the only cosmopolitan and pioneering species had found its proper home on every continent of the earth. Here he found his clue at the same time to the equality of man and to man's special destiny for the kind of work undertaken in America.

For antiequalitarians like John Adams, who were impressed by present disparities among men, all speculations on the source of the primeval migrations of men seemed purely academic:

Whether serpents' teeth were sown here and sprung up men; whether men and women dropped from the clouds upon this Atlantic island; whether the Almighty created them here, or whether they emigrated from Europe, are questions of no moment to the present or future happiness of man. Neither agriculture, commerce, manufactures, fisheries, science, literature, taste, religion, morals, nor any other good will be promoted, or any evil averted, by any discoveries that can be made in answer to these questions.

Voltaire, too, impatiently dismissed the attempt of equalitarian visionaries to confirm their visions by the hazy facts of primitive history. 'If it should be asked,' he said, 'from whence came the Americans, it should be asked from whence came the inhabitants of the Terra Australis; and it has been already answered, that the same providence which placed man in Norway, planted some also in America and under the antarctic circle, in the same manner as it planted trees and made grass to grow there. . . . It is no more surprising to find men in America, than it is to find flies there.' [10]

But the Jeffersonian betrayed no doubt that there had been a single original source for all mankind, from which men had anciently emigrated. Its precise location, however, seemed a matter over which intelligent men might differ. Barton, for example, in his *New Views of the Origin of the Tribes and Nations of America*, sharply contrasted the two classes of anthropologists: first, those superficial students who thought the American Indians were strictly speaking the aborigines of the soil, and not emigrants from other parts of the world; and second, the men of great learning and wisdom, including the clergy, and those like Joseph Acosta, Edward Brerewood, John de Laet, Hugo Grotius, George de Hornn and many others, who asserted that the American Indians were anciently derived from another continent. The men of this latter group understandably disagreed among themselves as to the residence of the parents of the species (some placing it in Asia, while others found it in Europe, in Africa, or in the unknown Atlantis). What according to Barton distinguished them from the other school was not where they had discovered the cradle of mankind, but that they all refused to doubt that there had been such a cradle.

Jefferson himself categorically denied the separate creation of the American Indians, but he was too cautious to swallow any of the simplistic theories of Indian origin. He could not accept

Moreton's deduction of the American Indians from the fugitive Trojans, Adair's derivation from the Hebrews, Reinold Foster's theory of their descent from the soldiers sent by Kouli Khan to conquer Japan, nor Brerewood's doctrine of their Tartar ancestry. While finding all these much less absurd than Romans' doctrine of separate creation, Jefferson was forced finally to admit that 'the question of Indian origin, like many others, pushed to a certain height must receive the same answer, "Ignoro." ' Barton, who himself insisted on the common ancient origin of mankind, was hardly less cautious than Jefferson. Men had immigrated to America, he said, at several different periods, for numerous reasons and from more than one source.

Even the warmest favourer of the doctrine of *separate creations* [of man] cannot but view the posterity of the *Greenlanders* in the wretched inhabitants of LABRADOR: he cannot but confess the amazing similitude of the *Iroquois* to some of the nations inhabiting the *north-east* parts of ASIA. Necessity sometimes, but, I believe, much more frequently the love of fame, and the love of money, have led mankind to migrate from those regions in which they have reposed for centuries. There can be little doubt that one of these motives, or possibly a combination of the three, as well as the accidents attending navigation, were the causes to which AMERICA owes her first inhabitants. We every day, at least see new reasons to suppose, that the new has been peopled from the old world.[11]

Yet the Jeffersonian lacked the capacity, the interest and the materials to reconstruct any detailed account of the dispersion of mankind. He had no flair for history. He was without the techniques of modern geology and archaeology. At the same time, his theology required that ethics be founded on natural facts. He therefore sought to confirm his equalitarianism without depending on the vagaries of ancient history.

He grasped any clues—however meager or ambiguous—in man's present social equipment which might show a trace of the ancient community of mankind. Any such fact seemed to increase the probability of the descent of all men from the same parents. For example, if it could be shown that the surviving languages (especially those remotest from the hypothetical ancient cradle of mankind) all stemmed from some common ancient source, the common origin of mankind would be corroborated. This helps explain the great interest in linguistics and etymology among Jeffersonian philosophers. Such implications of linguistics were clearly if somewhat extravagantly remarked by Barton in his 'Hints on the Etymology of certain English Words':

The books of Moses inform us, that mankind were created in Asia. Ever since I have busied myself, and I may add, rendered myself happy, with inquiries into the languages of the Americans, I have ceased to entertain any doubts of the accuracy of the scripture story, so far as regards the Asiatic origin of men, and their dispersion from a common centre. These two great facts, which constitute corner-stones in the history of the species, are supported by the more modern history of nations; and I am persuaded will bear the strictest scrutiny of every research of humanity. The original of nations may, in many instances, be determined solely by an attention to the languages of mankind. Had the books of Moses perished; had no memorials concerning them escaped the numerous revolutions of our globe; had no traditions concerning the origin of the species been transmitted to us, the researches of philosophers, through the medium of language (such is the pure certainty of science!) would have conducted them to the great historical truth, that Asia has been the cradle of the world.[12]

The American philosopher, toward the end of the eighteenth century, was admirably situated for such linguistic studies. Close at hand were the Indians whose languages were still to be recorded; and because they were the people geographically most remote from the Biblical cradle of mankind, their language was thought by some to provide the ultimate test of the descent of all modern languages from a common ancient origin. Sir William Jones' pioneer studies in Sanskrit, Arabic and Chinese, together with his *Grammar of the Persian Language* published in 1771, had just now made available to Western scholars new raw materials for a scientific answer to the fundamental linguistic question. The Philosophical Society, not unaware of the richness of this material, in 1799 listed among the principal duties of its permanent committee the inquiry into the languages of the American Indian. The discovery of such materials helped bring Barton by 1803 to the belief that 'the most finished *Anthropologia*' would be constructed to a considerable extent upon the affinities of languages. With his customary industry, Barton compared the languages of American Indians with the ancient languages of the Orient. Some of his observations, such as the similarity of the modern American word 'booze' (spelled 'bouse' in Barton's day) to the 'Asiatic word Boo, water,' were of purely antiquarian interest. But others concerned more common and significant words:

> Democratical. I think it has escaped the notice of the English Dictionary-makers, that *Demo* is the name for men, or people (*homines, populus*) in the language of the old Persians. I find a great number of English, French, and American (Indian) words in this old language, which Sir William Jones has shown to be Sanscrit. Philosophers will ultimately repose in the belief, that Asia 'has been the principal foundery of the human kind'; and Iràn, or Persia, will be considered as one of the cradles from which the species took their departure, to people the various regions of the earth.[13]

These resemblances, as Barton admitted, did not of themselves prove conclusively that men were all members of the same species; but they did suggest that the American Indian and the Persian had once lived in the same community. This surely increased the probability that they—and if they, probably all men—were descended from the same primeval parents.

Studies by other members of the Philosophical Society confirmed Barton's thesis. In a paper 'On the Language of Signs among certain North American Indians,' William Dunbar found a hint of common origin in the similarities of American Indian sign languages to the Chinese written language. Dr. Samuel Stanhope Smith, whose works we have already met, explained how diverse languages might have grown up after the Flood, as men were dispersed into different tribes living under different conditions. The Reverend Nicholas Collin concluded from his 'Philological View of some very Ancient Words in several Languages,' that languages of North America were more allied with the Asiatic and European than was generally known. When Barton himself came upon 'some striking affinities between the languages of the Yolofs (one of the blackest nations of Africa) and certain American tribes,' he could not restrain his enthusiasm:

What a field for investigation does this last mentioned circumstance open! Whilst philosophers are busied in investigating the influence of climate and food, and other physical agents, in varying the figure and complexion of mankind, they should not neglect inquiries into the resemblances of all languages. The farther we push our researches of this kind, the more we discover the proofs, if not of the absolute derivation of all mankind from one pair, at least of the ancient intercourse of all the nations of the earth.[14]

From the linguistic evidence—substantiated by Indian traditions and by the greater populousness of western North America when the first Europeans arrived here—Barton was inclined to believe that the common ancient source had been in Asia. His theory surely did not lack confusion, but whatever difficulties he encountered in locating the place of human origin did not shake his confidence in the essential fact.

It was a desire to confirm the common origin of men that drew Jefferson's own energies into linguistic studies. In his *Notes on Virginia*, he distinguished the different original stocks of Indians on the basis of their languages; he established the connection of American Indians with the eastern inhabitants of Asia; and he catalogued the Indian tribes for the benefit of future scholars. The strikingly large number of radical tongues found on this continent had led him to the novel conjecture that the American Indians might be older than the Asiatic peoples and that the original home of man might therefore have been in America. Throughout his life he studied Indian languages, always with an eye to the light they might throw on the source of mankind. It is true that he never reached an answer which satisfied him in detail. He always professed that his mind was open to any relevant facts. Yet while he eagerly examined evidence which might tell him where the common cradle of mankind had been, he never seriously questioned that such a cradle must have existed. His plan of study, formed early in life, to which he faithfully adhered, disclosed this framework of his inquiry: he sought to build up 'a vocabulary of such objects as, being present everywhere, would probably have a name in every language'; and he instructed his correspondents that it was not the current language, 'but it is their original languages I wish to obtain.' Even in the White House he found time to pursue his interest. He eagerly sought a copy of Pallas' learned volume, *Vocabulaires comparés des langues de toute la terre*. And in 1806, he declared that within a year or two he would give the public the fruits of his research. Unluckily, Jefferson's work was never to be published, for by an 'irreparable misfortune' (described at length in a letter to Barton), his Indian vocabularies, the fruit of thirty years' laborious collecting, were mysteriously stolen in 1809 from a chest being moved with the rest of his belongings from Washington to Monticello.[15]

It is not hard to understand why belief in a single original language should have been slow in dying—especially in this country. 'Some scalping heroes of America,' the Reverend Collin conjectured in 1798 from his study of words, 'may be kinsmen of Alexander, Caesar, and the proudest conquerors of Europe; as they probably are of Tamerlan and Ogus Chan.' Noah Webster, writing on the 'Origin of Language' in the introduction to his *American Dictionary* in 1828, still held that 'all languages have sprung from one source,' namely, the 'vocal sounds or words . . . used in . . . communications between God and the progenitors of the human race.' The vitality of this hypothetical language of Adam was closely tied to faith in human equality, and to the expectation that this faith would be confirmed by science.

3. Varieties of Mankind: the Indian and the Negro

THE Jeffersonian of course noticed among men, as among other representatives of any fixed biological type, the existence of varieties. By 'varieties' he meant something quite definite: variations not created in the beginning as a part of the original scheme of creation, but which had come into being more recently from environmental causes. This meaning of 'variety,' still in use when the first edition of the *American Dictionary* appeared in 1828, was succinctly stated by Noah Webster under the word *Species:*

> 1. In *zoology*, a collection of organized beings derived from one common parentage by natural generation, characterized by one peculiar form, liable to vary from the influence of circumstances only within certain narrow limits. These accidental and limited variations are *varieties*. Different races from the same parents are called *varieties*.

This was precisely the sense in which Jefferson himself used the words. In his *Notes on Virginia*, for example, he explained that there were 'varieties in the race of man, distinguished by their powers both of body and mind,' just as in the case of other animals. 'It is not against experience,' he added, 'to suppose that different species of the same genus, or varieties of the same species, may possess different qualifications. Will not a lover of natural history then, one who views the gradations in all the races of animals with the eye of philosophy, excuse

81

an effort to keep those in the department of man as distinct as nature has formed them?' Since these different 'varieties' were by definition nothing but accidental variations of a single primeval type, the American philosopher was prepared against allowing the existence of 'varieties' of man in any way to impugn the unity of the human species.

In this he was supported by the best authority. For his usage was plainly authorized by Linnaeus' *Systema Naturae* which had provided the vocabulary for Jeffersonian natural history. Opening the first volume of the *Systema Naturae*, we find beneath the Order of Primates the *Genus Homo* which is divided into two species: *homo* (*sapiens*) *diurnus* which includes all humankind; and *homo* (*troglodytes*) *nocturnus*, illustrated by the orang-outang (*homo sylvestris Orang Outang*). Within the human species Linnaeus distinguished several varieties: *Ferus, Americanus, Europaeus, Asiaticus, Afer,* and *Monstrosus*. Each of these (except 'Monstrosus' which was a kind of sport of nature) was designated by the environment in which it had developed. The 'Ferus' was a man who had become wild or savage by growing up alone in the wilderness; the others were distinguished by the continents which had brought them into being.

The large numbers of Indians and Negroes made this continent a nearly perfect laboratory of anthropology and enabled the Jeffersonian to scrutinize at least three (*Homo sapiens Americanus, Homo sapiens Europaeus,* and *Homo sapiens Afer*) of the six principal 'varieties' of the human species. Moreover, the axiomatic symmetry of the cosmos made it superfluous to examine the causes of every variation among men. The Jeffersonian was therefore ready to assume that if the peculiarities of the red man (probably a migrant from Asia) and of the black man (surely a migrant from Africa) which distinguished them both from the white man of Europe, could be shown to have arisen recently and through the influence of environment— if there was no difference of species among these—then evidence pertaining to unexamined varieties would not be likely to disprove the unity of mankind. The American philosopher built his generalizations on personal experience—in Jefferson's phrase, 'on what I have seen of man, white, red, and black.' Rush's extensive studies of the Indian were based on contemporary observations. It is hard to believe that Benjamin Smith Barton and his uncle, David Rittenhouse, had not actually encountered Indians on their surveying expedition to western Pennsylvania. Numerous articles in the *Transactions* of the Philosophical Society were illustrated by personal anecdotes of Indian manners and customs. John Adams recollected clearly the 'forms and figures' of the Indians who frequented his father's house in Massachusetts. Such observations were especially valuable because in western Europe, even at the time of the Declaration of Independence, reliable information about the physique, the nature and the habits of non-European races was extremely scarce. Two centuries earlier, Shakespeare had been attracted by tales of anthropophagi whose heads grew beneath their shoulders; in the eighteenth century, travel books told the even more marvelous tales of beautiful virgins who grew on trees.

When Jefferson undertook his study of the American Indian, he made it his first task to clear away the inventions of fanciful writers. He revealed a piquant satisfaction in showing how his predecessors (and particularly the opponents of human equality) had distorted the facts of anthropology. Most European tales about the Indian, he said, were no more true than Aesop's fables—and, he implied, no less guided by the preconceptions of their authors. From his ample first-hand experience he refuted each of the allegedly innate deficiencies of the Indian. In the Appendix to his *Notes on Virginia*, he disproved one by one the items on Buffon's list:

Monsieur Buffon has indeed given an afflicting picture of human nature in his description of the man of America. But sure I am there never was a picture more unlike the original. He grants indeed that his stature is the same as that of the man of Europe. He might have admitted, that the Iroquois were larger, and the Lenopi, or Delawares, taller than people in Europe generally are. But he says their organs of generation are smaller and weaker than those of Europeans. Is this a fact? I believe not; at least it is an observation I never heard before.—'They have no beard.' Had he known the pains and trouble it costs the men to pluck out by the roots the hair that grows on their faces, he would have seen that nature had not been deficient in that respect. Every nation has its customs. I have seen an Indian beau, with a looking-glass in his hand, examining his face for hours together, and plucking out by the roots every hair he could discover, with a kind of tweezer made of a piece of fine brass wire, that had been twisted round a stick, and which he used with great dexterity.—'They have no ardor for their females.' It is true they do not indulge those excesses, nor discover that fondness which is customary in Europe; but this is not owing to a defect in nature but to manners. Their soul is wholly bent upon war.

European philosophers said that because the Indian had little sexual passion, he felt less family affection, was less philanthropic than the white man, and ought for that reason to be distinguished as an inferior species. To support this, their main evidence was the alleged lack of the body hair which the European associated with strong sexual instincts. But even if their facts had been correct, Jefferson objected, their conclusion was unwarranted: Negroes, for example, actually had less hair than white men, and yet were notoriously more ardent. If philosophers would only gather enough facts, would weigh them impartially, and would take full account of the influence of environment, Jefferson believed that they would probably find the American Indian to be 'formed in mind as well as in body, on the same module with "Homo sapiens Europaeus."' To avoid any vagueness about his intention to speak in precise biological terms, he referred his reader to the 'Definition of a Man' in Linnaeus' *Systema Naturae*.[16]

After all the fanciful travelers' tales were discarded there still remained, as Jefferson admitted, a mass of obvious distinctions between the Indian and the white man. The more remarkable differences were in color, morals and social development. If the Jeffersonian belief in equality was to withstand the test of

84

facts, these distinctions would have to be accounted for without jeopardizing the axiom of a single human species.

Most Jeffersonian philosophers, including Jefferson himself, were not much troubled by the characteristic color of the Indian. They somehow found the Indian's copper skin so much like that of the white man as to suggest nothing more than a difference of 'variety.' When Rush did discuss the Indian's color he showed no hesitation in saying that it had been produced by environment.[17] Dr. Samuel Stanhope Smith, as we have seen, argued that anyone who denied the identity of human origin because one nation was red and another black, must on the same principle have denied to persons of different complexion an identity of family.

Yet the difference of complexion between white man and red man was nothing compared with the difference between their stages of civilization. Opponents of human equality simply asserted that the Indian had been created a species inferior to the European in intellectual and social endowments; but the equalitarian was committed to a more elaborate explanation. There was, for example, the sociological account of Dr. Samuel Stanhope Smith. After the Deluge, he observed, men found themselves in an immense wilderness where beasts multiplied faster than the human race. Although agriculture had been the employment of Noah and his immediate descendants (from whom the civilized states traced an uninterrupted descent), this was too laborious a mode of subsistence to satisfy all men. The less industrious, seeing the wilderness filled with beasts, readily abandoned the toils of clearing and cultivating the ground and sought an easier and more adventurous living from the chase. Hunting soon dispersed them over extensive regions; and single families, or collections of a few families, became independent tribes. Their remoteness from one another and their mode of procuring subsistence rendered them savage and made progress impossible.

While most of the Jeffersonians found the general features of this account acceptable, they were more reluctant than the pious Dr. Smith to adopt the Biblical history of the Deluge with all its consequences. Again, instead of attempting to reconstruct the details of ancient history, they preferred to interpret recent facts so as to disprove the strictures on the contemporary Indian. Barton, for example, easily refuted the charge that the Indians' unfriendliness to Christianity was evidence of their intellectual inferiority; the true explanation, he said, was the natural reluctance of rude nations to forsake the religions of their ancestors, and the improper means of persuasion used by Jesuit missionaries. Rush contradicted those who treated the phlegmatic character and unintelligent countenance of the Indian as evidence of his innate inferiority. Instead he found 'their vacant countenances, and their long disgusting taciturnity' to be the effects of a want of action in their brains, due to a deficiency of ideas, which was in turn caused by a lack of external stimuli. 'The weakness of the intellects in certain savage and barbarous nations . . . is as much the effect of the want of physical influence upon their minds, as a disagreeable colour and figure are of its action upon their bodies.' The savage environment, contrary to the accounts of Rousseau and others, was unfavorable to the development of lively minds and warm affections; for the stimuli of civilization and religion were universally needed. When one added unhealthy local customs and a numbing climate to the general deficiency of stimuli, no further explanation could be required for the Indian's peculiarities. Even the Indian's special susceptibility to certain diseases, which Rush did not fail to remark, was no evidence of a predisposing native weakness but simply registered the effect of circumstance. Thus Rush gladly disposed of 'the objection which has been urged against the Mosaic account of the whole human race being descended from a single pair.' [18]

Since the Jeffersonian had never pretended to distinguish the kind of acquired characteristics which could from those which could not become incorporated in the hereditary texture of a race, he was never troubled by the need to explain whether particular eighteenth-century peculiarities of the Indian or anyone else should be included within the inheritable class. Where facts were available he marshaled them to defend the Indian, but in difficult cases he relied on the presumption that any apparent inferiority of the Indian could eventually be explained by environmental and historical facts which were still hidden from the anthropologist. Be careful, he urged, not to argue from the qualities of the eighteenth-century Indian to the qualities of those men who first left the human cradle to settle on the American continent. By drawing hasty conclusions, you may be degrading a whole race from its intended equal rank with other human races. You may be overlooking environmental explanations which rest on facts which you do not know and may never know. All the while of course he had cast his own faith in human equality in the form of a presumption of fact which he dared his opponent to rebut by the scanty available evidence.

According to Jefferson, great allowance (how much was never clear) had to be made for those circumstances of the Indians' situation which called for a display of particular talents. In the Indian the faculties employed in tracking down an enemy or a wild beast were extraordinarily well developed; and this suggested that the lesser development in him of talents which he had no occasion to exercise was not evidence of native inferiority. From such facts, recounted in his *Notes on Virginia*, Jefferson had no hesitation in asserting the Indian in body and mind equal to the white man.[19] Where Indians had been reduced to physical and moral abjection it was always because of external circumstances. Examples of cowardice could be explained as the effect of subjugation and ill treatment. On the other hand, the virtues of the Indian, while characterized by the condition of his society, were by no means inconsiderable: he showed wisdom in council, and bravery and address in war. Logan's dying speech was a sufficient sample; and Jefferson's praise of the unlucky Mingo Chief was so effective that for many years American school boys were to memorize phrases of Indian eloquence.

The American philosopher was pleased, though hardly surprised, when he found buried in the American earth relics of an ancient Indian civilization of a high order. While not an

87

antiquarian by temperament, he showed avid interest in objects which could give solid support to his equalitarian argument. The Philosophical Society particularly instructed its permanent committee to obtain plans of ancient fortifications, tumuli and other Indian works of art. A correspondent who in 1792 reported to the Society his observations 'On the Ancient Works of Art, the Native Inhabitants, &c. of the Western-Country,' was glad to be able to draw the broad conclusion that these relics showed the Indian to be as capable as any other nation of learning any mechanical or liberal art. When Barton examined remains from the Northwest, he rejoiced at their testimony to the essential talents of the Indian, which confirmed 'the relations of man to God; and the relations of men to each other.' [20]

A skeptic might easily have seen in the vicissitudes of the American Indian some evidence of his inferiority to the white man. Had not the white man moved steadily upward toward a pinnacle of enlightenment and civilization in the eighteenth century? And had not the Indian shown himself unable even to preserve the intellectual and technological advances of his ancestors, much less to build upon them? But from the ups and downs of Indian civilization Barton drew quite a different moral:

Let it not be said, that they are incapable of improvement. Such an assertion can only suit those speculative philosophers who retire to their closets inveloped in a thick atmosphere of prejudices, which the strongest lights of truth cannot pervade. Natural History, which opens the door to so much precious knowledge concerning mankind, teaches us, that the physical differences between nations are but inconsiderable, and history informs us, that civilization has been constantly preceded by barbarity and rudeness. . . . The Americans are not, as some writers have supposed, specifically different from the Persians, and other improved nations of Asia. The inference from this discovery is interesting and important. We learn that the Americans are susceptible of improvement.[21]

The Negro presented the Jeffersonian anthropologist with a more difficult problem. The Indian was observed in autonomous communities which displayed a gamut of talents, including powers of organization and leadership: the white man perforce met him as an equal, if only in battle. But, in America at least, the Negro's servile condition concealed his talents. It would not be so easy to prove that the Negro's physical peculiarities and his primitive social development were nothing but environmental modifications on the original type of man. Virtually nothing was recorded of his African civilizations, and little could be learned from the Negro himself, or from buried relics like those which told of an ancient Indian culture. Since little was known of the native African languages, the student lacked still another kind of information that had been useful in demonstrating the Indian's membership in the single tribe of mankind.

It is not surprising then that the Jeffersonian who had committed his moral science to the data of natural history should betray uncertainty whether the Negro was the equal of other races of man. If we have understood his canons, we may be impressed that he was able to provide himself even such qualified assurance as he did. It would have been remarkable indeed if in this case a Southerner like Jefferson, for whom the Negro's status was intimately involved with economic and political interests, had not found the outlines of the Creator's original plan to be somewhat hazy. Yet from what we have already seen of Jeffersonian science—from the confidence with which facts were asserted and conclusions drawn about the great-claw, the mammoth, and even the Creation itself—it is hard not to believe that a broader and firmer equalitarian faith might have produced some unambiguous proof of the equality of the Negro. Our suspicion is confirmed when we note the American philosopher's facility at explaining away the most obvious and troublesome peculiarity of the Negro—his color.

After we have observed the ingenuity with which Rush (a Philadelphian and an undeviating abolitionist) shaped scanty facts to support his dogmatic assertion of the Negro's membership in the single human species, we may better judge Jefferson's excuses that his own final answer had to wait upon more evidence. In his 'Observations intended to favour a supposition that the Black Color (as it is called) of the Negroes is derived from the Leprosy,' [22] Rush reasoned, partly from his clinical observations in the Pennsylvania Hospital and partly from common experience, toward the conclusion that the so-called black color of the Negro was the effect not of any original difference in his nature, but of the affliction of his ancestors with leprosy. This disease, he noted, was accompanied in some instances by a black color of the skin. The big lips and flat nose typical of Negroes were actually symptoms of leprosy, which Rush himself had more than once observed. The inhabitants of the leper islands of the South Pacific possessed thick lips and woolly hair; and albinism (also found among American Negroes) was not unknown there. The same morbid insensibility of the nerves which was induced by leprosy was found peculiarly in Negroes, who, compared to white people, were able to endure surgical operations with ease. Rush recalled cases where Negroes had actually held the upper part of a limb during amputation. Such pathological insensibility was also apparent in the apathy with which Negroes exposed themselves to great heat, and the indifference with which they handled hot coals. Lepers were remarkable for their strong venereal desires; and so strong were these desires in Negroes that even the depressing circumstances of slavery had not prevented their extraordinary fruitfulness. When asked to account for the duration of the Negro's color through long centuries, Rush answered that leprosy was of all diseases the most permanently inherited. According to Rush, the fact that in the eighteenth century Negroes seldom infected others with the disease could not be held against his theory, because by now leprosy had nearly ceased to be infectious. And actually there were even instances where something like an infectious quality had appeared in the skin of Negroes. Since local diseases of the skin seldom affected the general health of the body or the duration of human life, the present health and longevity of the Negro constituted no objection to his thesis.

If the black color of the Negro had really been caused by leprosy, Rush found certain conclusions inevitable:

1. That all the claims of superiority of the whites over the blacks, on account of their color, are founded alike in ignorance and inhumanity. If the color of the negroes be the effect of a disease, instead of inviting us to tyrannise over them, it should entitle them to a double portion of our humanity, for disease all over the world has always been the signal for immediate and universal compassion.

2. The facts and principles which have been delivered, should teach white people the necessity of keeping up that prejudice against such connections with them, as would tend to infect posterity with any portion of their disorder. This may be done upon the ground I have mentioned without offering violence to humanity, or calling in question the sameness of descent, or natural equality of mankind.

3. Is the color of the negroes a disease? Then let science and humanity combine their efforts, and endeavor to discover a remedy for it. Nature has lately unfurled a banner upon this subject. She has begun spontaneous cures of this disease in several black people in this country.

Rush remarked that attempts to cure Negroes of this disease of their skin would be encouraged when philosophers understood how much it would increase human happiness. Such a cure would destroy an argument in favor of Negro slavery—both among the ignorant who supposed that the black color had marked Negroes as objects of divine judgment, and among the learned who urged that the pigmentation of the Negroes' skin had destined or qualified them for labor in hot and unwholesome climates. When cured of the disease, the Negroes would be much happier, for however well they sometimes appeared to be satisfied with their color, there were many proofs of their preferring that of the white people. And most important, Rush concluded, 'We shall render the belief of the whole human race being descended from one pair, easy, and universal, and thereby not only add weight to the Christian revelation, but remove a material obstacle to the exercise of that universal benevolence which is inculcated by it.'

Through this whole argument ran the assumption (the more significant because not explicitly avowed) that the norm for the color of a healthy member of the human species was *white*. It was inconceivable to Rush that when the Negro had been cured of his affliction and returned to his pristine condition, he would have the red complexion of the American Indian or the yellow of the Asiatic. One of his final arguments for redoubling the effort to perfect a cure was that the Negro might have the happiness of wearing the proper white color of the human skin. Jefferson himself betrayed this assumption in the *Notes on Virginia* (Query XIV) when he judged the color of the Negro to be aesthetically inferior to that of the white man: 'Are not the fine mixtures of red and white, the expressions of every passion by greater or less suffusions of color in the one, preferable to that eternal monotony, which reigns in the countenances, that immovable veil of black which covers the emotions of the other race?'

Jefferson's anthropological judgments on the Negro all betray a suspicion that color might very well have been among 'the real distinctions which nature has made.' [23] We must not forget that Jefferson, unlike Rush, was a Virginian. Although he was theoretically opposed to the institution of slavery, he had been reared in a society where there seemed little to confirm the equal talents of the Negro. While his relevant statements were uniformly and perhaps designedly ambiguous, Jefferson seemed inwardly driven to suggest that some original differences in color (which by hypothesis implied a hierarchy of color) must have been indelible in the Creator's design. Yet he never quite dared say that color variations were actually indices of a difference of species. His position was, of course, inadmissible according to the technical vocabulary of Linnaean natural history to which he was otherwise faithful. Within that system there could be no intermediate term between *species* brought into being by the hand of the Creator in the beginning, and *varieties* induced in more recent times by environment and accident. Still Jefferson wished to make just such an intermediate term of the Negro.

He was not sure enough of the irrelevance of the Negro's color to assign him the same ancient parents as the white man; yet he was too much of an equalitarian to suggest that the Negro might have been created a distinct species.

Partly because of this inner uncertainty, Jefferson's comments on the Negro were written in the optative mood, and therefore admirably illustrate the relation between his theology and his science. While he insisted that the axiomatic unity of the human species had to be confirmed by facts, he was willing finally to rely on a general presumption in favor of human equality.

The opinion that they [Negroes] are inferior in the faculties of reason and imagination, must be hazarded with great diffidence. To justify a general conclusion, requires many observations, even where the subject may be submitted to the anatomical knife, to optical glasses, to analysis by fire or by solvents. How much more then where it is a faculty, not a substance, we are examining; where it eludes the research of all the senses; where the conditions of its existence are various and variously combined; where the effects of those which are present or absent bid defiance to calculation; let me add too, as a circumstance of great tenderness, where our conclusion would degrade a whole race of men from the rank in the scale of beings which their Creator may perhaps have given them.[24]

The reader of such warnings cannot but be bewildered. On the one hand, Jefferson urged, be careful lest by overhasty conclusions from scanty evidence you assume that the present peculiarities of the Negro show an original difference of species; for this might mistake the Creator's design and thereby degrade a whole race from their destined rank. On the other hand, he insisted with barely less emphasis, be careful that you do not hastily ignore any visible distinctions, for these all may have a divine claim to social recognition.

In his *Notes on Virginia*, Jefferson (in the passage to which we have just referred) concluded after examining the evidence:

I advance it, therefore, as a suspicion only, that the blacks, whether originally a distinct race [Jefferson significantly does not say 'species'] or made distinct by time and circumstances, are inferior

93

to the whites in the endowments both of body and mind. It is not against experience to suppose that different species of the same genus, or varieties of the same species, may possess different qualifications. Will not a lover of natural history then, one who views the gradations in all the races of animals with the eye of philosophy, excuse an effort to keep those in the department of man as distinct as nature has formed them?

It would be hard to imagine a statement more tentative or ambiguous than this and still couched in the language of Linnaean natural history. Jefferson thus revealed both his determination to confirm his concept of man by the data of biology; and, at the same time, his reluctance to confide his feelings, where they were really uncertain, to the strict arbitration of unfriendly facts.

Again and again we find Jefferson on the Negro purporting to use the language of natural history, but seeking to save himself from its rigorous axioms. Consequently he plays fast and loose with the concepts on which he had built his whole science. For example, in 1785, only a few years after the passage just quoted, Jefferson wrote General Chastellux a long letter discussing at large the evidence for the equal endowments of the American Indian and the white man. 'I believe the Indian, then,' he concluded, 'to be, in body and mind, equal to the white man. I have supposed the black man, in his present state, might not be so; but it would be hazardous to affirm, that, equally cultivated for a few generations, he would not become so.' [25] In the context of Jeffersonian natural history and of his particular inquiry, no remark could have been more meaningless than this ostensibly scientific supposition which he urged in defense of the Negro. In his environmentalist defense of the Indian (in this same letter) Jefferson had already mentioned the irrelevance of the eighteenth-century characteristics of a race to the question of their original nature. Since the equality of creatures had been determined once and for all by the qualities of the species at the Creation, it was nonsensical to express a hope that the Negro after favorable influences might 'become' equal. Individuals not equals in the original order of creation could not by any later circumstances become so. It is unlikely that Jefferson meant here to propose the emergence of a new species; for this would have been unique in his copious writings on natural history and would have been at odds with his primary beliefs about the universe. What is more likely is that Jefferson was trying to preserve his large equalitarian faith and was willing to do so even at the expense of his science.

Similar doubts appear in his attempts to assess the effects of slavery on the Negro. In order fairly to judge the influence of environment on the Negro's capacities, Jefferson compared him, not with his white master, nor with his free Indian neighbor, but with the ancient Roman slave. Only after a long and circumstantial comparison, in which he considered the poetic and philosophic accomplishments of slaves in Roman times, did he conclude that the inferiority of the Negro might not be explained by his servile status. 'It is not their condition then,' Jefferson said, 'but nature, which has produced the distinction.' To say that the Negro lacked the genius of an Epictetus, a Terence, or a Phaedrus was, of course, highly ambiguous dispraise, and probably was meant as such. Yet Jefferson felt compelled to mitigate even these gentle strictures by adding that, whether or not further observations would verify 'the conjecture, that nature has been less bountiful to them in the endowments of the head . . . in those of the heart she will be found to have done them justice.' [26]

The 'fact' on which he relied to defend the Negroes against their allegedly congenital disposition to theft was little more than Jefferson's own unwillingness to believe that they lacked a moral sense; with the corollary (admittedly unsupported by facts directly concerning the Negro) that if the circumstances of the Negro were changed, his moral behavior would surely also change. After an ingenious evasion in which Jefferson questioned whether the slave might not be justified in taking a little property from his master when his master had already taken everything from him, he summed up the 'factual' foundation of his belief: 'That a change in the relations in which a

95

man is placed should change his ideas of moral right or wrong, is neither new, nor peculiar to the color of the blacks. Homer tells us it was so two thousand six hundred years ago.'

Jefferson remained apologetic for his uncertainty about Negro talents, because it seemed to him to imply uncertainty of human equality. Twenty-five years after the *Notes on Virginia*, he still sought to excuse his doubts, which he said had always been expressed with the greatest reluctance, and only on the basis of the limited and unfavorable opportunities for observation within the borders of Virginia. 'It was impossible for doubt to have been more tenderly or hesitatingly expressed than that was in the Notes of Virginia, and nothing was or is farther from my intentions, than to enlist myself as the champion of a fixed opinion, where I have only expressed a doubt.' What he always expressed was an open-minded hopefulness that the facts would some day produce unambiguous proof of the equality of the Negro. He never lost his eagerness for an entirely satisfactory demonstration 'that the want of talents observed in them is merely the effect of their degraded condition, and not proceeding from any difference in the structure of the parts on which intellect depends.' On this he expected the St. Domingo experiment to throw some light. 'Be assured,' he wrote to a correspondent who had sent him a disappointing anthology of Negro literature, 'that no person living wishes more sincerely than I do, to see a complete refutation of the doubts I have myself entertained and expressed on the grade of understanding allotted to them by nature, and to find that in this respect they are on a par with ourselves.' [27]

Both his apology and his hope attest how thoroughly Jefferson believed he had entrusted his ethics to the arbitration of natural history. Only in the case of the Negro did he seem quite ready to follow wherever facts might lead; and it is hard not to see this docility as a symptom of the weakness of his conviction. Yet even here his equalitarian faith was often strong enough to draw cosmology and natural history into its service. Consider, for example, Jefferson's characteristic way of denying the congenital laziness which had been widely attributed to the Negro. Noah Webster in his *Effects of Slavery on Morals and Industry* (1793) had refuted this accusation by the substantial facts of language: 'lazy,' he said, was derived from the Saxon 'lazzi,' which was a word for the lowest order of bondmen, and gradually had come to suggest the indolence always found among enslaved peoples. 'If slavery had this effect upon our own ancestors, the warlike heroes of the *north*, surely modern philosophers need not resort to an original difference of race, for the cause of that dullness and want of mental vigor, remarkable in the enslaved natives of the *torrid zone* and their degenerate descendants.' Compared to Webster's, Jefferson's argument was more devious. Some antiequalitarians had claimed that because of a congenital laziness the Negro would never (without the physical coercion of slavery) work hard enough to provide himself the necessities of life; and they said that this peculiarity itself marked the Negro as a distinct species. Jefferson answered by appealing to his axioms of the indestructibility of species and the economy of nature. Of course, he urged, the question would eventually have to be solved 'by experiment'; but the result of experiment could hardly be doubted. 'It would be a solecism,' he wrote Frances Wright, the British feminist and reformer (August 7, 1825), 'to suppose a race of animals created, without sufficient foresight and energy to preserve their own existence.'

On other occasions Jefferson actually violated the premises of his science, and retreated altogether from the realm of facts, because that realm had failed to resolve his doubts and confirm his equalitarian faith. Yet such retreat was for him a rare and desperate intellectual expedient. 'Whatever be their degree of talent,' Jefferson wrote of the Negro on one occasion, 'it is no measure of their rights. Because Sir Isaac Newton was superior to others in understanding, he was not therefore lord of the person or property of others.' [28] But in the very letter in which he stated this principle, he rejoiced at finding some new evidence of Negro talents which would help demonstrate the 'equality' of the Negro. Jefferson was surely fickle and unhappy in his professed willingness to demonstrate human equality by other than scientific evidence; and he unwittingly revealed his insecurity by appealing to the very example of Newton. Not only was Newton an unquestioned member of the human species and hence entitled to all the equality which anthropology could prove; but Jefferson's own doctrine of natural aristocracy betrayed more than a suspicion that a man's talents might actually give him some natural claim to political superiority over others.

We may find an irony and perhaps a moral in noting that where the Jeffersonian remained truest to his professed reliance on the facts of natural history, was where his ethical faith was least secure. Even while Rush (who was an abolitionist) proved that the black color of the Negro was no mark of the original divine displeasure, he urged the white to shun social equality with the Negro—at least until that distant day when the Negro's leprosy should have been cured. Jefferson himself guarded his own uncertainties, while reaffirming his large faith in human equality. That he saw his vivid promise of human equality in the axiomatic unity of the human species was never more apparent; nor was his faith ever more clear that the Creator could not have destined creatures for equality without equipping them equally for activity. He impatiently awaited more facts to show the accord of his faith with the indelible design of nature.

4. The Fulfillment of Human Equality

THE extreme environmentalism by which the Jeffersonian defended the Indian and the Negro against charges of inferiority actually opened the door to another possible argument against human equality. Had not the Creator in the beginning made all continents—all the different natural environments—as part of His original design? Without supposing that there had been a 'chosen' variety of the human species, one might conceive that some particular habitat had been intended to produce a superior breed of man. The American philosopher, as we have seen, could not ignore the fact that each continent seemed to show a different set of variations: the varieties of man (besides the *Ferus* or 'Wild' and the *Monstrosus* or 'Deformed') were 'American,' 'European,' 'Asiatic,' and 'African.'

For some time, European naturalists had observed a connection between climate and the temperaments and capacities of men. In 1748, the French philosopher Montesquieu had noted:

Cold air constringes the extremities of the external fibres of the body; this increases their elasticity, and favors the return of the blood from the extreme parts to the heart. It contracts those very fibres; consequently it increases also their force. On the contrary, warm air relaxes and lengthens the extremes of the fibres; of course it diminishes their force and elasticity. People are, therefore, more vigorous in cold climates. . . . This superiority of strength must produce various effects; for instance, a greater boldness, that is, more courage; a greater sense of superiority, that is, less desire of revenge; a greater opinion of security, that is, more frankness, less suspicion, policy, and cunning. . . . If we travel towards the North, we meet with people who have few vices, many virtues, and a great share of frankness and sincerity. If we draw near the South, we fancy ourselves entirely removed from the verge of morality; here the strongest passions are productive of all manner of crimes, each man endeavoring, let the means be what they will, to indulge his inordinate desires. In temperate climates we find the inhabitants inconstant in their manners, as well as in their vices and virtues: the climate has not a quality determinate enough to fix them.[29]

Was this not making environmentalism an argument against the equality of mankind? For the Creator had made the warm lands as well as the cold; having destined men to live everywhere, He must have intended the resulting inequalities.

Eighteenth-century naturalists like Montesquieu, who saw

symmetry in all nature, found it easy to imagine that each continent like each species had been assigned an homogeneous character. And the notion that Europe was the ideal habitat for the human species came to be suggested by some European philosophers who were struck by the 'fact' that America produced an inferior breed of all animals. By the end of the eighteenth century some of the best French naturalists had elaborated a thesis of the 'degeneracy' of life in the New World. The Count de Buffon had laboriously developed the notion with respect to animals generally and the Abbé Raynal had casually applied it to man. The doctrine had made such headway, and its implications seemed to Jefferson so disastrous that in his *Notes on Virginia* he actually organized his comprehensive description of the fauna of the country into a systematic refutation. Buffon's 'facts' which Jefferson set out to rebut were: (1) that the animals common to the Old and the New World were smaller in the latter; (2) that those peculiar to the New World were on a smaller scale; (3) that those which had been domesticated in both had degenerated in America; and (4) that on the whole America exhibited fewer species. The Creator, according to Buffon, had made this continent naturally deficient in fecundity and in the powers needed to make animals large, strong and numerous. Supposedly the American temperature had been made too warm and the atmosphere too humid to be the best habitat for animal life. Or, as Jefferson summed up Buffon's theory, it presupposed that heat was friendly and moisture adverse to the production of large quadrupeds. Jefferson found these suppositions contrary to the evidence.

The truth of this is inscrutable to us by reasonings *a priori*. Nature has hidden from us her *modus agendi*. Our only appeal on such questions is to experience; and I think that experience is against the supposition. It is by the assistance of *heat* and *moisture* that vegetables are elaborated from the elements of earth, air, water, and fire. We accordingly see the more humid climates produce the greater quantity of vegetables. Vegetables are mediately or immediately the food of every animal; and in proportion to the quantity of food, we see animals not only multiplied in their numbers, but improved in their bulk, as far as the laws of their nature will admit.[30]

Not only these obvious facts of botany and ecology, but numerous examples contained in Buffon's work actually contradicted his own thesis. Cattle, for example, grew especially large in Denmark, the Ukraine, and Tartary—cold and humid lands where, according to the theory, they should have been smaller.

Since man himself was part of the American fauna, Buffon's thesis held clear implications for the dogma of human equality. A general tendency of lower animals to degenerate in America might hint the Creator's intention that different local races of men too should hold unequal places in the scale of creation. Rush and Jefferson themselves had come dangerously close to such a suggestion when, arguing against multiple human species, they attributed the present inferiority of the Indian to the effect of his environment. Buffon, crudely applying his own environmentalist thesis to the American Indian, had discovered an actual degeneration of the species. The Abbé Raynal, who was principally responsible for applying Buffon's thesis to man, incautiously generalized the doctrine of degeneracy from the Indian to the much more difficult case of 'the race of Whites transplanted from Europe.' By this extension he had committed himself to a hypothesis virtually impossible of proof, especially since American philosophers who had the best access to the evidence would be personally offended by the hypothesis. According to Raynal—and his view was widely popularized—man in America was not free from the curse of the continent. Therefore, he said, the prudent course for Americans was 'to know how to make themselves happy by œconomy and with mediocrity,' never to expect genius and so never to be disappointed.[31]

Such an argument could not but embarrass the humble American philosopher. One appropriate reply was banter like that employed by Franklin in Paris, as recounted by Jefferson himself:

The Doctor [Franklin] . . . had a party to dine with him one day at Passy, of whom one half were Americans, the other half French, and among the last was the Abbé [Raynal]. During the dinner he got on his favorite theory of the degeneracy of animals, and even of man, in America, and urged it with his usual eloquence. The Doctor at length noticing the accidental stature and position of his guests, at table, 'Come,' says he, 'M. l'Abbé, let us try this question by the fact before us. We are here one half Americans, and one half French, and it happens that the Americans have placed themselves on one side of the table, and our French friends are on the other. Let both parties rise, and we will see on which side nature has degenerated.' It happened that his American guests were Carmichael, Harmer, Humphreys, and others of the finest stature and form; while those of the other side were remarkably diminutive, and the Abbé himself particularly, was a mere shrimp. He parried the appeal, however, by a complimentary admission of exceptions, among which the Doctor himself was a conspicuous one.[32]

Jefferson, lacking Franklin's sense of humor, could not dismiss Raynal's thesis with a dinner-party joke; and he offered a copiously documented refutation in his *Notes on Virginia* (Query VI). In the first place, he observed, Raynal would not be justified in reproaching America for not having produced a good poet, until the American people had existed as long as the Greeks had before producing a Homer, the Romans a Virgil, the French a Racine and Voltaire, and the English a Shakespeare and Milton. If the continent still should not have produced its poet, then and not until then would American anthropologists have anything to explain away. But according to Raynal, America suffered from more than a poetic deficiency: the continent had not produced 'one able mathematician, one man of genius in a single art or a single science.' Against this rash and malicious verdict, Jefferson found it sufficient to recall the great trinity of American genius (all still alive): Washington, a general with few equals in history; Franklin, the prodigy of modern philosophy; and Rittenhouse, who was not only the greatest living astronomer, but whose Orrery showed him to be as great a mechanical genius as the world had ever produced. No man of judgment could have classed any of these among 'the degeneracies of nature.' 'We calculate thus: The United States contains three millions of inhabitants; France twenty millions; and the British islands ten. We produce a Washington, a Franklin, a Rittenhouse. France then should have half a dozen in each of these lines, and Great Britain half that number, equally eminent.' These greatest models of American genius could be supplemented by still others of a high order, not only in philosophy, in war, in government and in oratory—but even in painting and sculpture, where the infancy of American civilization had offered peculiar obstacles. No one possessed of the facts could seriously argue that America had produced less than her share of the genius of the age.

We cannot be surprised that the American philosopher found the evidence inconsistent with a theory of American degeneracy. What was significant was that he usually stopped short of any countertheory asserting the biological superiority of the American habitat. Jefferson, for example, had actually gathered enough data convincingly to support a thesis that animals in America tended to be larger than related species in Europe; but he would not draw this conclusion. Even the vast bulk of the American mammoth was for Jefferson no evidence of the superior potency of the American environment. While admitting that the mammoth was 'the largest of all terrestrial beings,' he refused to say that America must therefore have the most fecund of all soils and climates. All that he would say was that the mammoth helped rescue the American soil and atmosphere from the imputations of Buffon and Voltaire, and helped refute their foolish suggestion that nature was less active or less energetic on one side of the globe than on the other. 'As if both sides were not warmed by the same genial sun; as if a soil of the same chemical composition was less capable of elaboration into animal nutriment; as if the fruits and grains from that soil and sun yielded a less rich chyle, gave less extension to the solids and fluids of the body, or produced sooner in the cartilages, membranes, and fibres, that rigidity which restrains all further extension, and terminates animal growth.' [33] It was the universal vitality of nature that he was determined to vindicate. Just as the diminutive size of certain breeds of domestic animals when transplanted to America showed no weakness in the powers of nature, but was rather the product of uniform causes operating on this continent; so, too, the bulk of the largest American animals showed universal laws producing opposite results. He attributed the popularity of the French hypothesis to the 'vivid imagination and bewitching language' with which the error had been supported. Jefferson wished to do nothing more than suggest a doubt whether the bulk and faculties of animals depended on the side of the Atlantic on which their food happened to grow. Had nature, he asked, enlisted herself as a Cis- or Trans-Atlantic partisan?

But Jefferson's question leads us inevitably to one of our own. If the existence of distinctions between kinds of creatures had been intended to provide variety, if each species stood in an hierarchical relation to the others, why should there not have been a similar scale among the parts of the earth? Since all animate creatures were connected in a chain from the lowliest mineral upward through the plants and insects to man himself, why did not the American philosopher entertain the possibility of a similar chain of continents? Surely this would have been harmonious with his conception of a workmanlike and designing Creator. Were not the arctic wastes the perfect environment for the mammoth and the tropical jungles for the elephant? Why was it not conceivable to the Jeffersonian that there was similarly some ideal habitat for man, and that the man who grew in that lucky environment would be superior by divine intent?

To have permitted this analogy would have jeopardized the Jeffersonian proof of equality. It might even have turned his whole environmentalist argument into a demonstration that the divinely intended inequalities among men were as great as the diversities of environment. This clearly would not do. In the case of man, therefore, the American philosopher extracted from the facts of environmental influence quite another moral. When he saw men living in the arctic, in the tropics, and in temperate zones, he felt no impulse to emphasize the superiority of temperate conditions. Instead he was impressed that men actually could survive in all climates, and he concluded that adaptability itself was man's specific characteristic. If the American wild turkey failed to flourish when transplanted to Europe, it was because the American continent was its ideal habitat; but if man succeeded in living at all (however poorly and unhappily) in the arctic, it showed that there was *no* limited habitat for the human species.

This 'conclusion' was actually of course nothing but a way of restating the assumption that all men were descended from the same ancient parents. The Jeffersonian knew from the outset that the distinguishing feature of the whole human family was its ability to adapt itself to changed circumstances (as Americans had done), and so to acquire characteristics different from those of its ancestors. He had thus presupposed the impossibility of cutting away the tangled overgrowth of acquired characteristics to see what lay beneath. His very inability to delineate Adam and Eve seemed to strengthen the presumption that such a single original pair must have existed. All the future variations among men would be further evidence.

The promise of human equality, as we have observed, was contained in that hypothetical fact—also an expression of faith—about all mankind: the first creation of a single species of man. In a sense, the intended equality of men had already been fulfilled by their original creation in the same mold; human equality was thus already realized in nature by the Creator's design. To the Jeffersonian, the force of his equalitarian faith thus derived in large measure from his belief that equality was no mere idea; that to deny the equality of mankind was to deny the very shape of nature. In this sense, his faith was strikingly different both from the otherworldly equalitarianism of early Christianity and from the this-worldly utopianism of modern communism. The fulfillment of Jeffersonian equality was not postponed to a future state when all souls would appear before the throne of God; nor to a distant age when all economic classes would disappear and each would be rewarded according to his needs. Equality was first and foremost a biological fact. To be otherworldly or utopian about equality seemed like looking wistfully forward to a day when men would have two arms and two legs.

The Jeffersonian never doubted that to discover a difference of species among men would automatically show the inferiority of the members of one species to those of another. But why so? Where had it been written in the Book of Creation that there could be no equal links in the chain of beings—especially at the very top of the chain, where man was supposed to have been placed? Why was it not conceivable that varieties *within* a species (themselves the product of forces which the Creator had made) had been intended to have moral significance? The assumptions which foreclosed this possibility were, of course, basic to Jeffersonian anthropology, and yet they were neither made explicit nor justified in any way. How could the American philosopher know which differences among creatures should be translated into ethical claims? This question, too, he left unanswered, while he reiterated that the answer was apparent in the facts themselves.

If the eighteenth-century American Negro should actually have possessed an intellect inferior to that of the white man (and even for such a statement the Jeffersonian admittedly lacked sufficient evidence) we would ask what this would prove about whether the Negro should be treated as an equal of the white man? Perhaps this inferiority was a symptom of his degenerate condition; perhaps it showed an original inferiority. Supposing the first, what 'facts' could then lead us from the original similarity of his mind and that of the white man, to the conclusion that he should be treated as the moral equal of the white man in the eighteenth century? Or supposing the second, what 'facts' showed that the moral equality of men was anyway dependent on the similarity of their minds? The ambiguity which seems obvious to us was one which the American philosopher's cosmology could not admit. That the facts might be scanty or uncertain, surely; but that their *meaning* could be unclear, never. Jeffersonian cosmology, by blending the world as it was with the world as it ought to be, had already identified the precepts of practical success with the divine design. The power of man to cope with nature—of prime importance in eighteenth-century America—had been made the test of his moral value. According to Jeffersonian anthropology, the foundation and proof of human equality was somatic; a metaphysic of equality seemed superfluous because all men had been cast in the same corporeal mold.

Yet the very argument by which that similarity was established had foreclosed the possibility that physical or social uniformity could be the ideal of human development. Since variability in response to environmental stimuli was from a purely biological point of view the specific sign of humanity, the fulfillment of the equality of mankind could never be in the creation of a uniform type. It was the striking diversity of human races—of their figures, complexions and cultures—that showed conclusively the membership of all in the single pioneering species, and hence the intended equality of all men. From the Jeffersonian point of view, this destined diversification of men was not the outward material counterpart of unique souls. It was rather the varied response to different environments by essentially similar biological units. The mission of any group of men came then not from an inward designation, not from a peculiar spirit of which they were messengers, but from the special opportunities of their environment.

This was the upshot of Jeffersonian efforts to avoid the ambiguities of ethical theory by a biological approach to the equality of man. They had made man's adaptability—his ability to pioneer in new environments and to seize the advantages of every climate and landscape—his supremely human quality which distinguished him from the lower animals and held the promise of a New World. It was therefore axiomatic for the Jeffersonians that the history of the species simply recorded the adaptation of branches of the human family to the different continents. All this showed that while it was one thing to praise the workmanship of God, it was quite another to apotheosize man the workman. For while God had made the environment, the Jeffersonians had to start from the environment as they found it. The environment was in a sense master of man.

Only by recognizing, acquiescing in, and—so far went the Jeffersonians!—making a virtue of this subservience to environment, could men fulfill their destiny to master the world. One consequence of such emphasis on adaptability was the dissolution of virtually all standards of what was human. Man became the mirror of nature; and nature was enormously variable and diverse. Such a way of thinking seemed to lead toward a happy pluralism. But the diversity and the development of man envisaged were again almost exclusively biological and material. We shall be better able to understand why the Jeffersonians could not find in man's spiritual qualities something characteristically human, and even how their view held within it the seeds of a dogmatic activism, when we have examined the Jeffersonian conception of the nature of thought.

CHAPTER THREE

The Physiology of Thought and Morals

'In looking at things spiritual, we are too much like oysters observing the sun through the water, and thinking that thick water the thinnest of air.' MELVILLE, Moby Dick

The Physiology of Thought and Morals

M UCH of American thought since Jefferson has boasted a flexible and experimental attitude in philosophy, metaphysics and religion. This complaisance has not however expressed a willingness to allow disagreement in the most important matters, because in our civilization action has seemed most important. The Jeffersonians could view the disputes of metaphysicians and theologians with detached amusement or indifference, because it is easy to tolerate anarchy in a realm where one has never really entered and which one is glad to see discredited. The facts and theories by which they fenced in their intellectual experience actually separated them from the schools and traditions of past philosophers. That very materialism which was the heart of their metaphysics was, according to the Jeffersonians, no philosophy but a 'fact.'

On the other hand, the experimental method which the Jeffersonians had to profess in order to get their practical scientific job done, carried with it (as it often has in our more recent history) an unconsidered dogmatism in matters of behavior and morals. While the easiest way in metaphysics is to condemn all metaphysics as nonsense, the easiest way in morals is to elevate the common practice of the community into a moral absolute. If the Jeffersonians discarded metaphysical speculation as insignificant, they avoided moral speculation as downright dangerous. And in morals they came close to being absolutists. They actually enlisted physiology to prove that their particular moral creed was a physical 'faculty,' and they even dared say that the very 'health' of the body was inseparable from obedience to the Jeffersonian code of behavior.

In equalitarian and democratic societies, and especially in the United States (as de Tocqueville pointed out over a hundred years ago), there has been a dangerous readiness to transform the principle of majority rule, which is a political necessity,

111

into a philosophical credo; and to confuse the dictates of public opinion with the voice of the individual conscience. The consequence has commonly been a tyranny of public opinion over personal faith and thought. This tyranny has been all the harder for us to perceive simply because it has been so willingly preferred to the travail of individual mind and conscience. Conformity and naïve faith in matters of morals and behavior—together with a distrust of all metaphysics—have seemed to save that much more effort for inquiry and progress in scientific matters. While this tyranny of public opinion is of course preferable to more institutionalized or better enforced tyrannies, it must nevertheless be combated if the spirit of free inquiry, which alone can reveal the perils of all tyrannies, is to be nourished. Against these perils only the most vigorous speculation, the broadest and most energetic search for foundations in metaphysics and theology of the tenets of behavior, can be an antidote.

1. 'The Mode of Action Called Thinking'

WHEN the Jeffersonian counted men not as 'souls' but as biological units of the human species, he meant to imply that the biological man was the whole man—the only man whom the naturalist and the philosopher needed to consider. This 'materialism' (as the Jeffersonian reluctantly called it) was, characteristically, to be found not in any metaphysical treatise but implicit in his particular investigations. Everything the historian or the philosopher could discover about the creation of life on this earth demonstrated, according to the Jeffersonian, that mind and body were not separate substances.

Thought was no proof of the existence of a nonmaterial realm, for thought itself was nothing but the interaction of material forces. What could show this more conclusively than that physical life and mental life had been created at one stroke and by the same physical stimuli? In his 'Inquiry into the Cause of Animal Life,' Rush recounted the historical facts in some detail:

'And the Lord God formed man of the dust of the ground, and breathed into his nostrils the breath of life, and man became a living soul.' The common explanation of this passage of Scripture is, that God, in this act, infused a soul into the torpid, or lifeless body of Adam, and that his soul became its principle of life, or in other words, that he thus changed a dead mass of animalized matter, into an animated being. That this was not the case I infer, not only from the existence of life in many persons in whom the soul is in a dormant or torpid state from diseases in the brain, but from a more liberal and correct translation of the above passage of Scripture. . . . It is as follows. 'And the Lord God breathed into his nostrils, the *air* of *lives*, and he became a living soul.' That is, he dilated his nostrils, and thereby inflated his lungs with air, and thus excited in him, animal, intellectual and spiritual life, in consequence of which he became an animated human creature. From this view of the origin of life in Adam, it appears that his soul and body were cast in the same mould, and at the same time, and that both were animated by the same act of Divine power by means of the same stream of air.[1]

At the birth of every infant Rush saw recapitulated the same creation of life and thought. The new-born baby did not possess a life of his own until his lungs had been filled with air; it was this physical stimulus that set the lungs in motion. The lungs in turn moved the heart, the heart the brain, the brain the 'mind,' and the reaction of brain and mind, according to Rush, moved every other part of the body. Priestley argued that a close study of the precise words of the second book of Genesis gave biblical confirmation to these physiological facts. For the scriptural account described *the whole man* as being made from the dust of the ground; there was no mention of any higher principle in his constitution. If a nonmaterial ingredient had been involved in the Creator's alchemy, surely it would not have been omitted from His story of the Creation. Yet even Priestley, who put more faith in Scripture than did his fellow philosophers, would not make exegesis do for science; and he rallied chemistry to show that breathing was all that made the difference between unanimated earth and the living soul. Man, he concluded, was an homogeneous and wholly material being.[2]

To have believed in the existence of a 'soul' with some reality apart from man's body would have carried a dangerous implication: perhaps there was in man some self-existent quality which had never required a God for its creation, and would not require a God to keep it alive. Moreover, belief in a non-material realm of being, Priestley further argued in his *Disquisitions Relating to Matter and Spirit*, would imply doubt of the very existence of a Creator; to say that God was a spiritual being was to say He might be *everywhere* at once, and this was nothing but a cowardly rhetorical way of stating that God really existed *nowhere*, and therefore did not exist at all. 'To say that the human soul, angels, God, are immaterial,' warned Jefferson, 'is to say, they are *nothings*, or that there is no God, no angels, no soul. I cannot reason otherwise.' The strength of this argument, as Jefferson and Priestley of course refused to confess, depended on the truth of the very assertion they were pretending to prove; namely, that the tangible world was the only world which existed. Even in Jeffersonian terms, this argument involved the fundamental contradiction of making the reality of a God whom man had never seen, prove the unreality of everything which was not visible. A similar 'argument' which Priestley urged was that materialism, by reminding man of his constant dependence on physical stimuli external to himself, made more vivid to him the reality of the God who was the ultimate source of all such stimuli. 'Self-existence,' Rush agreed, 'belongs only to God.'[3]

It was not permissible, Jefferson insisted, to make the truth of the doctrine of materialism depend on the philosopher's ability to explain how matter could be made to think; for this would assume that the devices of a divine workman were within the comprehension of the human mind. 'I can conceive *thought* to be an action of a particular organization of matter,' he explained, 'formed for that purpose by its Creator, as well as that *attraction* is an action of matter, or *magnetism* of loadstone. When he who denies to the Creator the power of endowing matter with the mode of action called *thinking*, shall show how He could endow the sun with the mode of action called *attraction*, which reins the planets in the track of their orbits, or how an absence of matter can have a will, and by that will put matter into motion, then the Materialist may be lawfully required to explain the process by which matter exercises the faculty of thinking.'[4] The logician's objection that such an argument used the very hypothesis in question to put the burden of proof on its opponents hardly seemed relevant, for the Jeffersonian meant to affirm his unshakeable belief in his God. The motto which Priestley chose for his *Matter and Spirit* declared that if anyone should successfully show that the soul was material, religious men ought not to be alarmed: here actually would be further cause to admire a Power which could endow matter with such a marvelous faculty.

This was, however, a slippery subject—especially for the philosopher who lacked a systematic metaphysic. Having made the incomprehensibility of the Creator's art the first defense of his materialism, Jefferson nevertheless made his second defense the precisely opposite axiom: that the Creator's ways were always simple, economical, and understandable to the meanest intelligence.

I should . . . prefer swallowing one incomprehensibility rather than two. It requires one effort only to admit the single incomprehensibility of matter endowed with thought, and two to believe, first that of an existence called spirit, of which we have neither evidence nor idea, and then secondly how that spirit, which has neither extension nor solidity, can put material organs into motion.[5]

In his materialism, as in many other dogmas which he asserted categorically, the Jeffersonian did not rest entirely easy. And when he tried to harmonize Newtonian physics with materialist philosophy, he brought to the surface his latent doubts. Rittenhouse, who attacked the method of the 'tyrant' Aristotle, praised Newton's method 'because it pretends not to be of Nature's privy council, or to have free access to her most inscrutable mysteries; but to attend carefully to her works, to discover the immediate causes of visible effects, to trace those causes to others more general and simple, advancing by slow and sure steps toward the great first cause of all things.' Priestley, the most explicit and systematic defender of Jeffersonian materialism, explained that when Newton showed that matter itself was not solid (but consisted of the attraction of minute particles perhaps with empty interstices) he had added greatly to the acceptability of materialist philosophy. Thus Newton, according to Priestley, had gone far toward wiping away the traditional 'reproach' of matter, namely that it was impenetrable. The materialist philosopher's denial of the existence of nonmaterial substance now no longer excluded altogether the reality of immaterial entities. For the 'matter' of which the universe was exclusively composed might have all the fine airiness of the idealist philosopher's most impalpable essences. The process of the original creation had become more understandable:

This supposition, of matter having no other properties besides those of attraction and repulsion, greatly relieves the difficulty which attends the supposition of the *creation of it out of nothing*, and also the continual moving of it by a being who has hitherto been supposed to have no common property with it. For, according to this hypothesis, both the creating mind, and the created substance are equally destitute of *solidity* or *impenetrability*; so that there can be no difficulty whatever in supposing that the latter may have been the offspring of the former.[6]

Yet to justify materialism by proving that it was really a form of idealism was not wholly satisfactory, for the Jeffersonian had made too much of the rest of his philosophy depend on materialism in a naïve form. Priestley and others sometimes actually argued that a great virtue of their philosophy was precisely the contrary of that just described. To deny reality to everything which was not tangible, was, they said on these occasions, to make the Creator by definition a material being: and because their God was solidly material He must therefore be more real than the God of the idealists.

Despite his satisfaction that Newtonian materialism had left the door open to immaterial entities, the Jeffersonian persistently claimed that his own philosophical edifice was built exclusively of the data of the senses. Jefferson himself found considerable reassurance in the current discoveries of experimental psychology. With the passing of the years and the accumulation of evidence he felt justified in giving his materialism increasingly explicit and dogmatic statement. During his stay in France just before the French Revolution, at Madame Helvétius' famous salon at Auteuil, Jefferson had met the pioneer positivist, Monsieur Cabanis. When Cabanis published the two volumes of his *Rapports du physique et du moral de l'homme* in 1802, he sent them to his American friend. Jefferson, acknowledging the volumes, noted that Cabanis' specific connections between thought and the human body had advanced the materialist argument a long way toward conclusive proof—'within reconnoitering distance of the citadel itself.' Ten years later, writing to another friend, the prominent materialist Dr. Thomas Cooper, Jefferson still called Cabanis' work the most profound of all human compositions.

Not until 1825, the year before Jefferson's death, did he find satisfactory confirmation for his lifelong materialism. Then he came upon 'the most extraordinary of all books,' the experiments of Monsieur Flourens, which had been first published in French just three years before. These extensive experiments on the nervous system of vertebrates, from Jefferson's point of view left very little to be desired. Flourens' conclusions were drawn from his delicate vivisection of fowls. First he had completely removed the cerebrum of some animals, leaving the cerebellum and the other parts of the brain uninjured; such animals lost all the senses of hearing, seeing, feeling, smelling and tasting, and the faculties of will, intelligence, memory and perception, but still could live for months in perfect health. They retained powers of motion, but would not move except on external excitement; and actually would starve while standing on a pile of grain unless food was crammed down their throats. Then Flourens, varying the operation, removed from other fowls the cerebellum, while leaving the cerebrum untouched; such animals retained all their senses, faculties, and understanding, but lost the powers of regulated motion, and exhibited the symptoms of drunkenness. Jefferson—'the materialist fortified with these new proofs of his own creed'—rejoiced at Flourens' discoveries. When he enthusiastically recounted these experiments in a letter to John Adams in 1825, he declared that Flourens had conveyed the philosopher actually within the citadel which Cabanis had brought into view. 'Cabanis had proved by the anatomical structure of certain portions of the human frame, that they might be capable of receiving from the hand of the Creator the faculty of thinking; Flourens proves that they have received it; that the cerebrum is the thinking organ. . . . I wish to see what the spiritualists will say to this.' [7]

Jefferson's delight at the final scientific demolition of 'spiritualism' is surely not hard to understand. His materialism was no appendage to the rest of his thought, but an assumption—or rather a predisposition—which colored all his ideas. Unless he had presupposed that the only realm of being was the realm of tangible things, he could not easily have believed that the nature of the Creator could be adequately sensed through the visible universe. And this belief (the first axiom of his theology) was the foundation of his natural history. Materialism was involved in all his principal beliefs about man. Had he believed that men possessed an immaterial entity or 'soul,' his anthropological demonstration of human equality would have been either superfluous or irrelevant. The equalitarian implications of materialism seemed obvious; for to demonstrate man's homogeneity with the material universe was to destroy arrogance. Rush remarked that man's constant dependence on physical stimuli from his Maker showed his essential resemblance to the lower creation, and the fact that he was of no higher substance than the simplest plant or the meanest insect seemed a proper motive for humility. 'A pigmy and a Patagonian, a mouse and a mammoth,' observed Jefferson, 'derive their dimensions from the same nutritive juices.' [8] And Priestley repeated the appropriate words of Ecclesiastes (3:19-20): 'As the one dieth, so dieth the other; yea, they have all one breath; so that a man hath no preeminence above a beast: for all is vanity. All go unto one place; all are of the dust, and all turn to dust again.'

2. The Happy Variety of Minds

BY demonstrating that men were wholly physical creatures, the Jeffersonian, as we have seen, had identified thought with action. Perhaps more important from his point of view, he had prepared himself to make his faith in the valuable variety of the material universe a refuge from all metaphysics. In the present section we shall see how he argued toward this comfortable conclusion. When the Jeffersonian had established that man shared the qualities of the inanimate and lower animate universe, he was ready to find in human thought the qualities of all physical nature, and to justify them as inevitable and good. Rush's substitute for metaphysics—a study which he called 'the anatomy of the human mind' or 'phrenology'— sought by the physical sciences to explain the diversities and conflicts in human thought. By calling man a 'homogeneous being' Priestley had affirmed not merely that man was purely material, but furthermore that men's minds like their bodies showed the qualities of the whole material creation.

In the universe as a whole the Jeffersonian philosopher, we have noted, admired the beautiful variety established by the

Creator. He could not conceive that human minds should fail to show the same manifoldness. 'It is obvious,' Rush remarked, 'there is the same variety in the texture of the minds, that there is in the bodies of men.' Jefferson agreed and drew an important conclusion: 'As the Creator has made no two faces alike, so no two minds, and probably no two creeds.' The experiments of Flourens had confirmed that the brain was an organ of such delicate texture that the slightest variation in its shape or the slightest lesion on its surface was immediately registered in the thoughts and sensations of the affected creature. Might not the differences in men's thoughts be explained then by physical differences in their thinking organs? To see the character of men's ideas determined by the shapes of their minds was thus to incorporate the variety of human thought into the indelible plan of the universe. 'Differences of opinion . . . ,' Jefferson remarked, 'like differences of face, are a law of our nature, and should be viewed with the same tolerance.' Again and again, when Jefferson had occasion to explain away the differences among thinking men, and when he was unwilling to assert categorically that his own opinion was the right one, he reasoned in just this manner. When John Randolph wrote him in 1803 concerning certain of their disagreements, Jefferson's friendly reply was that such explanations were not needed; for, he said, he had ceased to wonder at the differences of opinion on any subject, and acquiesced in them as readily as in the physical variations of the human form. In a letter to Rush in 1811 expressing eagerness to be reconciled to his old friend John Adams, Jefferson asked, 'Why should we be dissocialized by mere differences of opinion in politics, in religion, in philosophy, or anything else? His opinions are as honestly formed as my own. Our different views of the same subject are the result of a difference in our organization and experience.' Examples could be multiplied where Jefferson took refuge in the happy variety of nature: not merely in the more abstract philosophical problems, which never troubled Jefferson deeply anyway, but even in politics. 'The terms of whig and tory,' he often observed, 'belong to natural as well as to civil history. They denote the temper and constitution of mind of different individuals.' [9]

Was it not, then, as absurd to seek a metaphysical norm for human thought, as to ask in the abstract what should be the human figure or complexion? Why should 'the mode of action called thinking' be essentially different from other modes of action? Why should not the thoughts of men vary with the physical shape of their brains? The American philosopher's demonstration of the equality of men had been eased by the hypothetical impossibility of discovering any bodily norm for the parents of the human race: similarly now his ethical ideal of toleration rested on the meaninglessness of a norm for the mind of man. Who was to say that the aquiline nose of the Roman was to be preferred to the snub nose of the Irishman? Or that the dour mind of a John Adams was inferior to the sanguine mind of a Jefferson? Were not both products of the same Maker's craftsmanship? Were not both equally needed to express the Creator's love of variety?

The Jeffersonian, then, could in good conscience declare that men were not responsible for their opinions. As Rush proved from clinical evidence in his ingenious 'Inquiry into the Influence of Physical Causes upon the Moral Faculty,' and as others confirmed by commonplace examples, the particular opinions which men expressed were usually the effect of special physical causes. 'We think by force, as well as live by force. If any man doubt the truth of this assertion, let him suspend, for a moment, the operations of his mind, or, in other words, let him cease to think.' [10] In his *Introductory Lectures* he declared that reasoning was 'as much an involuntary act, as the pulsation of the heart and arteries.' Jefferson sometimes doubted whether any arguments could bring men to give up the opinions to which physical forces had predisposed them. 'I never saw an instance of one of two disputants convincing the other by argument,' he once facetiously remarked. 'I have seen many, on their getting warm, becoming rude, and shooting one another.' The Creator had not made human minds so that they were all equally and similarly moved by the pure force of reason. Minds were indeed machines, but each was unique, and in a sense followed its own internally-given laws. When Jefferson wrote Rush (March 6, 1813) that 'every man's own reason must be his oracle,' he was not professing faith in the power of an impartial logic, but was underlining the uniqueness of each man's brain. 'Our opinions,' he said, 'are not voluntary.'

If no man was responsible for the shape of his brain, and if that shape predetermined his opinions, there was surely no justification for praising, blaming, or punishing a man for what he thought. The standard of intellectual virtue obviously could not be the possession of 'truth,' for the Creator could not have required man to transcend his body. Yet the American philosopher refused to believe that there was no standard by which men's thinking could be judged. And he actually found one which seemed harmonious with his cosmology, with his belief in an orderly Creator, and even with his own unwillingness to commit himself explicitly to any absolute other than the Creator. The proper test, the Jeffersonian declared, was not what a man believed, but how accurately and honestly he avowed whatever the Creator had destined him to believe. The ideas which a man professed were less important than whether these ideas were the characteristic expression of the mind which the Creator had given him. Of course, according to a strict materialism, even a man's intellectual honesty was no choice of his own, but the simple effect of environmental influences on his thinking organ. Yet at this point the Jeffersonians were not too rigorous. 'Your own reason is the only oracle given you by heaven,' Jefferson advised his young friend Peter Carr, 'and you are answerable, not for the rightness, but uprightness of the decision.' Integrity of views more than their soundness, he told Gerry, was the proper basis of esteem.[11] The Creator desired above all that men be true to themselves. According to the preamble of Jefferson's Act for establishing Religious Freedom in Virginia, 'Almighty God hath created the mind free . . . all attempts to influence it by temporal punishments or burthens, or by civil incapacitations, tend only to beget habits of hypocrisy and meanness, and are a departure from the plan of the Holy author of our religion, who being Lord both of body and mind, yet chose not to propagate it by coercions on either, as was his Almighty power to do.'

The free interaction of variegated minds had been commanded by the Creator Himself. But Jeffersonian materialism had given to the 'freedom' of the human mind a dangerous ambiguity. In what sense was a man 'free' to think, if his ideas had been predetermined by the shape of his brain? Jefferson's own materialism and his theory of toleration were themselves theories. How could he prove them anything more than the product of his own peculiar brain? Yet it was by means of them that he sought to mediate among different views.

This problem did not much disturb the Jeffersonian. He was not anxious to escape the Pyrrhonist trap that awaits all materialist philosophies. As we have seen, thought from the Jeffersonian point of view was essentially a mode of action, rather than the intellectual pursuit of an absolute. Nothing could have seemed more futile than to seek a standard for thought when the Creator Himself had produced only varied ways of thinking. The task of the Jeffersonian philosopher, as he conceived it, was not to harmonize different concepts of truth, but to mediate among modes of mental action: not to bring consistency into the realm of thought but sociability into the world of thinkers.

In religion, for example, the Jeffersonian saw each man not in spiritual pursuit of a metaphysically accurate vision of the True God, but as engaging in an *act* of homage to his Creator. While it might have been impossible to make men's disparate theories of God logically consistent, the Jeffersonian had set himself quite another task, namely, to enable men sociably to perform their different acts of homage. There was no question of 'consistency' here: problems arose only when a clash of opinions became a clash of men. Paine portrayed in an eloquent metaphor the Creator's delight in the multiformity of men's minds and in the diversity of their acts of religious homage:

123

If we suppose a large family of children, who . . . made it a custom to present to their parents some token of their affection and gratitude, each of them would make a different offering, and most probably in a different manner. Some would pay their congratulations in themes of verse and prose, by some little devices, as their genius dictated, or according to what they thought would please; and, perhaps, the least of all, not able to do any of those things, would ramble into the garden, or the field, and gather what it thought the prettiest flower it could find, though, perhaps, it might be but a simple weed. The parent would be more gratified by such a variety, than if the whole of them had acted on a concerted plan, and each had made exactly the same offering. This would have the cold appearance of contrivance, or the harsh one of controul. But of all unwelcome things, nothing could more afflict the parent than to know, that the whole of them had afterwards gotten together by the ears, boys and girls, fighting, scratching, reviling, and abusing each other about which was the best or the worst present.

Why may we not suppose, that the great Father of all is pleased with variety of devotion; and that the greatest offence we can act, is that by which we seek to torment and render each other miserable? . . . I do not believe that any two men, on what are called doctrinal points, think alike who think at all. It is only those who have not thought that appear to agree.[12]

The very nature of ideas seemed to show that in the Creator's design sociability—the happy coexistence of the created variety of minds—had been more important than uniformity. For ideas had happily been made so that their discord never in itself produced physical injury: in Jefferson's succinct phrase, ideas were not like stones. 'It does me no injury for my neighbor to say there are twenty gods, or no God. It neither picks my pocket nor breaks my leg.' The Creator would surely not have given this peculiar undamaging quality to ideas unless He had intended each man to be free to publish the peculiar product of his brain. 'When I hear another express an opinion which is not mine, I say to myself, he has a right to his opinion, as I to mine; why should I question it?' asked Jefferson. 'His error does me no injury, and shall I become a Don Quixote, to bring all men by force of argument to one opinion? If a fact be misstated, it is probable he is gratified by a belief of it, and I have no right to deprive him of the gratification.' [13]

Jefferson's materialism led him to use natural science actually to discover the destined function of ideas. An interesting example of such reasoning is his discussion of Oliver Evans' claim for a patent on a grain elevator:

If nature has made any one thing less susceptible than all others of exclusive property, it is the action of the thinking power called an idea, which an individual may exclusively possess as long as he keeps it to himself; but the moment it is divulged, it forces itself into the possession of every one, and the receiver cannot dispossess himself of it. Its peculiar character, too, is that no one possesses the less, because every other possesses the whole of it. . . . That ideas should freely spread from one to another over the globe, for the moral and mutual instruction of man, and improvement of his condition, seems to have been peculiarly and benevolently designed by nature, when she made them, like fire, expansible over all space, without lessening their density in any point, and like the air in which we breathe, move, and have our physical being, incapable of confinement or exclusive appropriation.[14]

While to us it might seem that the obvious lesson from Jefferson's observations was the reality of some realm of being where the rules of physics were inapplicable, Jefferson could draw no such moral. Instead he saw his materialist criteria confirmed by their ability to show the role of ideas in the universal order.

The variety of minds served the economy of nature in many ways. The Creator, who designed the human brain for activity, had insured the restlessness of all minds by enabling no single one to envisage all the qualities of the creation. Since no one by himself could aspire to a serene knowledge of the whole truth, all men had been drawn into an active, exploratory and co-operative attitude. As Benjamin Smith Barton explained in the motto (borrowed from Akenside) for the first volume of his *Elements of Botany:*

But not alike to every mortal eye
Is this great scene unveil'd. For since the claims
Of social life, to different labours urge

The active powers of man; with wise intent
The hand of NATURE on peculiar minds
Imprints a different bias, and to each
Decrees its province in the common toil.

This different bias of different minds, by leading men to explore diverse aspects of nature, resulted in the whole being more thoroughly examined.

Even men's errors kept alive the spirit of inquiry. Rush urged that universities encourage differences of opinion to prevent them becoming (in Adam Smith's phrase) 'the dull repositories of exploded opinions.' Priestley acknowledged the debt of all to those who differed from them, when he dedicated his defense of the phlogiston theory to several French opponents of the doctrine. In primitive communities, where the absence of civilization, science and religion caused a deficiency of stimuli, the wholesome variety of opinion was lacking; and this in turn re-enforced that 'dull and disgusting sameness of mind,' which, according to Rush, characterized all savage nations. Such lack of variety itself explained why savages knew so little of science. 'Difference of opinion leads to inquiry,' Jefferson observed, 'and inquiry to truth.' [15]

Since successful inquiry was most important in the fundamental issues of human life, the diversity established by the Creator should, of course, be most encouraged in fundamental matters. In religion least of all would the Creator have intended uniformity of minds, for such uniformity might have prevented successful inquiry into the nature of the Creator Himself. On this most difficult of all subjects, Jefferson remarked in his *Notes on Virginia* (Query XVII), the mutual criticisms of men of honestly differing views were especially needed. 'Subject opinion to coercion: whom will you make your inquisitors? . . . And why subject it to coercion? To produce uniformity. But is uniformity of opinion desirable? No more than of face and stature. Introduce the bed of Procrustes then, and as there is danger that the large men may beat the small, make us all of a size, by lopping the former and stretching the latter. Difference of opinion is advantageous in religion. The several sects perform the office of a *censor morum.*' Priestley observed that unbelievers and even bigots had their use in the general plan: their assigned task, like that of the idolatrous Canaanites, was to exercise the faith of the Israelites, without having the power to drive the faithful out. It was by the objections of the obstinate, Priestley thought, that Christianity would be forced to purge itself and return to its primitive purity. 'A truth that has never been opposed,' he remarked, 'cannot acquire that firm and unwavering assent, which is given to that which has stood the test of a rigorous examination.' [16]

If the variety of minds was to forward the discovery of truth, there must indeed be a truth to be discovered. The Jeffersonian had actually argued that the happy variety of the mental world enabled men to discover a reality, stable and apart from the idiosyncrasy of each mind. But by declaring that the differences between brains explained the variety of ideas, he had merged ideas into the flux of the physical world and had seemingly deprived himself of criteria. This logical dilemma however could not discomfit the Jeffersonian mind in which the physical world always seemed an undeniably real and stable aspect of the cosmos. There might be many ways of doing homage to God; but there must be one right antidote to the poison of the rattlesnake. The American Philosophical Society, we must recall, existed for promoting '*useful* knowledge,' and knowledge could not be useful unless it corresponded to the facts of nature. Yet the Jeffersonian significantly never felt it necessary to demonstrate the existence or the singleness of the visible material universe: the concrete and constructive tasks of life were close upon him and pressed with an urgency which he did not need to prove real. If he was to master his environment, he dared not luxuriate in the exquisite manifoldness of the human mind.

3. The Perils of Metaphysics

THE American philosopher therefore made it his mission to warn men against the idiosyncrasies of their brains. What form did he give his warning, and what were its consequences? The world out there, which his cosmology assumed to have objective reality, was what every man must see if he was to know anything, and to do his job as Workman. Had there been no such objective reality, there would have been no design to evidence the existence and character of a Creator. The Jeffersonian never dared believe that the Creator's character varied with the point of view of the observer. While he did not worry over explaining the relationship between the true shape of nature (which must have been visible to the Creator) and that myopic shape which each man could see, he more than once betrayed his conviction that there was one and only one true shape. He sometimes suggested that the more 'accurate' and detailed was any man's view of the economy of nature, the more closely would the content of his mind approximate that of the Creator's. The highest praise which Rush could give Franklin was to call him 'that MAN whose mind like a mirror, has long reflected back upon the Deity a miniature picture of his own works.' The greatness of Rittenhouse was that his model of the solar system was a true representation of the Creator's original.

While men's minds might be infinitely varied, the external world had to be defined if men were to cope with it. The Jeffersonian could not doubt that there was a solid raw material to be grasped and put to use. 'Fact' was the Jeffersonian word for the elements in that fixed and absolute external reality. It was 'facts' alone which were capable of 'unadulterated purity,' and the Jeffersonian sought the uncontaminated fact much as the Platonist sought the pure idea—convinced that it alone gave access to the structure of the creation. 'In conducting a series of experiments,' Barton urged in his study of the rattlesnake, 'it is ever a matter of importance, that the mind of the experimentalist should be free from the dominion of prejudice and system. Perhaps, facts are never related in all their unadulterated purity except by those, who, intent upon the discovery of truth, keep system at a distance, regardless of its claims. The strong democracy of facts should exert its wholesome sway.' By a 'fact' the American philosopher meant anything recordable by man's physical senses. Information received through the senses was especially well suited for a refuge from the variety and vagary of particular brains; for, as Priestley noted, each sensation could remind man of his dependence on the single Creator. 'When once we quit the basis of sensation,' Jefferson warned John Adams (August 15, 1820), 'all is in the wind. To talk of *immaterial* existences, is to talk of *nothings*.' Or, in Paine's epigram, 'A fact is superior to reasoning.'

The primacy of facts, according to Rush, had been declared by the Creator in the Garden of Eden, when He made natural history the first study of Adam. The printing press, as Rush lamented, had encouraged men to rely more on 'opinions' than on 'facts,' more on the senses of other people than on their own; a pure scientific method now remained only among farmers, mechanics, and seamen who, seldom opening a book, had cultivated habits and talents of observation. Rush therefore carried in his coat pocket a small notebook in which he jotted the 'home remedies' which he encountered among the unlearned. Though he called this his 'Quack Recipe Book,' he always viewed these lay recipes with interest rather than contempt, for he expected to learn something from observers who were uncorrupted by medical theory. 'Hippocrates,' he remarked, '. . . copied only from the book of nature; and it is to the stability, which the truth and correctness of his facts have given

129

to his works, that they have descended to us in safety along the deep and rapid stream of time in spite of the constant tendency of his false reasonings to overset them.' [17] Facts were the raw material of all knowledge: they were in Rush's figure the juice of the grape while reasoning was nothing but a fermenting process. In the raw data of the senses there could be no human flaw, but in the process of individual fermentation, anything might happen. Thus it was not in the exercise of right reason, but in the collection and comparison of sensible experience that Jefferson, in a familiar passage of the *Notes on Virginia,* found the avenue to truth: 'A patient pursuit of facts, and cautious combination and comparison of them, is the drudgery to which man is subjected by his Maker, if he wishes to attain sure knowledge.'

The philosopher's only hope was to flee from the weakness, the partiality, and the factitious subtlety of his brain, to the pure data of his senses. In this aspect, Jeffersonian philosophy was an attempt to capture naïveté; to divest individual minds of their peculiarities that each might sense the visible universe with childish innocence. The large purpose was to save men from ideas and systems: to take them out of the cave where they saw nothing but the puppets of their own brains, into the open air where they could see the sensible objects which alone were real.

The shortcomings of Jeffersonian epistemology were not so much the weaknesses of an explicit system, as an example of the inevitable failure of naïveté. The Jeffersonian was not himself disheartened by his inability to explain the connection between the common universe of men's senses (facts) and the miscellaneous product of men's brains (ideas). He despised metaphysics and was himself surely no metaphysician. But that very materialism which seemed to him to have bridged the gap between mind and matter, idea and experience, had actually drawn him into a dualism no less metaphysical and no less obscure than that of the 'spiritualists' whom he despised.

The first element in the Jeffersonian dualism was the human mind. As we have seen, the variety of minds was the divine mandate that every man put upon the world the peculiar product of his brain. Here the American philosopher veered close to an ideal of self-expression which was foreign to much of the rest of his thought. But even here he unwittingly admitted that something more could be said: some minds functioned more satisfactorily than others; the perceptions of some might even be 'wrong' and the perceptions of others 'right.' His accounts of mental disorders which we shall presently examine implied some ideal of mental health. Without admitting in so many words that there was a universal criterion for the product of all brains, when he talked of 'healthy' functioning he was saying quite the same thing. 'The sickly, weakly, timid man, fears the people, and is a Tory by nature. The healthy, strong and bold, cherishes them, and is formed a Whig by nature.' [18] Was this not just another way of saying that Toryism was false, and Whiggery true?

The second element in Jeffersonian dualism was the physical universe. When he looked at the interpretations which different minds (and especially the most ingenious) had made of the universe, he was struck by the fact that even the best interpretations were always more transient and less complete than the universe itself. Man could never grasp within a theory the manifoldness of nature. But the Jeffersonian would not draw the moral that the human brain was incommensurable with the reality which underlay the physical universe; rather he said man must eschew all 'theory' in order to arrive at facts-in-themselves. This of course expressed an unquestioned belief that there was a texture of objective reality, which could—however partially—be grasped by the organs which the Creator had given to men.

The American philosopher saved himself from the more inconvenient consequences of this dualism by the way he stressed its elements. In theology and politics, where sociability was his aim, he emphasized the desirable diversity of men's ideas. In natural science he emphasized the community and the objective reality of the evidences of men's senses. The task which he assigned to philosophy, as we shall see, actually implied an external and absolute object of knowledge, while relieving the philosopher of defining its realm of being.

For the Jeffersonian, the major role of philosophy was prophylactic. 'The conquest of a man's prejudices,' remarked Priestley, 'is more honorable to him than the discovery, or the most successful defense, of any truth.' [19] The philosopher had no right (much less a duty) to 'standardize' thought. He was not to lead men to truth, but to save them from errors. In practice, then, the philosopher's task would be to warn against 'mistakes,' against perversions of the true and universal data of man's senses by the peculiarities of any man's brain.

'Abstraction,' which was the prime occupation and the essential sin of metaphysics, was the greatest menace to all true philosophy. It was a surrender to the human temptation to oversimplify, and the tantalizing complexity of nature made such vice understandable enough. Indolence induced men uncritically to adopt the views of others, so that they became hypocrites or purveyors of second-hand knowledge, frustrating the Creator's design. But whenever a man failed to realize that the brain which the Creator had given him was only an individual and peculiar organ, he was on the brink of intellectual arrogance. Both indolence and arrogance had drawn men away from careful observation of nature—the only true resource of theology and philosophy. Men were only too ready to believe in short and easy paths to nature's secrets. 'Candour,' lamented Barton, 'is too rare a virtue among philosophers; and the desire to establish systems has deluged the world with errors, and with fables.' [20] While the arrogant, the weak, or the cowardly mind abstracted aspects of nature, erected them into a system, and pushed out of view the magnificent artifice of the Creator, the true philosopher would try to describe the particular facts of the creation in all their complexity.

This concept of the philosopher's function expressed both reverence for the Creator, and a scrupulous respect for sensible experience: the perfect marriage of the 'ought' and the 'is.' Somehow, out of what men had seen and done would emerge a prescription for how men ought to think—or rather how they ought to interpret the physical universe. The lessons of philosophy were hardly to be distinguished from the fruits of experience; knowledge was indivisible. Attempts to divide 'reason and the senses, so happily paired by the Creator of the world' —like attempts to separate religion and morals, government and liberty—produced the evils which inevitably followed disregard of the divine symmetry.[21] 'Metaphysics' (which thrived on 'abstraction') always attempted precisely such a separation and for the Jeffersonian, therefore, it was not a branch of philosophy, but a mental disorder. The metaphysician suffered from narcissism: he admired his own cleverness rather than the magnificent creation. He was the egoist—or the dreamer—who had forgotten that what he saw was only the partial picture which one man's mind had abstracted from the manifold universe.

Characteristically, the Jeffersonian sought to unmask these common errors through experience. While the history of almost any science would have illustrated the sins of metaphysics, he found them most flagrant and their practical consequences most unhappy in the history of medicine. For centuries metaphysically minded doctors had been preoccupied with neat oversimplifications; and Rush found it necessary to devote much of his life to the reform of 'nosology' or the science of classifying diseases. The halting progress of medical science he laid to the readiness of physicians to generalize wildly from the peculiar circumstances of their place and generation. Such medical 'systems,' which purported to tell the whole truth about diseases, actually did nothing more than register the peculiar bias of their inventors. Thus, for example, Dr. Stahl had argued from the success of nature in curing the simple diseases of Saxony, to his peculiar *anima medica*, according to which nature had the power to cure all diseases; Dr. Boerhaave, observing only the diseases endemic to Holland, had said that all were caused by fluids; and Dr. Cullen, who had seen nothing but the prevailing nervous disorders of Great Britain, insisted that all diseases originated in the nerves. While Rush himself was not wholly innocent of oversimplifying all bodily disorders into the effects of a single cause, he was alert to see the error in others. And he did much to liberate the minds of his young medical students from a choice among simplistic theories. The only way the physician could ever rise above the passing fads of scientific terminology, Rush urged, was to turn from simple names to complex facts. 'There is the same difference between the knowledge of a physician who prescribes for diseases as limited by genera and species, and of one who prescribes under the direction of just principles,' Rush remarked, 'that there is between the knowledge we obtain of the nature and extent of the sky, by viewing a few feet of it from the bottom of a well, and viewing from the top of a mountain the whole canopy of heaven.' [22]

Jefferson was similarly outspoken against these errors of medical science. The moment a person formed a theory, he warned, the imagination could see in every object nothing but the traits which favored it. So ready were men to rely on their caricatures of nature that they had committed themselves without reserve to theories which were as transient as the fashions of ladies' gowns. In the curriculum of the University of Virginia, he therefore sought to divert students from these passing theories and toward the actual shape of nature. Jefferson opposed teaching the 'theory' of medicine which he said was the charlatanry of the body, as theology was the charlatanry of the mind.[23] Of course he favored teaching the *practice* of medicine, which was to be confined to the study of actual disorders and their actual symptoms in the animal body. Such symptoms, he wrote Dr. Caspar Wistar (June 21, 1807), were 'as various as the elements of which the body is composed. The combinations, too, of these symptoms are so infinitely diversified, that many associations of them appear too rarely to establish a definite disease; and to an unknown disease, there cannot be a known remedy. Here then, the judicious, the moral, the humane physician should stop.'

Jefferson's concept of the proper sphere of medical science is not a little puzzling. 'Facts,' he said, must displace 'theories.' The medical systems of Hoffmann, Boerhaave, Stahl, Cullen, and Brown, according to Jefferson, had passed 'like the shifting figures of a magic lantern . . . like the dresses of the annual doll-babies from Paris, becoming, from their novelty, the vogue of the day, and yielding to the next novelty their ephemeral favor.' Jefferson warned the student against systems which substituted presumption for knowledge, and indeed against any ingenious dream which promised 'to let him into all nature's secrets at short hand.' Yet the principal motive for his warning, as Jefferson declared to Rush, was a theory of his own which seems to us a still shorter shorthand than any of the rest. This was his belief in the *vis medicatrix naturae,* or healing power of nature. In most cases, Jefferson urged, man's knowledge of diseases was so scanty that rather than launch 'into the boundless region of what is unknown,' the wise physician would 'be a watchful, but quiet spectator of the operations of nature.' [24] He could not doubt that the Creator's economy would make its own adjustment.

The perils of metaphysics were not all of the metaphysicians' making. Many necessary social institutions threatened to interpose between the actual shape of nature and the senses of the observant individual. The very language which men used tempted them to abstraction. In all man's thought, in all his discussions with his fellow philosophers, he was misled by the seductive simplicity of words. An education built on languages was therefore particularly dangerous. 'We teach our sons words, at the expense of things,' Rush lamented. Paine explained in *The Age of Reason* that the schools of the Greeks had been schools of science and philosophy, and not of languages; but now men showed themselves most un-Greek by studying ancient words instead of modern things. The mind's natural predisposition to science was smothered 'by the barren study of a dead language,' and the philosopher was lost in the linguist.

Jefferson himself opposed linguistic 'purists' and argued for vitality in language. Words were too often the fossils of old ideas. Purists, he complained, would keep thought in old grooves, bolster outmoded systems and classifications, and make

135

it difficult for men to describe the perpetual novelty of their experience. To keep the language flexible was as important as to keep men free from other seductive certainties. A language could not be too rich. 'I am a friend to *neology*,' Jefferson declared. 'It is the only way to give to a language copiousness and euphony. . . . Dictionaries are but the depositories of words already legitimated by usage. Society is the workshop in which new ones are elaborated.' He had been unwilling in 1776 to undertake a thorough codification of the laws of Virginia because language was too imperfect and experience too varied to allow the expression in a few sentences of the shades of meaning which future situations would require; therefore, at least in that early period, he preferred the tentative and shifting phrases of the common law. He observed that Shakespeare's art would have been unthinkable without his free and magical creation of words, and that modern chemistry was possible only because men had transformed the antiquated terminology of Van Helmont, Stane, and Scheele. French science had progressed with the elaboration of the French language.[25]

By the flexibility of language Jefferson hoped to help ideas keep pace with the flux of the visible universe. This desire that mind should not be isolated from the physical world had been at the root of his materialism, and indeed had shaped his very conception of the philosopher's mission. For by warning against abstraction, by questioning systems, and by attacking purism, the philosopher saw himself bridging the gap between mind and matter, idea and experience.

When the American philosopher sought to be true to his antimetaphysical bias, to see pure facts-in-themselves, the consequence was not to reveal a higher meaning but rather to turn the universe into miscellany. As his merging of mind and body had made mind seem a display of the divine manifoldness, so now his relentless materialism seemed to dissolve even the axiomatic categories of his material universe. From the fact that every physical object was in some sense unique, his materialism drew him to the suspicion that there could be no natural classes of objects. As Jefferson remarked:

Nature has, in truth, produced units only through all her works. Classes, orders, genera, species, are not of her work. Her creation is of individuals. No two animals are exactly alike; no two plants, nor even two leaves or blades of grass; no two crystallizations. And if we may venture from what is within the cognizance of such organs as ours, to conclude on that beyond their powers, we must believe that no two particles of matter are of exact resemblance. This infinitude of units or individuals being far beyond the capacity of our memory, we are obliged, in aid of that, to distribute them into masses, throwing into each of these all the individuals which have a certain degree of resemblance; to subdivide these again into smaller groups, according to certain points of dissimilitude observable in them, and so on until we have formed what we call a system of classes, orders, genera and species. In doing this, we fix arbitrarily on such characteristic resemblances and differences as seem to us most prominent and invariable in the several subjects, and most likely to take a strong hold in our memories.[26]

Priestley, who agreed that nature exhibited nothing but particulars, went on to describe not merely all general terms, but all general propositions as 'artificial things'—crutches required by the weak human memory. To confirm the nonexistence of classes and species, the Jeffersonian appealed to random and peculiar examples. Jefferson himself pointed to the Australian Ornithorhynchus (duckbilled platypus, or duck mole) and the strange animals discovered by Alexander von Humboldt in his travels to South America, as among the striking anomalies by which nature sported with human classifications. The unknown diseases, which had made Jefferson and Rush distrust all systems of nosology, were made grounds for attacking all abstractions. And when Barton in his *Elements of Botany* noted the final difficulty of drawing a line between plant and animal life, he too ventured to doubt all the classes of the natural historian.

But general ideas and categories (like 'species') were necessary to the theology which held the Jeffersonian world together, and to the science by which he mastered his physical environment. He therefore could not permit himself finally to deny their reality. Despite the doubts bred by his materialism, the Jeffersonian refused to allow himself to be argued into absurdity, inaction, or ineffectiveness—by materialism any more than by any other philosophy. He would not deny the existence of implements which he had found so useful. In Jeffersonian thought as a whole we therefore hear nominalism expressed only in cautious and uncertain whispers, stifled by the louder demands of theology and science.

The American philosopher never dared directly and comprehensively deny the pervading order which his theology had expected and his science had confirmed. His denial of perceptible order was always piecemeal. Apart from passages like those already cited, his doubts of the order of nature are expressed only in his occasional complaints against Linnaean terminology; and even these disclosed his uneasiness in raising such questions. Having built his natural history and much of his anthropology and ethics on Linnaeus' *Systema Naturae*, he commonly expressed unstinting admiration for the Swedish naturalist. Benjamin Smith Barton, himself perhaps the most distinguished American taxonomist of the day, called Linnaeus the Swedish Pliny, the greatest of naturalists—'a mind which with respect to the arrangement of natural bodies has never been equalled.' Peale guided the visitor through his museum by the Linnaean terminology. Rush and Jefferson agreed that his work was without peer. But just as the pious Linnaeus himself had admitted that he had not arrived at a truly natural system, so, too, the American philosopher recognized his limitations. Jefferson insisted that Linnaeus' system and all his categories were artificial. And Barton thought Linnaeus' approach to a natural plan was only occasional. 'System is a slippery thing,' he warned; a truly 'natural' arrangement of vegetables would never be accomplished.[27]

Linnaeus had explained the defects of his system by the disproportion between human comprehension and the divine order. Similarly, the Jeffersonian, even while expressing his doubts of man's power to discover the order in the universe, affirmed his abiding faith in some such order. Jefferson himself anxiously denied the implication that the unreality of humanly defined 'orders' and 'species' was an imputation on the art of

138

the Creator. Any apparent chaos in nature seemed evidence of the incomprehensible intricacy of the Creator's art. 'The plan of creation,' he observed, 'is inscrutable to our limited faculties. Nature has not arranged her productions on a single and direct line. They branch at every step, and in every direction, and he who attempts to reduce them into departments, is left to do it by the lines of his own fancy . . . it has been necessary to draw arbitrary lines, in order to accommodate our limited views.' According to Barton, it was 'the many beautiful analogies' which the Creator had established between the plant and the animal kingdoms, that explained man's difficulty in defining the precise difference between plant and animal life. The very inability of individual men to comprehend the divine scheme thus seemed proof not merely of its existence, but of its infinite subtlety.

Desperately the Jeffersonian clung to his faith that there was an absolute order in the universe, independent of the perceptions of individual men. His materialism and his strong bias against metaphysics had made him unable to find this stability inwardly in logic, or above in some realm of pure ideas. The material world itself was his realm of order, actual and potential: and this was pregnant with implications for his ethical and political theory. Still he actually claimed for his philosophy many of the virtues of idealism, for he found in 'the facts' the same transcendental reality which he scorned in the 'spiritualist' world of idea. 'The facts,' though no man might ever see them clearly or gather them exhaustively (and his philosophy presupposed this impossibility), were the only reality. He had simply inverted the Platonic progress which was from all particulars upward toward the pure idea. The American philosopher's upward intellectual progression began with idiosyncratic 'ideas' and 'systems' of thought, rose through particular facts toward the desirable but unattainable totality of facts. In these terms—humanly satisfying, though not logically satisfactory— the Jeffersonian expressed his belief that men's lives might be peaceful, orderly and prosperous, even while there seemed no final hierarchy or systematic relation among ideas.

4. The Moral Sense
and the Life of Action

THE axiomatic order of the material universe and the axiomatic disorder of human thought led the Jeffersonian to believe that something other than thought must have been intended to guide the behavior of men. The anatomy of that other principle constituted his moral science, which we shall now examine. Jefferson himself explicitly connected his cosmology with his ethics: 'Assuming the fact, that the earth has been created in time, and consequently the dogma of final causes, we yield, of course, to this short syllogism. Man was created for social intercourse; but social intercourse cannot be maintained without a sense of justice; then man must have been created with a sense of justice.' [28] It was with intentional precision that he spoke here of a 'sense' and not a knowledge of justice.

Everything the American philosopher knew (or could not know) of the human mind, indicated that morals could not have been founded in thought. A cosmic necessity required some more reliable and less variable human faculty; and he found this faculty in a special 'moral sense' quite separate from the brain. The Creator, Jefferson said, had designedly separated reason from morals in order that the motives for action, which stabilized the economy of nature, should be preserved from the diversity and infirmity which characterized the minds of men. 'It must afford great pleasure to the lovers of virtue,' Rush remarked, 'to behold the depth and extent of this moral principle in the human mind. Happily for the human race, the

140

intimations of duty and the road to happiness are not left to the slow operations or doubtful inductions of reason, nor to the precarious decisions of taste.' Jefferson believed that the Creator had on purpose impressed these principles indelibly on men's hearts to prevent their being effaced by the subtleties of their brains. Even while the thoughts of men varied, the proper motives to human behavior were thus preserved intact.[29]

Avoiding the metaphysics of ethics, Jefferson preferred to study the natural history of the moral faculty. He advised his young friend Peter Carr:

Moral Philosophy. I think it lost time to attend lectures on this branch. He who made us would have been a pitiful bungler, if he had made the rules of our moral conduct a matter of science. For one man of science, there are thousands who are not. What would have become of them? Man was destined for society. His morality, therefore, was to be formed to this object. He was endowed with a sense of right and wrong, merely relative to this. This sense is as much a part of his nature, as the sense of hearing, seeing, feeling; it is the true foundation of morality, and not the τo $\kappa a \lambda o \nu$, truth, &c., as fanciful writers have imagined. The moral sense, or conscience, is as much a part of man as his leg or arm. It is given to all human beings in a stronger or weaker degree. . . . It may be strengthened by exercise, as may any particular limb of the body. This sense is submitted, indeed, in some degree, to the guidance of reason; but it is a small stock which is required for this: even a less one than what we call common sense. State a moral case to a ploughman and a professor. The former will decide it as well, and often better than the latter, because he has not been led astray by artificial rules.[30]

Would not the conclusive demonstration that justice was an activity of the moral faculty have been some experiment similar to that by which Flourens had shown thought to reside in the cerebrum? If an operation could be performed which deprived an animal of the sense of justice and left the creature otherwise normal, then the organ would be known. The American philosopher had assumed that thought was common to man and other animals.[31] Therefore the dissection of lower animals could teach something about man's thinking organ; it was in fowls that Flourens discovered the nature of all thought. In the case of the moral faculty, however, the Jeffersonian without amplifying his reasons made the contrary assumption: the moral sense was to be discovered only, or at least primarily, in man. As a practical matter, of course, this deprived the American philosopher of the opportunity for proof by vivisection.

The Jeffersonian's faith was so firm, however, and his expectations so sure, that he was satisfied to show that there was nothing in the behavior of men inconsistent with a hypothetical sense of justice. He would then, without further ado, be ready to believe that a moral faculty existed somewhere in the human body. If some individuals or races were weak in the moral faculty, or even lacked it entirely, this seemed no evidence that it was not natural to the human species. Were not some men, Jefferson asked, born without eyes or ears or hands? Yet it was surely bad natural history to say that *man* was born without these: and sight, hearing, and hands would have to be included in a general definition of man. Similarly with the moral sense; it was false reasoning which converted the exception into the rule. The 'low degrees of moral perception' discovered in certain African and Russian tribes, Rush insisted, was no more disproof of the universal existence of a moral faculty than the low state of their intellects proved that reason was not natural to man; nor was the fact that other savage nations were now totally devoid of the moral faculty any proof that originally or by nature they lacked it.[32]

Rush supported his argument by various analogies, each of which presupposed the existence of another 'faculty' no easier to prove than the moral faculty itself. The stomachs of some men, he noted, were so disordered by intemperance that they refused all simple and wholesome diet; but this did not mean that bread was not the natural food for man's uncorrupted appetite. Some savages destroyed their beauty by painting and cutting their faces; but still, according to Rush, everyone admitted that a principle of taste was natural to the human

142

mind. 'It would be as absurd to maintain, because olives become agreeable to many people from habit, that we have no natural appetites for any other kind of food, as to assert that any part of the human species exist without a moral principle, because in some of them it has wanted causes to excite it into action, or has been perverted by example.'

If such a moral sense actually existed in the human body, its operations like those of the brain itself must have been affected by environment. In his 'Inquiry into the Influence of Physical Causes upon the Moral Faculty,' Rush enumerated seventeen different causes of this kind:

1. Climate	9. Cleanliness
2. Diet	10. Solitude
3. Drinks	11. Silence
4. Hunger	12. Music
5. Diseases	13. Eloquence of the Pulpit
6. Idleness	14. Odours
7. Excessive Sleep	15. Light and Darkness
8. Bodily Pain	16. Airs
	17. Medicines

He illustrated every one from history or from his own clinical experience:

3. The effects of CERTAIN DRINKS upon the moral faculty are not less observable, than upon the intellectual powers of the mind. Fermented liquors, of a good quality, and taken in a moderate quantity, are favourable to the virtues of candour, benevolence, and generosity; but when they are taken in excess, or when they are of a bad quality, and taken even in a moderate quantity, they seldom fail of rousing every latent spark of vice into action.

The fate of the Cities of the Plain dramatized the effects of idleness. In the Old Testament bodily pain was actually described as a preventive against vice. The ceremonial rites of the Jews illustrated the use of cleanliness to promote morals.

By the very phenomenon of vice, Rush was reassured of the existence of the hypothetical moral faculty. For, he said, vices

143

were nothing but moral disorders; and was it not nonsensical to call anything disordered unless that thing actually existed? Did not a man's perverse relish for tobacco prove that he possessed a sense of taste? Did not his unwholesome delight in exotic odours prove that he had a sense of smell? Similarly, perversion and vice proved the existence of a moral sense.[33] Just as his epistemology was readier to point disorders of the mind than to describe the nature of truth, his ethics described perversions of the moral faculty while studiously avoiding any definition of virtue. Rush, for example, invented a technical vocabulary for diseases of the moral sense: *Micronomia* described a weakened moral faculty; *Anomia*, its total absence. But virtue was without a name.

Obviously the desirable condition of the moral faculty was its 'health.' The word was especially appropriate, because one could not imagine that the virtue of men was anything but harmonious with their effective physical functioning under American conditions.[34] By such language, the Jeffersonian declared the grounding of his morality in natural history, and justified his refusal to inquire directly into the nature of good and evil. He did not try to expound the positive content of his morality, because the health of the moral sense, like that of any other sense, could be discovered only indirectly by observing its disorders. No one but a metaphysician would want to define such an obvious (or abstract) quality as health. The Jeffersonian therefore refused to dogmatize on how men ought to behave. He preferred to describe circumstantially the impulses and some of the conditions which affected whatever patterns of behavior men had chosen—and especially to point the relation between the action of the moral sense and the whole economy of nature.

For example, Rush sometimes used 'sensibility'—a familiar eighteenth-century word—to describe the healthy condition of the moral sense. Just as hearing could be dulled by monotonous repetition of sounds, or the eardrums could be burst by loud noises; just as the eye was injured by glaring light, or loss of eyesight was caused by perpetual darkness, so with the moral sense: anything which dulled sensibility injured morals. The scenes of cruelty to which the Romans were exposed had blunted their moral sense. Who could witness cruelty to men and animals, the contests of gladiators, and the other scenes of public punishment, without becoming callous to all injustice and human hardship? As Rush recounted, the Emperor Domitian by torturing flies had prepared himself for all the bloody crimes which disgraced his reign. Rush observed the same forces at work in his own day: Hogarth's prints, he said, were true to the natural history of morals when they showed the young criminal mistreating animals. If a delicate moral sense was to be developed in young people, accounts of suicides and brutal crimes must be hidden from them (and especially kept out of the newspapers); and yet they should be shown enough scenes of poverty and distress to keep their sensibility alive. We cannot be surprised that Jefferson called the works of Laurence Sterne 'the best course of morality that ever was written.' For it was not by learning right principles, nor by becoming fixed in virtuous beliefs, but by exercising the sentiments that men became just. Good books were to be read, not because of the doctrines they contained, but because of the encouragement and exercise which they gave the moral feelings.[35]

The Jeffersonians were more interested in the processes of moral behavior than in the content of a moral law. They labored not toward perfecting the commandments but toward explaining the connection between a healthy moral sense and the well-being of the species. They produced not a decalogue, but a vade mecum—a guide to moral health. Jefferson described how exercise made virtuous dispositions habitual. In such works as Priestley's 'Discourse on Habitual Devotion,' and Rush's 'Inquiry into the Influence of Physical Causes upon the Moral Faculty' and 'Account of the state of the Body and Mind in Old Age,' the role of habit in ethical behavior was elaborately discussed. By the fact that atheists were often very moral men, Rush sought to prove that just actions were not the effect of knowing the truth, but of having a sensitive and well-developed moral faculty. The aged were often more virtuous than the young, not because they knew more, but because their moral faculty had been better trained by habit. The strength of mental associations in cultivating habits of moral behavior was illustrated by many familiar cases. The master troubled by a servant who pilfered his liquors should not lecture him on honesty. Rather he should secretly dissolve a bit of tartar emetic in one of his bottles; when the servant had drunk this bottle, he would be cured not only of theft but of drunkenness as well. 'The recollection of the pain and sickness excited by the emetic naturally associates itself with the spirits, so as to render them both equally the objects of aversion.' According to Rush's interpretation of the Bible, Moses himself had employed this principle when he ground the golden calf into powder, dissolved it (probably by means of *hepar sulphuris*) in water, and compelled the idolators to drink it. 'This mixture is bitter and nauseating in the highest degree. An inclination to idolatry, therefore, could not be felt, without being associated with the remembrance of this disagreeable mixture, and of course being rejected, with equal abhorrence.' Rush urged that corporal penalties be administered immediately after a crime and near its scene, so that the past criminal act would always be associated with physical pain. Without metaphysical speculation on whether or why men should be sensitive, pious, honest and sober, the Jeffersonian had thus immersed himself directly in the practical tasks of making men aware of the sufferings of their neighbors, and punishing them effectively for drunkenness and theft. Untroubled himself by the ultimate questions of ethics, he preferred to advance the physiology of morals.

It was in his tentative and unsystematic asceticism that the Jeffersonian came closest to defining the positive content of ethics. But even his asceticism was a form of antisepsis rather than a prescription for the good life. Not a sure path to virtue, but a likely way to avoid vice. While varying somewhat with the temperament and personality of the particular philosopher, Jeffersonian asceticism was essentially an opposition to excess, whether in drink, tobacco, sexual passion, or other physical indulgence; and an advocacy of physical exercise, moderation, and the frugal and strenuous life. Rush, for example, was one of the earliest American enemies of spirituous liquors—and was immoderate enough to earn adoption as a patron saint of latter-day prohibitionists. In his 'Inquiry into the Effects of Ardent Spirits upon the Human Body and Mind,' he showed how alcohol deranged the body and caused illness, vice, crime and death. The vicious consequences of drink were quite direct: the effect of a chemical on the brain and the moral faculty. 'The effects of wine,' Rush observed, 'like tyranny in a well formed government, are felt first in the extremities: while spirits, like a bold invader, seize at once upon the vitals of the constitution.' Luxury and dissipation were the universal attractions of cities and provided the strongest moral argument against an urban civilization. Men went to cities to satisfy their factitious wants and to seek novel and superfluous sensations. 'The general desire of men to live by their heads rather than their hands,' observed Jefferson, 'and the strong allurements of great cities to those who have any turn for dissipation, threaten to make them here, as in Europe, the sinks of voluntary misery.' Artificers were the panders of vice, and the instruments by which the liberties of a country were overturned; and greed for wealth, which was the peculiar vice of commerce, could eventually degrade the vigor and morals of a whole citizenry.[36]

Jefferson often noted that most vices could not take root in country soil: he therefore expressed 'moral and physical preference of the agricultural, over the manufacturing, man.' According to John Taylor of Caroline, the rural life 'by the exercise it gives both to the body and to the mind . . . secures health and vigour to both; and by combining a thorough knowledge of the real affairs of life, with a necessity for investigating the arcana of nature, and the strongest invitations to the practice of morality, it becomes the best architect of a complete man.' [37] Although the Jeffersonians were for the most part enthusiastic agrarians, they usually did not elaborate the virtues of the farmer, nor defend his as the good life; it was enough that the farmer was safe from the grosser vices.

Men who did not work seemed especially susceptible to

147

diseases of the moral faculty. Idleness, according to Rush, was 'the parent of every vice'; while labor of all kinds facilitated the practice of virtue. This explained why the laborious country life was so desirable. 'If the habits of virtue, contracted by means of . . . labour, are purely mechanical, their effects are, nevertheless, the same upon the happiness of society, as if they flowed from principle. The mind, moreover, when preserved by these means from weeds, becomes a more mellow soil, afterwards, for moral and rational improvement.' If only the weeds were rooted out, then the seeds of virtue which the Creator himself had planted would surely flourish. In his *Diseases of the Mind*, Rush detailed the use of activity of all kinds in promoting mental and moral health:

Is debility the predisposing cause of disease in the body? so it is of vice in the mind. This debility in the mind consists in indolence, or a want of occupation. Bunyan has justly said, in support of this remark, that 'an idle man's brain is the devil's work shop.' The young woman, whose moral derangement I mentioned a little while ago, was always inoffensive when she was busy. The employment contrived for her by her parents was, to mix two or three papers of pins of different sizes together, and afterwards, to oblige her to separate, and sort them. The near relation of debility and vice has been expressed by the schoolmen in the following words 'non posse, est *malum* posse.' To do nothing, is generally to do evil.

These were cheering facts to the Jeffersonians—men immersed in action, who were reticent and inexplicit about the ends of their own activity.

This notion that evil somehow defined itself automatically out of man's relation to his environment, while giving vice the quality of concreteness, also somehow made vice less abhorrent. Man's moral faculty was liable to corruption simply because it was a part of his body, but this susceptibility seemed hardly more noteworthy or reprehensible than the body's need for air and food. When the Jeffersonian came upon the concept of evil in theology or moral philosophy, he naturalized it into just another bodily disease: a disease, indeed, of the moral sense, but essentially no different from others. To reproach a

148

man because his moral sense was corruptible was like blaming him for susceptibility to yellow fever—like reproaching a wagon for its broken wheel. 'All the moral, as well as physical evil of the world,' observed Rush, 'consists in predisposing weakness, and in subsequent derangement of action or motion.' The Miltonic epic of man's first disobedience could for him be nothing more than a dramatic summary of the consequences of being a physical creature; and the tragedy of the fall of man became cold allegory. Evil could not be explained as the intrusion of an external Satanic force on a pure human nature: as Rush put it, 'Physical and moral evil began together.' Once man had been created a physical being, there remained no hope of his freedom from disease; it was meaningless to think of him as originally spotless, but later fallen from grace. Vice like disease could not have been superimposed after the Creation, but must have been potential in every created being. 'With respect to the fall of Adam,' Priestley wrote, 'all that we can learn from the Scriptures, interpreted literally, is, that the laborious cultivation of the earth, and the mortality of his race, were the consequence of it.' [38]

How thoroughly the Jeffersonian had emptied his universe of dramatic conflict between good and evil—the vast distance by which he had separated himself from the Calvinist—appeared when he actually detailed the uses of evil in the economy of nature. Earlier theodicies had justified evil as a foil for good; the Jeffersonian explained evil, not as intended to magnify good, but as designed indirectly to promote activity. We could want no better evidence that he had made action paramount to any metaphysical value. The 'evils' which ensued from the fall, he saw necessary to the proper operation of the animal economy. Rush explained:

The necessity of exercise to animal life is indicated, by its being kindly imposed upon man in paradise. The change which the human body underwent by the fall, rendered the same salutary stimulus necessary to its life, in the more active form of labour. . . . By the loss of his innocence, he has subjected himself to the dominion of passions and emotions of a malignant nature; but they possess, in common with such as are good, a stimulus which renders them subservient to the purpose of promoting animal life.[39]

If, as Rush concluded, the fall simply dramatized the uniform laws of the whole animal creation, the greatest human tragedy could be nothing but a zoology lesson.

That kind of poignant and personal reality which the Calvinist had sensed in the existence of evil, the Jeffersonian sensed in the order of the natural universe. For him the processes of action were immediately and undeniably good. The Puritan was overwhelmed by the intensity of an inward struggle, which his theology explained as the omnipresent conflict between metaphysical forces. But the Jeffersonian had thoroughly externalized his struggle. He was therefore unwilling to reduce the variegated possibilities of material disorder to simple metaphysical categories. He had dissolved good and evil into the myriad qualities of the physical universe. By that dissolution he had deprived vice and sin of such fixity as had enabled medieval man to catalogue the deadly sins. Since Jeffersonian sins like diseases were unlimited in number, they could not be aptly represented by any fixed symbol. Evil for the Jeffersonian could not be a 'forbidden tree' whose poisonous apples were all ripe at the Creation; new diseases of the moral sense would surely emerge from time to time.[40]

Like the modern psychiatrist, the Jeffersonian philosopher made himself not a judge of good and evil, but an arbiter between man and his environment. He, too, always sought the least painful form of adjustment. In a sense, indeed, the Jeffersonian was equipped to be still more neutral than the modern psychiatrist, because his natural history (being also a theology) had explicitly justified the existence of every evil in the world. He had found benevolent design in swamps, in yellow fever and the rattlesnake. Why not also in the diseases of the moral faculty?

To hypostatize men's weakness into a devil or to make the good life a struggle against evil would obscure the essential harmony in the world of action. Life for the Jeffersonian, rather than being a war against evil, was a test of workmanship: not a battle but a job. When metaphysicians abstracted moral diseases into a Satanic personality or when they employed the notion of man being 'essentially evil,' they were pompously overstating the simple fact that physical creatures were not always perfectly healthy. As Paine remarked in *The Age of Reason*, such theological inventions seduced man to contemplate himself an outcast, at an immense distance from his Creator, so that he lost his sense for true religion. 'His prayers are reproaches. His humility is ingratitude. He calls himself a worm, and the fertile earth a dunghill; and all the blessings of life by the thankless name of vanities.' Preoccupation with moral disorder, like obsessive fear of other bodily diseases, was pure hypochondria, and could not but dull the motives for action.

5. Jeffersonian Christianity

OF the divergent tendencies in traditional Christianity, we cannot be surprised that the Jeffersonians found piety or the abstract love of God uncongenial, and morality or the ordering of men's social relations most meaningful. The Augustinian strain of piety, which was central in the Puritan way of thought, had little to say to the Jeffersonian: for traditionally this strain of Christianity had built its teachings both on profound inward revelations and on an elaborate structure of metaphysics and theology. It was precisely in these realms that Jeffersonians found rational discourse, agreement and the sharing of experience to be hardest. But the moral and reformist strain in Christianity they found appealing. The Jeffersonian God, like the Franciscan, was not so much to be worshiped as to be imitated.

Such a way of thought implied, of course, that the Jeffersonian had found in his God what he most admired in men. We have already seen that by conceiving his God as Supreme Workman, he had made Him the American beau ideal; and this conception had grounded much of his natural history and his ethics. When the Jeffersonian came to the traditional subject matter of religion, he showed a similar disposition to humanize his God into a beneficent being, and to make the primary quality of religion the exposition and inculcation of that benevolence. Paine, for example, asserted:

That the moral duty of man consists in imitating the moral goodness and beneficence of God manifested in the creation towards all his creatures. That seeing as we daily do the goodness of God to all men, it is an example calling upon all men to practise the same towards each other; and, consequently, that everything of persecution and revenge between man and man, and everything of cruelty to animals, is a violation of moral duty.

Since it was axiomatic that God's conduct must provide the example for man's morals, God could be neither unpredictable nor malevolent. His will and the precepts of His conduct must be benign and intelligible. Jefferson, for example, asserted that the apocalyptic books of the Bible could not be sacred or genuine: for it would have been blasphemy to impute to the Creator a revelation couched in terms which could never be understood by those to whom it was addressed. The burden of Paine's attack on the Bible in *The Age of Reason* was that it attributed to God a misanthropic and capricious character. A God whose ways were not reducible to a humanly intelligible principle must have been useless, and hence false, as an object of human emulation. The Jeffersonian was especially wary (perhaps because his materialism seemed to point in that direction) against anything like a predestinarian theology. Jefferson himself was bitter against 'the demoralizing dogmas of Calvin,' and especially against those which would have made man powerless to affect his moral destiny.[41]

152

Jefferson declared his moral theory to rest on his concept of God. 'He has formed us moral agents. Not that, in the perfection of His state, He can feel pain or pleasure in anything we may do; He is far above our power; but that we may promote the happiness of those with whom He has placed us in society, by acting honestly towards all, benevolently to those who fall within our way, respecting sacredly their rights, bodily and mental, and cherishing especially their freedom of conscience, as we value our own.' [42] The Creator, Rush explained, had implanted conscience in man 'on purpose to show His property in all intelligent creatures, and their original resemblance to Himself.' Another correspondent of the Philosophical Society described the sense of justice as 'a divine ray in the human mind.' Paine had declared that by exercising the moral faculty man imitated the character of the Creator. That all men possessed the same Creator explained quite simply the universal similarity of the perceptions of their moral sense.

According to Priestley, the character of the Creator also supported the argument that men must be free moral agents:

He that made man, certainly knew what he was capable of, and would never command him to do what he had not enabled him to perform; so as to propose to him a *reward* which he knew he could never attain, and a punishment which he knew he had no power of avoiding. If it be worth our while to inquire at all into the government under which we live, we must begin with assuming these first principles.[43]

Moreover, he argued, men had to believe they were free, because to believe otherwise might have had disastrous effects on behavior. Rush, too, forbade anyone to draw from materialism the conclusion that men were not voluntarily good or evil.

The cosmic design, revealed in natural history, also showed that some kind of religion was needed to make men healthy. Man seemed to Rush as naturally a religious, as he was a social and domestic animal. He demonstrated both the necessity of religion and the peculiar value of Christian morality by their effect on the human body.

153

The necessary and immutable connection between the texture of the human mind, and the worship of an object of some kind, has lately been demonstrated by the atheists of Europe, who, after rejecting the true God, have instituted the worship of nature, of fortune, and of human reason; and, in some instances, with ceremonies of the most expensive and splendid kind. Religions are friendly to animal life, in proportion as they elevate the understanding, and act upon the passions of hope and love. It will readily occur to you, that Christianity, when believed and obeyed, according to its original consistency with itself, and with the divine attributes, is more calculated to produce those effects than any other religion in the world. Such is the salutary operation of its doctrines and precepts upon health and life, that if its divine authority rested upon no other argument, this alone would be sufficient to recommend it to our belief.[44]

The accord of Christian morality with the economy of creation was proved by the numerous instances of its therapeutic influence. Persons oppressed by debt, disappointment, or a sense of guilt, could sometimes find temporary relief in wine, opium, or ardent spirits; but clinical experience showed that religion was the only sure and lasting remedy. Rush noted in his 'Inquiry into the Effects of Ardent Spirits upon the Human Body and Mind' that there were hundreds of cases throughout the United States of drunkards who had been cured by belief in the wholesome Christian doctrine.

Since the moral behavior of men was essential to the economy of nature and the continuation of life processes, such behavior obviously could not have required any deep theoretical knowledge. No man was so stupid as to be unable to cultivate grain, nor any woman so unintelligent that she could not learn to bake bread; it would then surely have been incongruous, Rush observed, if the motives to moral behavior had required the support of a subtle mind. From the design of the creation, Paine argued that a religion containing anything that shocked the mind of a child could not be true. 'As for morality,' he observed, 'the knowledge of it exists in every man's conscience.' [45] We have seen that Jefferson, too, believed that the operations of the moral faculty required almost no assistance from the brain.

Now the biological unity of the human species was itself made an argument in favor of the existence of uniform and objective moral principles; although, conversely, the absurdity of conceiving different moral rules for different men had actually been used to disprove the specific diversity of mankind. It seemed most unlikely that an efficient Creator would have governed the actions of similar creatures by diverse rules. By hypothesis, then, the essential truth of any religion must be contained in those moral precepts in which it agreed with all others. 'What all agree in, is probably right. What no two agree in, most probably wrong.' The plan of nature required that these be the only genuine precepts. The moral branch, Jefferson more than once declared, was the same in all religions. 'He who steadily observes those moral precepts in which all religions concur, will never be questioned at the gates of heaven, as to the dogmas in which they all differ.' [46]

The essence of religion was not theology, but morality; not what men thought, but how they acted. Every religion was good, Paine wrote, that taught men to be good, and every religion bad that failed to do so. Properly all religion was a quest for 'the natural dictates of conscience'; an attempt to recognize the Creator in 'the universal display of himself in the works of the creation and by that repugnance we feel in ourselves to bad actions, and disposition to do good ones.' Even Priestley, who personally had suffered the *odium theologicum*, declared that no theological doctrine could be dangerous so long as it did not affect the moral behavior of men. '*By their fruits shall ye know them*. . . . They cannot be bad principles with which men lead godly, righteous, and sober lives.' Never was Jefferson more emphatic: it was in men's lives and not in their words or ideas that their religion must be read.[47] The Creator Himself was known not through His metaphysical essence, or verbal revelation, but only through His works. Why should men not be similarly judged?

By this criterion, the Jeffersonian saw no reason not to be a

Christian. In his Virginia Act for establishing Religious Freedom, Jefferson listed as the first item in the prerogatives of a
religiously free man 'the comfortable liberty of giving his contributions to the particular pastor whose morals he would make
his pattern.' It was not difficult in eighteenth-century America
to find many Christian pastors whose moral conduct met the
exacting Jeffersonian standards. Christianity then had been
experimentally proven in the only possible manner: it had made
good lives. John Adams spoke for the Jeffersonian view when he
praised Christianity not as a source or sanction for knowledge
but as a useful method of propagating principles that derived
their validity from nature. 'One great advantage of the Christian
religion,' Adams wrote in his diary (August 14, 1796), 'is, that
it brings the great principle of the law of nature and nations,—
Love your neighbor as yourself, and do to others as you would
that others should do to you,—to the knowledge, belief, and
veneration of the whole people. Children, servants, women, and
men, are all professors in the science of public and private
morality. No other institution for education, no kind of political discipline, could diffuse this kind of necessary information,
so universally among all ranks and descriptions of citizens. The
duties and rights of the man and the citizen are thus taught
from early infancy to every creature.' Both Trinitarianism and
Unitarianism had made honest men, observed Jefferson, and
that was the only point to be considered. The American philosopher therefore was willing to accept Christianity—but in spite
of its theology. It is misleading to call his belief 'deism,' for
that is a theological word: more appropriate was Paine's 'Religion of Humanity.'

The pure and simple Christian morality had surely been
overladen by dogma and superstition; but the same was true of
Buddhism, Mohammedanism and all other religions—even (as
Rush and Jefferson remarked) Atheism. If purified Christianity
could promote moral health in the actual setting of eighteenth-
century America, that was enough to make the Jeffersonian
sympathetic. Jefferson more than once called himself a Christian—'a *real* Christian'—that is, an adherent of the morality of

Jesus.[48] Rittenhouse called himself a Christian. Priestley, while he was himself an ordained nonconformist minister and an apostle of Unitarianism, warned against the dangers of considering any one sect exclusively Christian. Rush, who was always a professing and outspoken Christian and urged the values of Christianity on his medical students, was at one time or another a member of nearly every large sect in contemporary Philadelphia: born a Quaker, antagonized by their political views, and especially their attitude to the Stamp Act, he became a Presbyterian for several years until his conversion to Unitarianism; in 1788 he was confirmed in the Episcopal Church; his children were baptized Presbyterian. Paine, alone of the Jeffersonian philosophers, would have called himself anti-Christian, but even in *The Age of Reason* he praised Jesus as the great moral reformer.

The hope that the major problems of life would be solved directly out of the experiences of the sensible world was revealed in the whole Jeffersonian approach to Christianity (which was primarily historical); and especially in the active and reformist role assigned to Jesus. The Jeffersonian had projected his own qualities and limitations into Jesus, whose career became his vivid symbol of the superfluity and perils of speculative philosophy. He credited Jesus and the Apostles with an admirably practical, simple and intelligible morality, growing out of everyday experience. Against them he saw pitted the theologians and metaphysicians.

Jesus had been a great 'philosopher'—in the strict Jeffersonian sense. He was not a system builder, but a reformer. He had cleared away the fabrications of priests and metaphysicians, bringing men back to simple facts which all could and should have known for themselves. While the ancient philosophers had improved men's understanding of themselves, and developed the control of their passions, they had been defective in a sense of duty to others. The Jews had moved forward toward a purer view of the Creator, but their ethics were still imperfect. Jesus' achievement was fourfold: he corrected some of the crude Jewish ideas of the attributes of God; he

157

improved the moral doctrines of the ancients regarding kindred and friends, and went beyond these to a universal philanthropy; where the Jews had been concerned with actions only, he 'pushed his scrutinies into the heart of man; erected his tribunal in the region of his thoughts, and purified the waters at the fountainhead'; and, finally, 'he taught, emphatically, the doctrines of a future state . . . and wielded it with efficacy, as an important incentive, supplementary to the other motives to moral conduct.' Jesus' ethics were thus eclectic and progressive, combining the best tenets of his predecessors, and improving them by bold reforms. The result, according to Jefferson, was that of all the systems of morality, ancient and modern, none was so pure as that of Jesus.[49]

The simplicity and universality of Jesus' teachings stood out in sharp contrast against those of the greatest moralists who had preceded him. In a little volume entitled *Socrates and Jesus Compared* (1803), much praised by Jefferson, Priestley showed the inferiority of the Greek to the Christian moralist. While Priestley, unlike Jefferson, considered Jesus actually an instrument of divine revelation, even he praised Jesus mainly as an ethical propagandist. Socrates had taught a few adult men of the upper classes; women and children were not in his audience, and he had given scant attention to the middle and lower classes though they were actually in the greatest need of instruction. The sophisticated Socratic rhetoric could communicate very little to uneducated minds. Jesus, on the other hand, never took account of class, sex, or age: poor and rich, weak and strong, he instructed with equal zeal; and his simple parables could be understood by everybody. Jesus' stature as a moralist was all the more impressive, since, as Jefferson and Paine recalled, he had died at thirty-three years of age, before his talents were fully developed.[50] Even in this short career, and despite the fragmentary and inaccurate historical record, intentionally mutilated and misstated by his followers, Jesus had established himself as the greatest moral reformer in all history.

Jefferson went to considerable trouble, twice in his life, to collect from the books of the New Testament, 'The Life and Morals of Jesus of Nazareth.'

In extracting the pure principles which he taught, we should have to strip off the artificial vestments in which they have been muffled by priests, who have travestied them into various forms, as instruments of riches and power to themselves. We must dismiss the Platonists and Plotinists, the Stagyrites and Gamalielites, the Eclectics, the Gnostics and Scholastics, their essences and emanations, their Logos and Demiurgos, Aeons and Daemons, male and female, with a long train of etc., etc., etc., or, shall I say at once, of nonsense. We must reduce our volume to the simple evangelists, select, even from them, the very words only of Jesus, paring off the amphibologisms into which they have been led, by forgetting often, or not understanding, what had fallen from him, by giving their own misconceptions as his dicta, and expressing unintelligibly for others what they had not understood themselves. There will be found remaining the most sublime and benevolent code of morals which has ever been offered to man. I have performed this operation for my own use, by cutting verse by verse out of the printed book, and arranging the matter which is evidently his, and which is as easily distinguishable as diamonds in a dunghill. The result is an octavo of forty-six pages, of pure and unsophisticated doctrines, such as were professed and acted on by the *unlettered* Apostles, the Apostolic Fathers, and the Christians of the first century.[51]

The degradation of the Christian doctrine was recounted in Priestley's *History of the Corruptions of Christianity*, which Jefferson read 'over and over again' and which was one of the few theological books on which he rested his faith.

The story which Priestley tells—and which Jefferson and others retold—is really an allegory of the Jeffersonian mind. The heroic figure is Jesus himself, a simple unlettered man: moved by no theology more complex than faith in a God, he observed acutely the conditions of his generation. His lessons came from sheer clarity of perception, and his vigorous moral sense guided a program of comprehensive reforms. The American philosopher was impressed with Jesus' success in achieving that intellectual naïveté for which he himself yearned. Jesus' enemies, the corrupters of his simple truths, were both the over-subtle metaphysicians and the inspired visionaries: the spinners of abstraction and the believers in mysteries. After Jesus, the heroic figures were the unlettered primitive Christians who still founded their science on observation and their morality in a healthy moral faculty; these primitive Christians, too, were opposed by Platonizing philosophers and schismatizing priests, who mistook their own theories for facts, who pushed out of view the actual shape of nature and the self-evident demands of active life. The conflict between Christianity and 'metaphysics' was the leitmotif of Jeffersonian history of the religion.

Systematic theology—itself a form of 'metaphysics'—seemed at odds with the spirit of Jesus. For Jefferson, theology as a separate study was mere 'mystery and *charlatanerie*.' [52] He said he would as soon have written for Bedlam as for the world of religious sects. The cobwebs of theologians were not involuntary private illusions: they had been spun by greedy and ambitious men on purpose to catch the unwary. The metaphysical distinctions of the priesthood had been especially designed to enlist the financial support of disciples. How, for example had sensible common people ever been brought to accept the fanciful notion of the divinity of Jesus? Such a doctrine had never been taught by Jesus himself; but, as Priestley explained, 'it was introduced by those who had had a philosophical education,' as a way of elevating the dignity of their Saviour, and gradually it was passed off on the illiterate masses. The idolatry of saints and the worship of relics had been similarly invented. In early times men had met at the tombs of martyrs, not to worship the dead, but because they thought their devotion to God was better excited there. This useful custom had been perverted by the immaterialist dogmas of priests who desired a remunerative traffic in the good will of departed 'spirits.'

The simple materialism of the Book of Genesis, confirmed by the common experience of men everywhere, had been the doctrine of primitive Christianity. But before long, ambitious theologians, partly inventing the idea and partly borrowing it from the heathen, propagated the false and profitable dogma that mind and body were separate substances. 'At what age of the Christian Church this heresy of *immaterialism*, or masked atheism, crept in, I do not exactly know,' Jefferson wrote to John Adams. 'But a heresy it certainly is. Jesus taught nothing of it.' Priestley found beginnings of this cancerous belief in the immateriality of the soul as early as the fifth century. The heresy of immaterialism, like other metaphysical inventions, had been neither innocent nor accidental: by supporting belief in essences and entities, priests had popularized the notion that God Himself was nothing but a spirit for them to conjure with. In innumerable other ways the abracadabra of theology had been used to mystify the unlearned. For example, by spinning out the doctrine of the Eucharist some priests claimed even more power than the Blessed Virgin herself; because, Priestley remarked, they pretended to create their Creator whenever they pleased whereas she had conceived him but once.[53]

From the Jeffersonian point of view Plato admirably suited the role of Anti-Christ. Plato was the patron saint of 'abstraction' who had actually invested the prime metaphysical vice with the dignity of philosophical method. He taught men to use poetry to clothe the whimsies of their brains; and his doctrines above all others had diverted men from the sensible shape of nature. As Jefferson explained:

The Christian priesthood, finding the doctrines of Christ levelled to every understanding, and too plain to need explanation, saw in the mysticism of Plato materials with which they might build up an artificial system, which might, from its indistinctness, admit everlasting controversy, give employment for their order, and introduce it to profit, power and preëminence. The doctrines which flowed from the lips of Jesus himself are within the comprehension of a child; but thousands of volumes have not yet explained the Platonisms engrafted on them; and for this obvious reason, that nonsense can never be explained.[54]

John Adams, who was blessed with a sense of humor, tried to calm Jefferson by observing that all he himself had ever learned from Plato was where Franklin had plagiarized some of his ideas, and how to cure the hiccups. For Jefferson, however,

Platonism was no laughing matter. He was convinced that no writer ancient or modern had bewildered the world with more *ignes fatui*: and after wading through 'the whimsies, the puerilities and unintelligible jargon' of *The Republic*, he was more than ever bewildered that the world had given reputation to such nonsense. Priestley had shown in detail how every corruption of Christian doctrine had been aided by Platonic texts. All this increased Jefferson's distrust not only of the foggy conceptions of Plato, but of the whole metaphysical method of which he had been godfather. As Jefferson grew older, he became increasingly bitter against those Platonizing Christians who would 'give up morals for mysteries, and Jesus for Plato.'

The history of Christianity thus reinforced the Jeffersonian determination to keep men naïve—finding the precepts of behavior directly in their experience of the physical universe. Jefferson insisted that God had shared this determination: God had intended that while thought even about Himself should be motley, varied and unreliable, action could be orderly and uniform. The view of religion which we have been describing was itself a denial of the relevance of thought to action. Jefferson summarized the drift of his argument:

We should not intermeddle with the particular dogmas in which all religions differ, and which are totally unconnected with morality. In all of them we see good men, and as many in one as another. The varieties in the structure and action of the human mind as in those of the body, are the work of our Creator, against which it cannot be a religious duty to erect the standard of uniformity. The practice of morality being necessary for the well-being of society, he has taken care to impress its precepts so indelibly on our hearts that they shall not be effaced by the subtleties of our brain.[55]

But this immunity of the visible world from the anarchy of ideas was not easy to prove. Since the beginning of history, men had believed that what they thought made a difference to how they behaved. They had customarily traced definite if sometimes devious connections between their theology and metaphysics, and their program for man and society. History had been not merely a hand-to-hand battle, but also a debate between pagan and Christian, idealist and materialist, absolutist and relativist—and even Trinitarian and Unitarian. For the most part, the metaphysical disputants had believed that their choice of sides affected not only their private vision of the truth, but actually held implications for personal and political action. Were they all deceived in believing that the figments of their brains could make any difference in a divinely ordered universe?

The Jeffersonian was inclined to answer yes. He had himself found a refuge from the diversity of ideas in the satisfying concreteness of experience. Still this refuge would be unsafe if the gap between thought and action could ever be bridged. And even his own theology and metaphysics would not permit him to believe that there was no intelligible relation between man's thought and his action, his reason and his morals. However convinced he may have been that a metaphysic of morals was dangerous, he could not restrain his own effort to build one. Rush, for example, in his 'Inquiry into the Influence of Physical Causes upon the Moral Faculty,' developed some definitions which were supposed to show the relation between reason and morals. He described in the first place 'the moral faculty' proper, which was the power in the human mind of distinguishing good from evil, virtue from vice; it was a native principle, and, though capable of improvement by experience and reflection, was derived from neither. This faculty was the 'law' mentioned by St. Paul, which enabled the Gentiles to do by nature the things contained in the law, though they themselves did not possess the law. It was important, Rush said, to see clearly the difference between this moral faculty and the 'conscience,' which was 'a distinct and independent capacity of the mind'—the *regula regulata* of the medieval schoolmen in contrast to the *regula regulans* or moral faculty.

To speak in more modern terms, the moral faculty performs the office of a law-giver, while the business of conscience is to perform the duty of a judge. The moral faculty is to the conscience, what taste is to the judgment, and sensation to perception. It is quick in its operations, and, like the sensitive plant, acts without reflection,

163

while conscience follows with deliberate steps, and measures all her actions by the unerring square of right and wrong.[56]

Through this veil of elegant metaphor it is hard to discern the sharp outlines of any ethical theory; but it is clear enough that Rush was uneasy at leaving the sensations of the moral faculty entirely unrelated to the calculations of the brain.

This uneasiness could be expressed in many different ways. We recognize it in Jefferson's own gropings for a utilitarian morality:

> Some have argued against the existence of a moral sense, by saying that if nature had given us such a sense, . . . then nature would also have designated, by some particular ear-marks, the two sets of actions which are, in themselves, the one virtuous and the other vicious. Whereas, we find, in fact, that the same actions are deemed virtuous in one country and vicious in another. The answer is, that nature has constituted *utility* to man, the standard and test of virtue. Men living in different countries, under different circumstances, different habits and regimens, may have different utilities.[57]

Yet if the dictates of the moral sense varied as widely as Jefferson suggested, how could man ever surely know what they were? Was not the Jeffersonian rule-of-thumb (to find the moral common denominator of all religions) then of little use? Might not moral 'health' require one kind of behavior from the African cannibal and quite another from the American democrat? Jefferson knew that he could not avoid some such consequence; but he chose again to emphasize the similarities rather than the differences among men. Any man confronted with a moral problem could be assured that the right rule would be the one which served his real interest. Jefferson thus implied that to calculate one's 'interest' (the ambiguities of the word did not trouble him) was to be led to the conclusions dictated by a healthy moral sense.

But what if thought conflicted with instinct? 'So invariably do the laws of nature create our duties and interests,' replied Jefferson, 'that when they seem to be at variance, we ought to suspect some fallacy in our reasonings.' [58] Not the instinct, but the intellect, should generally be assumed defective. It was inconceivable that the Creator had not calculated utilities when he shaped the moral faculty and implanted it in man. But it would have been more surprising still if that calculus had been wholly intelligible to any one of his creatures, even man. As John Adams wrote to Jefferson (December 25, 1813), 'There is, there was, and there will be but one master of philosophy in the universe. Portions of it, in different degrees, are revealed to creatures.' Jefferson's utilitarianism therefore evaded metaphysical elaboration of the relation between reason and morals, between thought and action. Mastery of the utilitarian calculus was attributed only to God. And the Jeffersonian attempt to describe the relation of reason to morals issued finally in an affirmation of the axiom on which their universe rested—the orderly benevolence of the Creator and the intrinsic perfection of natural process. The ethical corollary of this axiom was that the solution of moral problems was implicit in the successful life of action.

It was enough that man had been qualified to act properly and effectively; this the Jeffersonians never doubted. But they were still awed by their environment and impressed by their smallness before the nature which surrounded them. They felt a certain humility before the vastness and intricacy of what they saw. If this humility led them to distrust all metaphysics and all theory, it hardly produced tentativeness in their approach to plans of action. For the challenge of that physical environment seemed an invitation to man's bold and decisive action: a clue that the Creator intended man to build rapidly and on a large scale, even while he could not comprehend the mystery of his own thought. This kind of intellectual humility became a form of philosophical indifference, which dulled the motives to self-scrutiny and contemplation. At the same time, the very materialism by which the Jeffersonians demonstrated the inadequacy of any one mind to grasp the essential nature of the universe was asserted with dogmatism, as if they had entered the secrets of thought and of the universe. The Jeffersonian moral creed itself expressed a confidence in every man's

165

instinct for action, which was neither humble nor tentative. All this we should hardly have expected had the Jeffersonians fully accepted the implications of their belief that man was a mere creature. It was the athletic, and not the spiritual, side of man's nature that in America had become impatient of any limitations. Not a Faust but a Paul Bunyan was to become the appropriate symbol of megalomania on this continent.

By taking man's relation to nature—rather than his inward consciousness or his relation to God or to his fellow men—as their starting point, the Jeffersonians had already in large measure shaped and limited their view of society. They had already decided that when they talked about community they would be less concerned with traditions, institutions and values, than with instincts, needs and physical health. In a sense they had brought the discussion of man's social life into a realm of discourse that was more concerned with what was animal than with what was human about man. They had thus provided a framework for political thought which qualified them to build a strong New World in an age when vigorous men could hardly have ignored such an opportunity. Yet at the same time they built a traditional framework in which their intellectual disciples and descendants were to be unwittingly confined.

CHAPTER FOUR

The
Natural History
of a New
Society

'States, even more than individuals, should practise virtues and avoid crimes, for a godless and
wicked man may die before he suffers punishment, but states are immortal and survive until
they suffer punishment both from the hands of
men and of gods.' ISOCRATES, On the Peace

FOR the Jeffersonians, man in the eighteenth century seemed essentially what he had been when he first came from the hand of his Creator in the ancient cradle of mankind. If this was so, then one might have expected man's past to be an invaluable aid to man's present. Actually, however, the Jeffersonians reasoned that man, like the other animals, had no significant past. For they were more concerned with the human species than with humanity, more with biological than spiritual continuity. The biological past seemed to have no meaning for the human present. By merging man into the whole natural universe, the Jeffersonians had in fact alienated themselves from the humanistic past. Driven back on the resources of their generation, they became unreceptive to the help and wisdom of their ancestors. They were insensitive to the value of traditions and institutions, which are the characteristically human means of enlarging the consciousness and the vision of individual creatures. The very ideas of tradition and institution were hard for them to comprehend. Their political science, which now concerns us, therefore dealt less with institutions than with those biological and demographic qualities of the human species which seemed to make institutions insignificant. Law, either in the Hebrew sense of a Torah or revealed truth perpetuated and enriched by tradition, or in the common-law sense of the ancient custom of the community, was quite foreign to them.

Whatever of novelty or of interest there might be in the history of man seemed to come from his relation to his natural environment. All this sharpened the Jeffersonians' sense of the special opportunities offered by each environment, and confirmed their belief in the uniqueness of the American task. Having left whole worlds outside their philosophical experience, they designed an educational program which would simi-

169

larly focus and limit the attention of posterity. Jeffersonian schemes for Americanizing education made education integral with the plan for cultivating the continent, and at the same time impotent to draw men into an assessment of what they were doing, or to a discovery of what makes men human. This spirit stifled the very desire of men to know the goal toward which they were moving. From the Jeffersonians such inadequacies were concealed by their peculiar sense of destiny, stated paradoxically in naturalistic terms, and confirmed and encouraged by American conditions in their day. The whole temper of their thought allowed them to hide from themselves the source, the sanction and the implication of their method of prophecy.

The antipathy to speculative thought, in which we are the heirs of the Jeffersonians, has helped conceal from us the fact that their tradition represents a way of thinking and prophesying as well as a plan of action. Of all parts of the Jeffersonian mind, their political thought has perhaps been the least understood—precisely because it has had the most immediate practical significance. One of the peculiar notions encouraged by democratic political institutions is that, since everybody is entitled to a voice in political matters and since most people lack an articulate political philosophy, democratic peoples can think without major premises. It is even suggested that some kind of institutional contrivance, such as allowing the people nothing but a veto on the plans of policy makers, can save the people from the consequences of lacking a philosophy. Such belief—which is encouraged by the pragmatic frame of mind—leads people to commit themselves to inarticulate and unknown philosophies, without at all freeing themselves from bondage to philosophy. The pragmatic spirit may save us some of the unhappiness and doubt which come from seeing the inadequacies of our own thought; it cannot free us from the necessity of being thinkers. It can make us readier to allow our thinking to be done for us by others, and thus make us more patient of leaders who take us toward unknown and unknowable destinations. The more conscious we become of the philosophical assumptions underlying our action, the more do we see the ways in which philosophy can give us freedom. We may, perhaps, discover the obscurity of our own political ideas in the mirror of Jeffersonianism.

1. Natural History and Political Science

NATURE, at once everywhere and nowhere, was the Jeffersonian City of God. While St. Augustine believed that the material universe only imperfectly hinted the potentialities of man and of God, Jefferson found there the superlative testimony of his Creator. What he asked of his political theory therefore was no blueprint for society, but a way of discovering the plan implicit in nature. His method of discovering this plan, and the large outlines of the plan itself are the subject of the present section.

To the Jeffersonians, political thought seemed to be a by-product rather than a cause of social activity. If men would but fulfill the natural potentialities of the species on this continent, their highest social possibilities would automatically be realized. Only 'metaphysical men' could think otherwise. Speculative thought threatened to sap man's virility and misdirect human efforts towards a merely human end: not political theory, but natural history was the way to harmony and prosperity. For the Creator surely could not have required the consummation of American philosophy to precede the exploitation of the American continent. As the Jeffersonian task was external, it seemed reasonable to assume that the Creator had externally defined its scope and limits. What man was destined to do in

171

America must have been obvious from the qualities of the species and the nature of the environment. The political writings of Paine and Jefferson therefore implied denial (if sometimes covert and indirect) of the importance of political theory.

By hypothesis human society could not be held together through common acceptance of a theory. All individual minds were too idiosyncratic, all 'theories' too personal, to have been intended by the Creator as the cement for community. The physical shape of the species made futile any hope for uniformity in men's social theories: the differing shapes of men's minds had caused inevitable differences in political as in all other thought. 'Political difference . . . ,' Jefferson remarked, 'is inseparable from the different constitutions of the human mind, and that degree of human freedom which permits unrestrained expression.' Wherever dissension was not artificially suppressed, men would be divided into opposed political parties. Even after the defeat of the Federalists, Jefferson never expected that the rightness of Republican views would conquer all opposition. 'An association of men who will not quarrel with one another is a thing which never yet existed, from the greatest confederacy of nations down to a town meeting or a vestry.' We have already noted that Jefferson considered the terms whig and tory to belong to natural as well as to civil history. Essentially the same parties found in America in 1800 had been seen in ancient Greece and Rome, and wherever the human species lived.[1]

It was, therefore, the divinely ordained principles of society and not humanly devised political theories that must have enabled men to live together. Action, not thought, drew men into community. Most of the order found in the human species, Paine observed, was not the result of government, but had its origin 'in the principles of society and the natural constitution of man.' It existed before government, and would remain if government were abolished.

Formal government makes but a small part of civilised life; and when even the best that human wisdom can devise is established, it is a thing more in name and idea than in fact. It is to the great and fundamental principles of society and civilisation . . . to the unceasing circulation of interest, which, passing through its million channels, invigorates the whole mass of civilised man—it is to these things, infinitely more than to anything which even the best instituted government can perform, that the safety and prosperity of the individual, and of the whole depends. . . . All the great laws of society are laws of nature. . . . But how often is the natural propensity to society disturbed or destroyed by the operations of government![2]

Jefferson's often quoted aphorism that the people were governed best who were governed least was simply another way of insisting on this distinction between imperfect human institutions and the Creator's perfect rule.

The obvious first step toward a science of society was to abandon that fruitless comparing of institutions which had preoccupied most historians and political metaphysicians, and to see man instead in the pure context of nature. Any dimness or ambiguity in Jeffersonian political thought would then be due to the difficulty of reading the Book of the Creation. Whatever was to be learned about government must come from the study of 'society'—from observing man not as the subject of human laws, but as a part of the divine economy; not as a citizen, but as a member of the species.

His sense of creaturehood or integration into nature made the Jeffersonian optimistic about the drift of social process. But his optimism, unlike that of Rousseau, was not founded in naïveté about human nature. Quite the contrary. The Jeffersonian actually combined a realistic and rather uncomplimentary view of the nature of man with a general hopefulness about society—and he made this combination convincing precisely because he viewed man in the large context of nature. His naturalistic equivalent of the concept of sin did not disorder his universe, simply because man seemed such a small part of the cosmos. He was prepared to believe that man's social behavior could not be justified from a short-run or narrowly anthropocentric point of view.

The eye of the Jeffersonian was arrested by a fact which al-

173

ready hinted his preoccupation with action, and suggested the negative role which he would give to government: *man was the only animal which levied war against its kind.* Jefferson himself observed this again and again.

In truth I do not recollect in all the animal kingdom a single species but man which is eternally and systematically engaged in the destruction of its own species. What is called civilization seems to have no other effect on him than to teach him to pursue the principle of *bellum omnium in omnia* on a larger scale, and in place of the little contests of tribe against tribe, to engage all the quarters of the earth in the same work of destruction . . . add to this that as to the other species of animals, the lions and tigers are mere lambs compared with man as a destroyer.[3]

Even among the most vicious 'inferior species,' Peale observed, there were no examples of an animal preying on its own kind: the lion did not destroy the lion, the hawk did not prey upon the hawk, and even sharks did not levy war against one another. Whenever explorers had come upon an isolated settlement of any single species, they found the animals living in perfect harmony, and rapidly increasing in numbers. Colonies of sea lions and sea wolves, discovered by traders to the Falkland Islands off the coast of Patagonia, flourished in their isolation; so peaceful was their life, Peale noted, that they had become unsuspecting and trustful of all creatures, and a man with a short bludgeon could kill hundreds of them before breakfast. The still lower species showed a similar harmony: the peace prevailing within each type of insect explained why they had become more numerous than any other class of animals. In contrast to all these, the human species was divided belligerently against itself.

If this was indeed a peculiarity of man, as the American philosopher did not doubt, it must serve some purpose in the economy of nature. Consider the phenomenon, the Jeffersonian urged, from the point of view of the Creator: to preserve all links in the chain of beings, He needed somehow to insure against any species becoming so numerous as to crowd out the rest. Among the lower animals this was done by allowing each species to prey upon others; for the Jeffersonian believed that the lower species were in some sense equals in the struggle for existence. 'That one species of animals should prey upon another,' Peale remarked, 'is perfectly consistent with the order of things, and it is wisely provided, that the number of each kind should correspond, so as to keep up that equilibrium of supply, which constantly prevails.' But the great power and ingenuity of man gave him a larger equilibrating force than had any of the other animals. If, for example, man wished to reduce the numbers of a particular species of noxious insect, Barton explained in his *Fragments of the Natural History of Pennsylvania*, he could simply increase the populations of those species of birds which preyed on that insect. Man's industry gave him 'an immense, an almost unlimited, command over all the living objects of this earth.' What was to prevent the human species from overrunning the earth, from destroying other species for limited human purposes? One obvious preventive which Rush noted in his *Introductory Lectures* was that the Creator had made man dependent on other animals (especially domestic animals) in order to give him an interest in protecting them. Still this seemed a curiously weak motive on which to hang the whole order of nature.

Man's dominion, described in the Book of Genesis, had meant also his own freedom from decimation by the lower animals; and his industry, adaptability, and reason saved him from many other natural perils. The Creator, therefore, must have made some special and substantial provision against human overpopulation. It was to attain this purpose that He had set man against his own species. As we have seen, Jefferson considered man the Creator's barrier against the too great multiplication of other animals; and against the fecundity of man himself, He had ordained the human species to be eternally and systematically engaged in its own decimation. From his study of the American Indians, Rush had concluded that wars, as well as fevers, old age, and casualties, were 'natural outlets' of human life, presumably designed to prevent an excess of the human species which might disorder the universe.[4]

The American philosopher thus charged to the benevolence of his Creator the major inconveniences of human society. His faith in that benevolence justified his pessimism about the nature of man. But Jeffersonian (unlike Puritan) pessimism did not presuppose the reality of evil. The life of action was essentially not a struggle between the just and the unjust; theodicy was no longer a vast moral paradox, but a mere balance of physical forces. War became euthanasia, and men's heroic struggles the effect of zoological law. The carnivorousness of the human species expressed the 'destructive passions' which had been implanted in man: the desire to dominate or devour one's neighbor was a congenital and incurable disease of human nature. The observant philosopher, according to Jefferson, might hope conceivably to see man 'softened,' but anyone who knew the facts would never hope for more.

It seemed obvious to the Jeffersonians that these destructive passions had not been confined to the sphere of international relations. If the British destroyed the French, then within Great Britain and France, too, many men must be ready to destroy their countrymen. War had a counterpart within every nation—namely, government. Jefferson tore off the paternal mask in which the European governing classes had disguised themselves. He saw wolves who had set themselves up as guards over sheep, kites pretending to protect the pigeons, hyenas who called themselves 'trustees' of the carrion. The figure varied, but the purport was always the same: the traditional governments of Europe were nothing but the institutions by which the ruling predators fattened their prey. Paine heartily agreed, and traced the origins of European government (except that of revolutionary France) to the perpetual internal war within the species:

It could have been no difficult thing in the early and solitary ages of the world, while the chief employment of men was that of attending flocks and herds, for a banditti of ruffians to overrun a country, and lay it under contributions. Their power being thus established, the chief of the band contrived to lose the name of Robber in that of Monarch; and hence the origin of Monarchy and

Kings. . . . From such beginning of governments, what could be expected but a continued system of war and extortion? It has established itself into a trade. The vice is not peculiar to one more than to another, but is the common principle of all.[5]

Such ideas strongly recall the Marxist view that 'the state is the product and the manifestation of the irreconcilability of class antagonisms.' Lenin and Marx, like Paine, saw government as conceived in sin: it was the symbol and the instrument of the exploitation of one class by another. But the Marxist imagined that by changing institutions, by abolishing economic classes, the state itself might be abolished, and with it the exploitation which it symbolized. Jefferson's pessimism precluded any such simple expedients, for the nature of man had made exploitation and institutions inevitable. He was concerned less with the imperfection of institutions than with the prior limitations of human nature. The social facts which most concerned the Jeffersonian were therefore drawn not from political but from natural history. Only secondarily did he come to the problem of institutions; he was seeking the science of society—the society which existed before government and would outlive governments.

In the predatory societies of Europe, Jefferson discerned the indelible characteristics of the whole species. His primary question was not what was the matter with European institutions, but what quality of the human animal had made such institutions possible. In 1787, Jefferson wrote from Paris:

Under pretence of governing, they have divided their nations into two classes, wolves and sheep. I do not exaggerate. This is a true picture of Europe. Cherish, therefore, the spirit of our people, and keep alive their attention. Do not be too severe upon their errors, but reclaim them by enlightening them. If once they become inattentive to the public affairs, you and I, and Congress and Assemblies, Judges and Governors, shall all become wolves. It seems to be the law of our general nature, in spite of individual exceptions; and experience declares that man is the only animal which devours his own kind; for I can apply no milder term to the governments of Europe, and to the general prey of the rich on the poor.[6]

177

In America no less than elsewhere man's instinct to exploit and dominate his fellows had to be the starting point of social science.

Anyone who ignored the essentially carnivorous nature of man, the Jeffersonian insisted, would mistake the order of the Creator. Institutions were nothing but human machinery operating within the Creator's laws. No ingenuity in the machine could change the substance of which it was made or the laws by which it was ruled. 'In every government on earth is some trace of human weakness, some germ of corruption and degeneracy, which cunning will discover, and wickedness insensibly open, cultivate and improve.' [7] Ultimately it was not governments but the species that contained the fatal flaw. How could one ever talk of a good society, when all societies were made of men, and men were designed by their Maker to prey upon each other?

Not the peaceful and harmonious, but the predatory condition of man was normal. More than once Jefferson reminded Washington that he was not immortal, and that his successors would possess the normal human vices of ambition and avarice. There could be no insurance against the reappearance of Caesars and George IIIs. Jefferson refused to pin his hopes on the occasional success of honest and unambitious men; on the contrary, the great danger was that philosophers would be lulled into complacence by the accidental rise of a Franklin or a Washington. Any government which made the welfare of men depend on the character of their governors was a delusion. This Jefferson observed in criticizing the imperfect separation of powers in the Virginia Constitution of 1776:

Mankind soon learn to make interested uses of every right and power which they possess, or may assume. . . . With money we will get men, said Caesar, and with men we will get money. Nor should our assembly be deluded by the integrity of their own purposes, and conclude that these unlimited powers will never be abused, because themselves are not disposed to abuse them. They should look forward to a time, and that not a distant one, when a corruption in this, as in the country from which we derive our

178

origin, will have seized the heads of government, and be spread by them through the body of the people; when they will purchase the voices of the people, and make them pay the price. Human nature is the same on every side of the Atlantic, and will be alike influenced by the same causes. The time to guard against corruption and tyranny, is before they shall have gotten hold of us. It is better to keep the wolf out of the fold, than to trust to drawing his teeth and claws after he shall have entered.[8]

Without denying the discomfiting facts which we have already recounted, the Jeffersonian laid alongside them another aspect of nature which pushed virtually all else out of view. The Creator, he said, loved life and action, and every quality of man was designed to that end. Even thought was a physical activity: men's brains, their bodies, and ideas themselves had been so constructed that any defects in 'the mode of action called thinking' should not interfere with other modes of action. The moral sense which guided action had been made true and sure, and was bound up with the health of the whole man, to keep the natural economy going. Man's 'destructive' passions seemed to hold nature in equilibrium. The Jeffersonian had made man a strange and motley animal: his mind had the crude individuality of any other piece of physical machinery, his moral faculty had the purity of a divine essence, and his social behavior showed the character of a cannibal.

Yet the Jeffersonian did not develop any such notion as that of 'the survival of the fittest.' For several reasons he could not explicitly idealize power and the predatory talents. In the first place, of course, there was his strong humanitarianism, growing out of primitive Christian morality, English and American Quakerism, and the European enlightenment generally. Rush was one of the most thorough and outspoken humanitarians of his day; he worked for the abolition of slavery and of capital punishment, the reform of prisons and the reduction of penalties, the gentler treatment of the insane, and the provision of free medical dispensaries for the poor. Paine and Priestley shared many of these objectives, and Jefferson worked actively for the reform of the criminal code of Virginia. But

179

more immediate and perhaps more peculiarly American reasons restrained the Jeffersonian from blatantly declaring the divine preference for the winners in the ancient *bellum omnium in omnia*. Such a notion as the survival of the fittest would have looked to Europe where the battle had been raging for centuries rather than to America where it had just begun. He preferred to judge men by their destiny rather than by their history. Moreover, the competition for survival between individuals was by no means the most prominent feature of his America. It was thus the general fitness of the environment for the health and welfare of the species, rather than the special fitness of any particular survivors, which preoccupied Jeffersonian thought. He saw the inevitable social struggle not as a universal competitive scramble, but primarily as a grappling of man with his environment, and secondarily as a conspiracy of the few against the many.

The struggle of the few against the many had been designed to secure a demographic equilibrium; but the fact that man's predatory instinct served this ulterior purpose in no way signified the benevolent Creator's approval of the predator. If men were not able to govern themselves, Jefferson confessed, he would have had to conclude either that there was no God or that He was a malevolent being. It was surely not conceivable that the Creator had made man in His wrath; to show that man was destined to govern himself was therefore to vindicate God from 'blasphemy.' 'It would have been inconsistent in creation,' Jefferson remarked, 'to have formed man for the social state, and not to have provided virtue and wisdom enough to manage the concerns of the society.' [9] He even went on from here to insist (perilous though this was to the axiomatic equality of men) that the Creator must have provided an aristocracy of talents—'the most precious gift of nature, for the instruction, the trusts, and government of society.' How otherwise could society function? And while Jefferson sometimes described the natural aristocracy as a providential means to save the common people from their own weakness, he frequently affirmed the still more optimistic belief that the people had been made competent for self-government.

To show that man was not doomed to be ruled by his enemies, that God had not left the sheep helpless before the wolves, would surely vindicate the divine plan; but in itself it provided no model for human institutions. The Jeffersonian significantly did not claim divine sanction for any particular form of government. The Creator could not have intended to confine man's activities within any particular institution: surely He must have meant to leave institutions flexible as the needs of life. In place of seeking a divine model for government, the Jeffersonian therefore sought the universal connections between bodily health and social well-being. While he studiously avoided the metaphysical quest for the good society, he had no scruples which prevented his anatomizing the healthy society. Jeffersonian political theory was dominated by this essentially practical notion: that the biological, the psychological, and the moral adjustment of man to his environment were all one. They were all equal and inseparable symptoms of harmony with the divine plan.

According to the American philosopher, the Creator had made the human body so that it would flourish when it lived in a happy community or was motivated by a noble social purpose; and conversely, He had framed all good political institutions so that they favored the health of the human body. An explicit demonstration was Rush's 'Account of the Influence of the Military and Political events of the American Revolution upon the Human Body.' [10] While the ostensible object of the essay was to examine all the physiological effects of the Revolution, it actually emphasized the connection between individual and social well-being, and right political principles—such as those of the rebels. Any general social disorder produced its accompanying bodily diseases; thus the political anxieties of 1774-1775 in Philadelphia, as Rush noted, had brought on an epidemic of apoplexy. He significantly stressed the differences between the physiological condition of the friends and that of the enemies of the American cause. The Loyalists who obstructed the Revolution tended to suffer from a disease which Rush christened 'revolutiana.' The common people had called this the 'protection fever,' since its main cause seemed to be the Loyalists' obsessive concern for protection of their persons and property. This obsession had caused bodily disorders which were accentuated by such incidental factors as inflation, the destruction of credit, the suspension of the English church, legal and extra-legal oppressions, and the Loyalists' sudden fall from wealth and influence to ostracism and penury. 'Revolutiana' was often a mortal disease. In South Carolina, for example, several Loyalists who had protected their estates by swearing allegiance to the British Government contracted the ailment and died soon after the evacuation of Charleston by the British Army. In other cases which Rush noted, the disease brought on death indirectly because the victims sought relief in exile, in seclusion or in spirituous liquors. As the aristocratic obstinacy of the Loyalists was naturally accompanied by physical disease, so too was an immoderate libertarianism. Rush observed that after the Peace of 1783, the people of the United States were not prepared for their new situation:

The excess of the passion for liberty, inflamed by the successful issue of the war, produced, in many people, opinions and conduct, which could not be removed by reason nor restrained by government. . . . The extensive influence which these opinions had upon the understandings, passions, and morals of many of the citizens of the United States, constituted a form of insanity, which I shall take the liberty of distinguishing by the name of *anarchia*.

Sharply contrasted with the mental and physical diseases of the monarchist and of the anarchist, was the remarkable health which symptomized the proper political enthusiasms. The friends of the Revolution generally showed an uncommon cheerfulness, enabling them to forget their defeats, their loss of property, and even the deaths of close relatives. Rush recorded that women who favored the Revolutionary cause were cured of hysteria. Any invigorating circumstance, such as a military victory, produced prodigious physical stamina among men inspired by a

182

noble cause. For example, the Philadelphia militia which joined the remnants of Washington's army in December, 1776, and had helped capture numerous Hessians at Trenton, underwent the rigors of outdoor life for six weeks of a hard winter. Yet of 1,500 men, most of whom had grown up in the debilitating city environment, only one died and only two fell ill. 'The patience, firmness and magnanimity,' observed Rush, 'with which the officers and soldiers of the American army endured the complicated evils of hunger, cold and nakedness, can only be ascribed to an insensibility of body produced by an uncommon tone of mind, excited by the love of liberty and their country.' So harmonious was the Revolutionary cause with the physical requirements of human life that, he noted, during the war marriages were more fruitful than before and a considerable number of women suddenly became able to bear children.

The Revolution was only one example of the reciprocal relation of social and physical health. Whenever society was well-ordered and happy, the human species seemed to flourish; conversely, if men were obsessed by unwholesome ideas or lived amidst oppression and social maladjustment, the species became ill. Jefferson himself observed that when, as in 1816, society suffered from a mania for speculation, there appeared a kind of feverish disorder of the brain, causing illusions which could not be dissipated by reason, facts, or argument. Rush remarked that the gambling in the paper of the Bank of the United States in Philadelphia in August, 1791, produced a 'paroxysm of avarice' which caused 'febrile diseases' in three of his own patients—one of whom, having acquired twelve thousand dollars in a few minutes, became mad and died several days later. Similarly, in France under the *ancien régime*, the physical disorders of the ruling class symptomized the general social evils. As Jefferson noted in Paris, the younger men there suffered from excessive love of pleasure, and the older from the disordering passion of ambition. Rush found such excesses of passion, succeeding in just this order, to be common in the human species: the body no sooner became insensible to the stimuli of pleasure, than a substitute was found in the stimuli of ambition. The

183

excess of either caused a disequilibrium in the human body, bringing with it proportionate social discord.[11]

Since the health of the body and the health of society were thus closely and positively correlated, whenever the Jeffersonian found his society vigorous, growing and prospering, he was ready to assume that the social order was natural and moral. It seemed obvious, for example, that the multiplication and elongation of human life was a sign of health; and whatever social conditions strengthened human life in this way must have been approved by the Creator. In his 'Inquiry into the Cause of Animal Life' (concerned with man as well as other animals), Rush observed:

In no part of the human species, is animal life in a more perfect state than in the inhabitants of Great Britain, and the United States of America. With all the natural stimuli that have been mentioned, they are constantly under the invigorating influence of liberty. There is an indissoluble union between moral, political, and physical happiness; and if it be true, that elective and representative governments are most favourable to individual, as well as national prosperity, it follows of course, that they are most favourable to animal life. But this opinion does not rest upon an induction derived from the relation, which truths upon all subjects bear to each other. Many facts prove animal life to exist in a larger quantity and for a longer time, in the enlightened and happy state of Connecticut, in which republican liberty has existed above one hundred and fifty years, than in any other country upon the surface of the globe.[12]

According to Rush, this naturally healthful effect of republicanism made it superfluous for free governments to use artificial expedients to increase their population or to lengthen human life. Contrariwise, despotic governments which had to try such methods, would inevitably be frustrated. Rush's observations were confirmed by those of less cautious students. For example, William Barton, nephew of the great botanist, communicated to the Philosophical Society in 1791 some 'Observations on the probabilities of the Duration of Human Life, and the progress of Population, in the United States of America.' This paper, a brilliant triumph of enthusiasm over science, marshaled copious statistics and numerous haphazard observations—such as that Mrs. Abigail Mayo of Cambridge, Massachusetts, had lived to the age of 106. The author came to the happy conclusion that life expectancy at every stage from infancy to old age was greater in the United States than in any European country, and that nowhere else in the world would population progress at so fast a rate.

The Jeffersonians had thus made demography a touchstone of political philosophy. What better evidence of the approval of the life-loving Creator than that the human species flourished and multiplied? When Jefferson foresaw on this continent a nation of one hundred million people, or when he envisaged the United States as 'the nest, from which all America, North and South, is to be peopled,' he was therefore expressing his faith in the principles of American society. If agriculture would make America prosper the Creator must have desired an American community of farmers. Conversely, that the life of the farmer favored the health of the moral sense was proof that the agrarian society would be prosperous. We have already noted Jefferson's 'moral and physical preference of the agricultural, over the manufacturing, man.' Rush, too, implied the general accord of social and individual well-being when he called agriculture 'the true basis of national health, riches, and populousness.' But Jefferson explicitly denied that the manufacturing life was necessarily worse than the life of the farmer; he meant simply that cities and manufactures were undesirable whenever they did not foster the health of the whole man.[13] Political science, like all philosophy, was merely prophylactic: its aim was not the good society, but a healthy society. We must now see how the Jeffersonians thought that political institutions might help them toward this goal.

2. The Use of Government

'HEALTH'—social or individual—was not to be attained by an elixir. It was only to be secured piecemeal, by treating symptoms as they appeared. To understand the Jeffersonian method for treating diseases of the political body, and the Jeffersonian fear that medicines might prove worse than the diseases, we must at the outset grasp the dualism which underlay Jeffersonian social science. In this dualism, 'society' and 'institutions' were antithetical terms. 'Society'—or the divinely ordered community—functioned because of the motives and incentives implanted by the Creator; in this realm there was no effective government except that of the Creator. 'Institutions' were nothing but the expedients by which diverse and feeble human minds grappled with transient problems. Between these two there could be little or no interaction. To attribute to human institutions the power to affect the divine economy would have given all nature the taint of human weakness; and to ascribe perfection to any human institution would have denied the material quality of the human mind, and have put creature on a level with Creator. A profound theological necessity thus kept the Jeffersonian from making society and institutions commensurable, for the divine plan had to remain untouched by human hand.

A century before Jefferson, the Puritans had felt a theological and metaphysical compulsion to make their institutions the instrument of the divine order. But even by the middle of the seventeenth century the conditions of life on a new continent, the raising of a generation without the near-by anchorage of ancient institutions, had led New England leaders to take their
186

cue increasingly from the American environment. The 'half-way covenant' was their way of facing the problems of a new society. By Jefferson's day the perils of the new continent no longer seemed Satan's traps set to try God's children in the wilderness, but were His challenge to His highest creatures. For the Jeffersonian, God's government did not need to be imposed on nature since it was actually revealed there. Now it seemed that man's role was to realize all natural potentialities, rather than to shape or restrain them. The corollary in political theory of this Jeffersonian theology was that man's mission in America was not so much to build institutions as to fulfill a species and a continent. The prime, if not the only, essential to this end was the healthy functioning of the species in this environment.

When man came from the hand of the Creator he was naked of institutions. Types of government, unlike types of living creatures, had not been made in the beginning. Whatever institutions men had clothed themselves with were their own handiwork; it was inconceivable that their present motley and tattered dress was actually the work of their Creator. What was man, Paine asked, when he came from the hand of his Maker? He was surely not 'citizen' nor 'subject' nor 'ruler'—nor anything else in relation to institutions. 'Man,' he insisted, 'was his high and only title, and a higher cannot be given him.' The error of Burke and other European political theorists—'metaphysicians,' Paine called them—was that they had overlooked this distinction and attributed imperfect institutions to the perfect Creator. This was unscientific because it ignored facts about the human species; and blasphemous because it mistook the character of God. By treating particular institutions as if they had divine sanction, Paine objected, 'man, considered as man, is thrown back to a vast distance from his Maker, and the artificial chasm filled up with a succession of barriers, or sort of turnpike gates, through which he has to pass.' Actually all institutional turnpikes, with their tickets and rules, were mere human fabrications: to include them in the Creator's scheme was to intrude into nature an unimaginable confusion. 'As there is but one species of man,' declared Paine, 'there

187

can be but one element of human power; and that element is man himself. Monarchy, aristocracy, and democracy, are but creatures of imagination; and a thousand such may be contrived as well as three.' [14]

Such order as there was in human society was necessarily the work of the Creator and not of his creatures. As Paine remarked in the familiar passage in *Common Sense*, 'Society in every state is a blessing, but Government, even in its best state, is but a necessary evil; in its worst state an intolerable one. . . . Government, like dress, is the badge of lost innocence; the palaces of kings are built upon the ruins of the bowers of paradise.' All political institutions were therefore given an essentially negative function. The statesman had been assigned a weak and undramatic role; he could be no Moses, since men were already in the Promised Land. Surely it is not surprising that Jeffersonian thought did not apotheosize the statesman.

The Jeffersonian imagination was stirred less by the building of institutions than by the fructifying of environment. In this respect too he had made his God a candid reflection of his aspirations for man. The Creator had himself given man no legacy of institutions but had spent His energy molding physical nature and facilitating its processes. Man could not do better than make the Creator his model: to recognize that the productivity of society resided in the processes of nature rather than in institutional constructs. Man's inevitable efforts to govern himself should not be allowed to obscure this fact. 'A wise and frugal government,' Jefferson in his First Inaugural Address defined as one 'which shall restrain men from injuring one another, which shall leave them otherwise free to regulate their own pursuits of industry and improvement, and shall not take from the mouth of labor the bread it has earned. This is the sum of good government, and this is necessary to close the circle of our felicities.'

But why was any human help needed to keep the natural economy running? Did this not impute imperfection to the machinery which the Creator had made for society? Did He indeed require any assistance from man? Obviously not, the

Jeffersonian declared; yet his political thought revealed more than a little doubt. The raw facts, as he saw them, showed man to be a beast of prey. Men everywhere attacked foreigners and enslaved their countrymen. Jefferson, we must recall, had lived under the rule of George III in America, had seen the *ancien régime* in France, and had observed continual destruction in Europe from the rise of Napoleon to the Congress of Vienna. In France he had seen a great popular revolution frustrated by the ambition and avarice of a few; and in the United States he had witnessed Federalists who had fought the tyranny of a British king seek to impose what was (at least in his opinion) a new tyranny of their own. The War of 1812 seemed itself evidence that tyrants would never be conquered, and that every generation would have to fight its own battle against fellow human predators. Whatever hope there was, had to be derived from the devious uses of war and misery in maintaining the equilibrium of species.

While the Jeffersonian was too pious to overlook such uses, he was too sensible to find much comfort in them alone. Here indeed was a serious weakness in his theodicy which he never thoroughly repaired. But he supported his conviction that man had in him something of the divine Workman and that the human species had been made for fruitful action, when he underlined another aspect of nature—the beneficent accord between the animal and the political economy. As we have already seen, the Jeffersonian was struck by the fact that the noble principles of the American Revolution actually invigorated the body; the happy republican government of the United States caused longevity of the species; the agrarian community, which was the most prosperous, seemed also to be the most moral. Such facts justified his hope that by building some institutions men might be serving a good end. Theoretically, his distinction between 'society' and 'institutions' had denied any interaction between the design of nature and the devices of man. But actually the American philosopher treated human institutions as a kind of mediating factor between the discomfiting necessities of the whole natural economy and the special needs of human activity. The proper work of government was to protect men from some of the unhappy (but necessary) qualities of the species.

Jefferson thus took his cue for political science not from any vast preconceived purpose, but from the struggle already going on among men. When he observed war and tyranny he could not but conclude, in the *Notes on Virginia*, 'that the sheep are happier of themselves, than under care of the wolves.' If the choice was between the absence of law found among the American Indians and the 'too much law' of civilized Europeans, he surely favored the former. But, Jefferson said, these were not the only alternatives: he aimed to devise a government too weak to aid the wolves, and yet strong enough to protect the sheep.

Political liberty amounted to guarding each man against the evil passions of his associates, and them against him; to secure such liberty was the whole end of government. The Revolution, according to Jefferson, had been fought to save man from the 'corrupt will' of his neighbors. 'Free government,' he wrote in the famous Kentucky Resolutions of 1798, 'is founded in jealousy, and not in confidence. . . . In questions of power, then, let no more be said of confidence in man, but bind him down from mischief, by the chains of the Constitution.' For Paine, the purpose of all constitutions (explained in *Rights of Man*, Part II) was 'to restrain and regulate the wild impulse of power.' By restraining these impulses, by keeping men from injuring one another, good governments might prevent ambitious men from obstructing the Creator's beneficence. But even while ascribing these uses to government, the American philosopher insisted on that distinction between 'society' and 'government' from which he had begun. Although the Creator had provided a 'natural aristocracy' specially qualified for governing, such an élite were by no means to be philosopher kings; they were not responsible for defining the ends of society. Such human definition was quite superfluous, for the ends had already been defined by the Creator and revealed in nature. The best human government might guard the divine order, but it could do no more. It might preserve what God had made, but was never to set itself up in place of God. Tyrants alone could believe otherwise.

To defend representative government, it was enough to show the use of republican institutions against the worst communal evils. Since the proper end of government was not in any case the attainment of the good society, the intractability or incoherence of the public mind was no objection to popular institutions. Nothing could have been further from the doctrine *vox populi, vox dei*. Since every tyranny had succeeded only by using the people against themselves, if only the people resisted being so used, they would be the effective barrier against tyrants. The people were the largest and most immovable obstacle in the path of ambition: their virtue was thus not qualitative but quantitative. Jefferson's argument made plain that he attributed no peculiar goodness or incorruptibility to the people. 'The evils flowing from the duperies of the people, are less injurious than those from the egoism of their agents.' It was not that the people could not be bribed, but that the cost of bribing so many was beyond the means of anyone or even several men. As he wrote in the *Notes on Virginia*:

The influence over government must be shared among all the people. If every individual which composes their mass participates of the ultimate authority, the government will be safe; because the corrupting the whole mass will exceed any private resources of wealth; and public ones cannot be provided but by levies on the people. . . . It has been thought that corruption is restrained by confining the right of suffrage to a few of the wealthier people; but it would be more effectually restrained by an extension of that right to such members as would bid defiance to the means of corruption.[15]

The corruptibility, the fickleness, the ignorance, and the crudity of the popular mass would surely prevent their conceiving or carrying through any grand design. This however was actually something in their favor, since only the Creator was qualified to make the blueprint for community.

The capacity of the people to 'control and enchain the aristocratic spirit of the government,' did not qualify them to conduct its complex daily affairs. Their active participation should be proportioned to their education and intelligence. When Jefferson professed faith in the 'good sense' of the masses, he was simply declaring them the best bloodhounds against tyrants: 'the tendency of power to degenerate into abuse' appeared in the common people as well as elsewhere. There is no better evidence of the prophylactic emphasis of his political thought, and of his refusal to find divine right in the popular will, than Jefferson's insistence that a good government had to guard against the corruption and excesses of the majority.[16]

Montesquieu had argued in his *Spirit of Laws* (Book VIII) that a republic could endure only if confined to a small territory. The public interests of such an area, he said, would be simple enough so that the people might comprehend them. For Jefferson, however, the problem could not be stated in this way, because it was no responsibility of government to insure the welfare of society. He simply asked how large a geographical extent would best enable government to achieve its limited prophylactic purpose. For this he preferred the larger area: 'local egoisms' could then be played off against each other and no endemic poison could infect the whole. 'Had our territory been even a third only of what it is,' Jefferson declared after the defeat of the Federalists in 1800, 'we were gone. But while frenzy and delusion like an epidemic, gained certain parts, the residue remained sound and untouched, and held on till their brethren could recover from the temporary delusion; and that circumstance has given me great comfort.' [17] A century before Frederick Jackson Turner, Jefferson saw the Western extent of the continent insuring against the local conflicts which had destroyed smaller republics.

In Jeffersonian thought the principle of federalism was supported less by a desire to leave local governments free to bring happiness to their citizens, than by the anxiety to fragment political power so that no institutions would attempt more than was within human power. 'It is as impossible,' John Taylor of Caroline observed, 'that politicians can extend the intellectual powers of men beyond their natural limits, as that priests can turn bread and wine into flesh and blood. The incapacity of one mind for securing the liberty and happiness of an extensive country, dictates the wisdom of dividing power.' [18] Whether the rulers of a government had the power to give adequate trial to their large designs did not (at least while he remained out of power) much trouble the Jeffersonian. Governments did not exist for such purpose; they were medicines and not elixirs. The 'divinity' of kings, Taylor remarked, had been invented to shield concentrated power against the resentments inspired by tyranny; the way to avoid tyranny was not to declare the 'divine right' of the people, for this pretension, too, could shield tyranny. Men must rather deny the divinity of all political institutions and make an energetic effort to draw the fangs of human power.

If the body politic was preserved from the unnatural tyranny of any of its parts, if it could be saved from the ambition and the avarice of the few and of the many, the Jeffersonian had little doubt that it would prosper. He was satisfied to point in the general direction of the Creator's plan; and he vowed war against any man who tried to frustrate it. He was the enthusiastic defender of a beautiful lady whom he had never seen and never would see, but who was somehow already incarnate and veiled in nature. This comprised one of the striking paradoxes of Jeffersonian thought. For the main difficulty in the way of the Jeffersonian construction of a systematic political theory was not the vagueness and remoteness of the divine plan but its omnipresence and concreteness. While all particular theories and institutions were relegated into the transient and unsubstantial world of idea, in political science as elsewhere in his thought, the actual shape of nature had been idealized into a materialist utopia. His political model was not in some inaccessible empyrean realm, not in some nowhere, but in the much too accessible everywhere. The Jeffersonian was overwhelmed by an excess of concrete material. His ideal for community could not be adequately defined until all the facts were gathered; but since this could never be accomplished, the Jeffersonian 'society' possessed a tantalizing vagueness.

193

3. A Philosophy of Rights

THE Declaration of Independence asserted it to be self-evident that men are 'endowed by their Creator with certain unalienable Rights.' These discrete claims of individuals to 'Life, Liberty and the pursuit of Happiness' logically preceded all Jeffersonian institutions. Paine's major work of political theory was entitled *Rights of Man*. All the Jeffersonians were great believers in 'Bills of Rights,' and the word 'rights' is the most familiar and most significant word in their political idiom. Contrary to general belief, this emphasis did not express a conscious reliance on metaphysical foundations, nor a 'rationalistic' or abstract basis of the state. It revealed, rather, the unsystematic and inarticulate character of Jeffersonian political theory. A list of 'rights' substituted for a systematic theory of government. 'Rights' are indefinitely enumerable, and (in the absence of a comprehensive theory of 'right') the addition or subtraction of any one does not necessarily require the subtraction or addition of others.

For the Jeffersonian, this approach to political theory, to be explored in the present section, seemed to provide at once a transcendental sanction and a sufficient definiteness for the social claims of men. The word 'right' was always a signpost pointing back to the divine plan of the Creation. The items in the list of rights, and the scope of each item, were to be discovered by enumerating the particular protections required to enable man to fit into the economy of nature. Even in the heavy irony which Paine directed against Burke, we discern the assumption that man's rights become obvious in the context of natural history.

194

Generally speaking, we know of no other creatures that inhabit the earth than man and beast; and in all cases, where only two things offer themselves, and one must be admitted, a negation proved on any one, amounts to an affirmative on the other; and therefore, Mr. Burke, by proving against the Rights of *Man*, proves in behalf of the *beast*; and consequently, proves that government is a beast; and as difficult things sometimes explain each other, we now see the origin of keeping wild beasts in the Tower; for they certainly can be of no other use than to shew the origin of the government.

Assuming, as the Jeffersonians did in all seriousness, that man's role in government was to be discovered from the quality and position of *homo sapiens diurnus*, the definition could be sharpened only by discovering the practical task which the Creator had assigned to man on this earth. Whatever rights were necessary to make individuals competent to these tasks would have the sanction of divinity. 'Every man wishes to pursue his occupation, and to enjoy the fruits of his labours and the produce of his property in peace and safety, and with the least possible expence. When these things are accomplished, all the objects for which government ought to be established are answered.' [19]

The Jeffersonian natural 'rights' philosophy was thus a declaration of inability or unwillingness to give positive form to the concept of community, or to face the need for defining explicitly the moral ends to be served by government. From the point of view of the individual, 'rights' have a positive enough look: they validate his power under certain circumstances and in certain ways to express his individuality without hindrance. But from the point of view of the community, 'rights' have a negative implication: they prescribe what the community *cannot* do. They warn where government dare not go, without suggesting where it ought to go. In Jefferson's own draft of the Declaration of Independence, he asserted as 'sacred & undeniable . . . that all men are created equal & independent.' [20] From his point of view the document should have been considered a declaration of independence, not merely of the American colonies from Great Britain, but of each man from all others. His 'natural rights' theory of government left all men naturally free from duties to their neighbors: no claims could be validated except by the Creator's plan, and the Creator seemed to have made no duties but only rights.

We cannot be surprised that the Jeffersonian found this metaphysical apparatus adequate for his political program. The individual claims which seemed necessary for man's mastery of his environment in Jefferson's day were socially innocuous: man's struggle was still more against nature than against his fellow men. The Jeffersonian 'rights' thus happened to coincide with the claims which many of us would be willing to give permanent validity. There seemed no inconsistency between declaring men's 'independence' of each other while insisting on their 'rights' against each other, for human independence subsisted in the ambiguous realm of nature where one creature's gain was not another's loss. Faith in the Creator's design was what saved the persistent iteration of 'rights' from seeming an anarchic individualism.

But the weakness of Jeffersonian political theory appeared even in its own day wherever the fulfillment of a right opened the question of the positive moral values to be affirmed by society. Consider slavery, for example. The Jeffersonian had no difficulty in discerning that the institution violated the sacred individuality of its victims: in fact he saw that slavery was the most thorough denial of God-given rights. 'Happy people!' Rittenhouse enviously addressed the inhabitants of other planets, 'and perhaps more happy still, that all communication with us is denied. We have neither corrupted you with our vices nor injured you by violence. None of your sons and daughters, degraded from their native dignity, have been doomed to endless slavery, by us in America, merely because *their* bodies may be disposed to reflect or absorb the rays of light, in a way different from ours.' Jefferson had included in his draft of the Declaration of Independence a solemn indictment of George III for encouraging the slave trade; Rush was a founder of the antislavery movement in Pennsylvania; Peale voted for the abolition of slavery. In the pages of his *Elements*

196

of Botany Barton lamented the incongruity between the beautiful symmetry found in the class Hexandria (which included the rice plant), and the social disorder revealed in the slavery of the Negroes who cultivated it. The gist of the Jeffersonian objection was that slavery allowed one half of the citizens to trample on the rights of the others. In the very course of violating the Negro's rights the white man was disordering his own and his children's morals. Jefferson could not believe that such flagrant violation of the Creator's plan would be permitted long duration.[21]

So far, so good. Beyond this protest, the Jeffersonian could not go. Of course, the Negroes were not yet freed, and to free them was surely his primary task. Even his abolitionism, however, was weakened because he was unsure what kind of community ought to emerge or what place the Negro should have in it. What was the Negro's proper place in the human, or more especially in the American community? Did other men have duties toward the Negro? Jeffersonian political science could not answer these questions because it was not concerned with duties. And it was not concerned with duties because it had left the moral ends of the human community vaguely implicit in nature.

Having referred his question to anthropology, the most the American philosopher could say (and even this without assurance) was that the Negro was probably a member of the single human species. Granting this to be true, the implication for political theory was nothing but an uncertain warning that it might be improper to treat the Negro differently than other varieties of mankind. From his actual demonstration of the Negro's membership in the human species, Rush's moral was that physicians should try to remedy the congenital leprosy of the Negro; meanwhile the Negro should be kept in social quarantine. While Jefferson himself was vigorous enough in proclaiming that slavery violated the rights of the Negro, he was quite unable to say how the Negro should be treated after freedom. Jefferson's fear of the consequences of his attacks on slavery was among the principal reasons why he delayed publishing his *Notes on Virginia*. Even in that volume, however, he explicitly opposed incorporating free Negroes into the population of Virginia. When colonization later became a practical issue, Jefferson objected to allowing the Negroes to colonize on the American continent, and suggested their transportation to foreign islands in the West Indies. He was happy at a proposal for African colonization which would result in 'drawing off this part of our population, most advantageously for themselves as well as for us.' [22]

The attitude of the Jeffersonian toward the Negro illustrates both the strength and the weakness of his philosophical method. A philosophy which marks off its problems mainly, if not exclusively, by contemporary urgencies may readily make the short-run satisfaction of the particular claims of individuals the highest term in its hierarchy of values. While such a temper may smooth the way for the abolition of a great moral evil like slavery, it is apt to judge those social claims best which speak in the loudest contemporary voice. Such a view may too easily be satisfied with the forms, while overlooking the substance of justice. It may frustrate its own larger end because it lacks foresight or concern for the new conflicts always bred by the satisfaction of discrete claims.

We discern these same features in the Jeffersonian theory of property, which affirmed the right of every man to the fruit of his labor. In the American context, this meant the right to acquire and accumulate property; the opportunity here seemed unique since the stock of land seemed boundless. The definition of ends seemed superfluous because the claims of different men seemed for ages still unlikely to interfere with each other. The large store of undistributed land and the great demand for labor in America made it possible for the worker from Europe to become independent of the will of any employer. The common man on this continent was therefore free of the 'moral coercion of want' which had constrained the poverty-stricken masses of Europe. St. John Crèvecoeur, a member of the Philosophical Society and a correspondent of Jefferson, gave a mythological generality to this phenomenon in his *Letters from an American Farmer,* first published in 1782. 'Andrew the Hebridean' was a poor man, bred in the servile atmosphere of Europe, who had come to the new continent to secure 'that manly confidence which property confers'; before he died this farmer, who in Europe had never had a will of his own, actually became embarrassed by his new-found independence. But neither Crèvecoeur nor Jefferson hinted how Andrew and his fellow immigrants should have used their independence. The great use of property was purely and simply that it enabled a man (and his children) to avoid dependence. As Jefferson wrote in his eulogy of the farmer's life, 'Dependence begets subservience and venality, suffocates the germ of virtue, and prepares fit tools for the designs of ambition.' [23]

But what of those men who had more than enough to secure independence? What should they do with their property? In the contemporary American economy this question could not have seemed urgent, because accumulations of great wealth were still rare; and the Jeffersonian did not concern himself with the social responsibilities of property. He gave his only directions in the negative form of his asceticism. He would not argue that some men be allowed to accumulate wealth so that they might use it for the benefit of society: the public benefactor, like the statesman, was a figure alien to Jeffersonian thought. Wealthy men had too often used their wealth to restrict the independence of their neighbors. It was Jefferson's fear of the predatory instinct in man—of 'the luxury, the riot, the domination and the vicious happiness of the aristocracy' —that came closest to providing a moral direction to the Jeffersonian economy. He saw the true choice to be *'economy and liberty,* or *profusion and servitude.'* Everywhere Paine saw 'luxurious indolence' associated with the splendor of a throne and the corruption of the state. 'Let our harbours, our doors, our hearts,' Rittenhouse had prayed in 1775, 'be shut against luxury.' Jefferson often looked back wistfully to the spartan frugality of Revolutionary days.[24]

Concepts of the 'public interest' and of 'welfare' were strikingly absent from Jeffersonian political thought; and circumstances made it difficult for him even to be aware of their absence. This weakness was illustrated in his attitude not only toward property but also toward education and travel. While Jefferson's own travels in France had provided him an opportunity to study diseases of the body politic, he warned that such observations were not to be risked by young men. They might be infected by the very germs they should have been studying. Foreign education and travel might corrupt the student by 'voluptuary pleasures' and alien manners, and therefore were to be avoided. The young traveler abroad was apt to develop tastes which could be satisfied only by infringing the rights of his neighbors.[25] Jefferson never seriously suggested that cosmopolitanism and breadth of mind might fit a man to discover the proper ends of society.

The Jeffersonian approach to political thought had the great virtue of immunizing the American republican against such doctrinaire schemes of government as those which plagued his French contemporaries. Unlike them, he never so thoroughly identified himself with his Creator as to hold himself responsible for design in the community. Consistency was a concept irrelevant to Jeffersonian institutions; their only test was external. The current needs of 'nature'—or society—expressed the paramount demands on government. The Jeffersonian never quite left himself at the mercy of a pragmatic necessity, because his vision of the divine economy was clear enough to define some inviolable rights of man.

At the same time, his preoccupation with action and nature gave a certain fickleness to the Jeffersonian concept of the state and a feebleness to his concept of law. The pragmatic temper of his political philosophy weakened all bulwarks against power. Jefferson's personal contribution to American political institutions (despite his insistence on preserving rights and fragmenting power) was his model of a strong Presidency. And this apparent inconsistency was not so much a violation of his political theory as a symptom of its incompleteness. Once in power, Jefferson could not but recognize that his negative concept of government was imaginary. He now easily presumed that whatever measures served prosperity or the 'needs' of the time must by definition serve the Creator's purpose. He found it hard to realize that he had left government without trammels, having weakened those very restrictions on power which he had called the prime end of all government.

Jefferson's 'natural rights' political philosophy thus threw him back on successful action as the final test of human institutions. Although his Kentucky Resolutions of 1798 had described constitutions as the chains to bind rulers, barely five years later he justified his unexampled executive act of the Louisiana Purchase:

The Constitution has made no provision for our holding foreign territory, still less for incorporating foreign nations into our Union. The executive in seizing the fugitive occurrence which so much advances the good of their country, have done an act beyond the Constitution. The Legislature in casting behind them metaphysical subtleties, and risking themselves like faithful servants, must ratify and pay for it, and throw themselves on their country for doing for them unauthorized, what we know they would have done for themselves had they been in a situation to do it . . . we shall not be disavowed by the nation, and their act of indemnity will confirm and not weaken the Constitution, by more strongly marking out its lines.[26]

When the exigencies of international affairs made even a belated appeal to the nation on this issue impolitic, Jefferson (who himself recognized that his course went far to make the Constitution 'a blank paper by construction') acquiesced in the partisan attempt to suppress the whole issue. Jefferson's persecution of Aaron Burr also showed a straining, if not a violation, of those limitations on power which ostensibly justified all Jeffersonian government. The contempt for the judiciary which Jefferson expressed freely and repeatedly had been occasioned by immediate political irritations, but it did betray his inability to feel respect for law. When judges crossed Jefferson's political aims, they became 'the corps of sappers and miners' working to undermine the independence of the states and to consolidate political power. He could not imagine that in the long run a strong and independent judiciary might fortify the restraints on political power; he had not wholly purged himself of that desire for power of which he accused his 'monocratic' enemies. In his own thinking, Jefferson had made political and legal questions indistinguishable.

The reduction of all questions to a final 'practical' test was made the easier because the American philosopher had denied the existence of 'forms' of government, each of which might have its proper order and balance. In the beginning the Creator had made creatures and society, but had cast no molds for institutions. Even republicanism Jefferson never hypostatized as an ideal political type. 'What is called a *republic*,' observed Paine, 'is not any *particular form* of government. It is wholly characteristical of the purport, matter or object for which government ought to be instituted, and on which it is to be employed, RES-PUBLICA, the public affairs, or the public good; or, literally translated, the *public thing*.' [27] To deny that there were forms of government threatened to render government formless: to weaken that sense for order, proportion and limit which might restrain power. Then how otherwise test institutions but by their use for an immediate practical program? John Adams' eloquent warning to Jefferson (February 2, 1816) was surely pertinent:

Power always thinks it has a great soul, and vast views, beyond the comprehension of the weak; and that it is doing God service, when it is violating all His laws. Our passions, ambition, avarice, love, resentment, etc., possess so much metaphysical subtlety, and so much overpowering eloquence, that they insinuate themselves into the understanding and the conscience, and convert both to their party.

Might not the needs of 'the public thing' always supply a handy argument for men who saw no inner laws or limitations growing out of their own nature or the nature of institutions themselves?

Jefferson had surely meant his appeal to his Creator to justify his own humble refusal to restrain men within any social design. But actually, by refusing to declare the *duties* of man, by refusing to face the large question of social purpose, he had presupposed the whole end to be prosperity and the perpetuation of the species. What then could close the door to the subtle pragmatic arguments of men in power? Any deficiency or incompleteness in Jeffersonian political theory (at least on Jeffersonian premises) was at the same time put beyond the pale of criticism because of the hypothetical perfection of the Creator's political thought.

The motto which Jefferson chose for his seal, 'Rebellion to Tyrants is Obedience to God,' comes close to summing up his whole political philosophy. Rebellion was the ultimate appeal against violated rights, and seemed their adequate symbolic affirmation. He believed in the divine right of revolutions; but no duties had sanction from the Creator. It is significant and appropriate that the American philosopher's classic political text should have been the Declaration of Independence. Jefferson and his fellows were among the great protagonists and polemicists of the Revolution: they knew that the rights of the colonists must be vindicated against the British tyrant; but they were not equally well equipped philosophically for building a new government. Jefferson was abroad at the time of the Constitutional Convention, and it is doubtful if the Constitution was much the worse for it. When he learned of the work of the Convention, he did not on the whole disapprove, but he was anxious that the government 'not be too energetic.' His only recommendations were that the constitution be changed to prohibit the re-election of the President, and that a bill of rights be added.[28] Jefferson himself was pleased to consider his accession to power in 1801 as a 'revolution.' When the Jeffersonian party controlled government (and therefore had no cause to fear its misuse) they were full of particular projects, but at a loss to incorporate them in a general theory.

The American philosopher imagined that by dogmatically asserting rights and revolutions he was not committing himself to any human pattern for government. 'A little rebellion, now and then,' remarked Jefferson, 'is a good thing, and as necessary in the political world as storms in the physical. . . . It is a medicine necessary for the sound health of government.' [29] Revolutions always seemed a way of giving government back to the Creator—of wiping the slate clean of distorted and obsolete human designs, so that the divine pattern might become visible.

4. The Sovereignty of the Present Generation

THE American philosopher found stability in the here-and-now. He felt at home in the contemporary as he did in the material world and he was sure that world must have broad and clear boundaries. He could not think of the present as a kind of overflowing of the past, nor as an Augustinian moment which fled speedily from futurity into history. His strong sense of separation from the past, which we shall now examine, made it hard for him to grasp firmly the concept of a tradition or an institution, both of which seemed illusory and transitory.

The past seemed both uninteresting and unreal. Only the present seemed unique. Jeffersonian anthropology became the substitute for history. The animal qualities of the species, unalterably fixed by the Creator in the beginning, had determined human experience. Even the life of Jesus—because it had occurred after the Creation and within the realm of institutions —seemed less important than the simplest biological facts. What interest could there be in human vicissitudes when the full meaning of the universe appeared in the unvarying shape of nature? Time and human fluctuations were no concern of the Creator; past and present operated according to the same inflexible laws. After the first creation, species never were born nor died, laws were never added, and human institutions had no active role. Each man, like an insect or an elephant, might have a 'life history'; but the history of the species could tell nothing more than the emergence of varieties and their adjustment to environment. Since the Jeffersonian was interested in the human stereotype which had not changed for six thousand years and would not change till the end of time, it seemed only common sense to study that stereotype in the bright light of the present. For such a study the American was admirably situated. As Paine observed:

In viewing this subject, the case and circumstances of America present themselves as in the beginning of the world; and our inquiry into the origin of government is shortened, by referring to the facts that have arisen in our own day. We have no occasion to roam for information into the obscure field of antiquity, nor hazard ourselves upon conjecture. We are brought at once to the point of seeing government begin, as if we had lived in the beginning of time. The real volume, not of history, but of facts, is directly before us, unmutilated by contrivance, or the errors of tradition.[30]

If the present was not an infinitesimal moment swallowed up by history at the instant of its birth, it had to be a chronological sphere with precise dimensions. To leave the present for the past, then, would be as clearly a physical act as crossing the Canadian border, or leaving life for death. Existence was, after all, a physical fact analogous to those which gave every man membership in the species. Mere physical coexistence established a fellowship which no abstract moral purpose could give. The present, Jefferson said, was a corporation as separate from the past as was England from the United States; it was as absurd to say that the dead should have a hand in governing the living as to say that Britons should govern Americans. 'We may consider each generation as a distinct nation,' he observed, 'with a right, by the will of its majority, to bind themselves, but none to bind the succeeding generation, more than the inhabitants of another country.' His mode of argument recalls that by which he supported his materialism: 'These are axioms so self-evident that no explanation can make them plainer; for he is not to be reasoned with who says that non-existence can control existence, or that nothing can move something.' [31]

If the end of institutions was only the protection of the 'rights' with which the Creator had invested individuals, then when anyone died the Creator extinguished automatically any possible relationship between him and future generations. 'The dead have no rights,' insisted Jefferson. 'They are nothing; and nothing cannot own something. Where there is no substance, there can be no accident. This corporeal globe, and everything upon it, belongs to its present corporeal inhabitants, during their generation.' The fact that the dead had no 'rights' conclusively demonstrated to the Jeffersonian his own lack of political connection with his ancestors. 'Our Creator made the earth for the use of the living and not of the dead . . . those who exist not can have no use nor right in it, no authority or power over it . . . one generation of men cannot foreclose or burden its use to another, which comes to it in its own right and by the same divine beneficence.' Since a man's powers and wants died with him, Paine observed, after death he could have no place in the concerns of the world, and therefore had no right to a voice in its affairs.[32]

If living men were not united by any idea of community, it was surely absurd to think that the living and the dead could be so united. In this sense a political 'tradition' or 'institution' was a contradiction in terms: this paradox lay at the heart of Jeffersonian political philosophy. And the 'fact' of the Creation became a myth newly enacted in every age. Paine explained:

The illuminating and divine principle of the equal rights of man (for it has its origin from the Maker of man) relates, not only to the living individuals, but to generations of men succeeding each other. Every generation is equal in rights to generations which preceded it, by the same rule that every individual is born equal in rights with his contemporary. Every history of the creation, and every traditionary account . . . all agree in establishing one point, *the unity of man*; by which I mean . . . that all men are born equal, and with equal natural right, in the same manner as if posterity had been continued by *creation* instead of *generation*, the

206

latter being the only mode by which the former is carried forward; and consequently every child born into the world must be considered as deriving its existence from God. The world is as new to him as it was to the first man that existed, and his natural right in it is of the same kind.[33]

Just as the material origin of all human life was recapitulated at the birth of each infant, so every birth symbolized the Creator's intention to provide a fresh opportunity to realize the possibilities of the species.

To deny the reality of 'generations' and their equality in rights would have been as unscientific as to deny the existence of species. The Jeffersonian theory of society was as much dependent on one as on the other. The cautious political scientist would always take care that the real rights of the living and not the illusory rights of the dead were being protected. A popular government in the precise materialist sense of the word had to represent the will of the *living* majority. To overlook this distinction was to substitute one form of tyranny for another. 'Every age and generation,' Paine remarked, 'must be as free to act for itself *in all cases* as the age and generations which preceded it. The vanity and presumption of governing beyond the grave is the most ridiculous and insolent of all tyrannies. Man has no property in man; neither has any generation a property in the generations which are to follow.' A whole dead generation, argued Jefferson, could have no more right or wisdom than a single dead individual; each of them came to nothing, and an infinite aggregate of nothings added up to the same.[34]

This principle could not be useful unless the boundaries of the present were precisely defined. In a long letter written to Madison from Paris in 1789, Jefferson showed how the answer to this basic problem of political theory was to be derived from simple demographic facts; and twenty-five years later he was still using the same method for delineating the boundaries of generations.[35] From Buffon's mortality tables which analyzed 23,994 deaths, Jefferson had observed that of all the persons of all ages living at any moment, half would be dead within

207

24 years and 8 months. By leaving out of account all minors and considering only the adults (21 years or older) who had the power to act for the society, Jefferson figured that one-half of the voting population alive at any moment would be dead within 18 years and 8 months. This, then, was the natural span of a political generation, from which Jefferson deduced a host of practical consequences.

Since within nineteen years a majority of the lawmakers would be dead, their laws, too, should then rightfully be dead. No generation should be bound in any way by the disposition of power, property or honors made by its predecessors. All ecclesiastical and feudal privileges, all entails, hereditary offices, jurisdictions and titles, and perpetual monopolies of every kind could be rightfully abolished whenever a majority of living men so desired. Whether the community would compensate individuals for such losses would always be a question of generosity and never of right. Most important, no generation had a right to contract a public debt which could not be retired within nineteen years; thereafter the debt was nullified by the natural law of society.

Had this principle been declared in the British bill of rights, England would have been placed under the happy disability of waging eternal war, and of contracting her thousand millions of public debt. In seeking, then, for an ultimate term for the redemption of our debts, let us rally to this principle, and provide for their payment within the term of nineteen years at the farthest. . . . Not that it is expected that Congress should formally declare such a principle. They wisely enough avoid deciding on abstract questions. But they may be induced to keep themselves within its limits.[36]

Each generation was supposed to come into the world fully clothed with rights, but naked of duties, whether to ancestors, to contemporaries, or to descendants. It was a function of political institutions to prevent men being stripped of these primeval rights. 'The first principle of civilization,' Paine asserted in his *Agrarian Justice*, 'ought to have been, and ought still to be, that the condition of every person born into the world, after a state of civilization commences, ought not to be worse than if he had been born before that period.' In that work Paine proposed (England was his example) that a national fund be set up to help vindicate the rights of the living. From this fund every person at the age of twenty-one would receive the lump sum of fifteen pounds sterling, and every person after the age of fifty would receive ten pounds per annum for life—'as a compensation in part, for the loss of his or her natural inheritance, by the introduction of the system of landed property.'

Starting from the always predominant rights of the present age, the Jeffersonian came into conflict with the traditional common-law theory. According to that theory (given classic form in the late Middle Ages), the binding force o.̇ institutions was roughly proportionate to their antiquity: custom acquired legal validity by being handed down from time immemorial—'a time whereof the memory of man runneth not to the contrary.' At least in the Middle Ages, such antiquity suggested a higher than human origin. Blackstone in late eighteenth-century England saw the mere survival of an institution through many centuries as evidence of the cumulative approval of many generations. Any ancient institution therefore seemed deeply rooted in the popular will; and neither antiquity nor desuetude could wither an act of the legislature. The Jeffersonian, on the contrary, declared a natural presumption *against* laws in proportion to their antiquity. 'The generality of . . . precedents,' observed Paine, 'are founded on principles and opinions, the reverse of what they ought; and the greater distance of time they are drawn from, the more they are to be suspected. . . . Either the doctrine of precedents is policy to keep a man in a state of ignorance, or it is a practical confession that wisdom degenerates in governments as governments increase in age, and can only hobble along by the stilts and crutches of precedents.' Even the right of repeal (always, of course, possessed by the present legislature) seemed no adequate safeguard against the tyranny of dead men over living. As Jefferson observed, legislatures were hard to convene, representation was unequal, parliamentary procedure cumbersome, bribery common—and worst of all, vested interests were hard to up-root. 'Impediments arise, so as to prove to every practical man, that a law of limited duration is much more manageable than one which needs a repeal.' Habit, moreover, was a numbing force which made men unable to distinguish their own will from that of their predecessors. 'A long Habit of not thinking a Thing *wrong*,' Paine remarked in *Common Sense*, 'gives it a superficial appearance of being *right*, and raises at first a formi-dable outcry in defence of Custom.' Jefferson therefore urged men to remain aware that, although it might often be conven-ient to leave ancient laws stand as if they had been re-enacted, this did not lessen one whit the right of the living majority to repeal them 'whenever a change of circumstances or of will calls for it. Habit alone confounds what is civil practice with natural right.' Of course the right of revolution provided a final resource against all kinds of usurpation. But revolutions would be needed less often if all public contracts, all laws and constitutions declared on their face that they were to be void in a limited time, not over nineteen years from their date of enactment.[37]

Constitutions might be distinguished from laws by their function and by the immediacy of their relation to the popular will; but they could not differ in the length of their natural du-ration. 'The laws which are enacted by governments,' Paine re-marked, 'controul men only as individuals, but the nation, through its constitution, controuls the whole government, and has a natural ability to do so. The final controuling power, therefore, and the original constituting power, are one and the same power.' Constitutions, no more than laws, had any natural capacity to outlive the men who had authorized them. As Jefferson observed:

No society can make a perpetual constitution, or even a perpetual law. The earth belongs always to the living generation: they may manage it, then, and what proceeds from it, as they please, during their usufruct. They are masters, too, of their own persons, and consequently may govern them as they please. But persons and property make the sum of the objects of government. The constitution and the laws of their predecessors are extinguished then, in their natural course, with those whose will gave them being. . . . If it be enforced longer, it is an act of force, and not of right.[38]

To the Jeffersonian this principle seemed neither utopian nor anarchic. Since every government was nothing but a congeries of expedients to combat current evils, it could be added to or whittled away without any loss of proportion or effectiveness and without fundamentally affecting the social order. The recurrent reconstruction of institutions could not amount to a reformation of society. In March, 1801, soon after his first inauguration as President, Jefferson declared that his 'Revolution of 1800' would not make the quixotic effort to rebuild the social machine: all he dared expect was to drive away the vultures who preyed upon the public funds, to improve a little the old routines, and to build 'some new fences for securing constitutional rights.' [39] The recurring usefulness of revolutions arose from the need to break the congealing shapes of institutions before they petrified, and thus to leave society free to follow its natural laws of development. Revolution seemed not a way of introducing a new model for institutions but rather of affirming every generation's right to be preserved from old models.

Since the Creator had intended each generation to be sovereign over its own affairs, He must have provided each generation with sufficient talent to govern itself. Each age therefore must be endowed with a natural aristocracy whose contemporary experience would be adequate to contemporary needs. 'Every generation,' insisted Paine, 'is, and must be, competent to all the purposes which its occasions require.' The commerce of the present with the past was never meant to be by way of human precedents, traditions, or institutions, but only through the indelible Book of the Creation. 'Between society and society, or generation and generation,' observed Jefferson, 'there is no municipal obligation, no umpire but the law of nature.' Unlike Burke, the Jeffersonian feared to enrich his political science by drawing on 'the general bank and capital of nations and of ages,' lest he put himself in debt to the past, and thereby limit his freedom to deal with the present.

While this complacent attitude alienated the Jeffersonians from some of the richest sources of political philosophy, it proclaimed an approach to institutions which seemed specially relevant to the unknown conditions of a new continent. In Jefferson's words, all government was an 'experiment.' The complexity and variability of men's interests, observed Priestley, made it unsafe to conclude anything *a priori* with respect to government. The circumstances, prejudices, and habits of different nations and ages would require different constitutions to suit their needs. Therefore, Jefferson found ancient writings like Aristotle's *Politics* of little use: 'So different was the style of society then, and with those people, from what it is now and with us, that I think little edification can be obtained from their writings on the subject of government.' Institutions had to be continually reformed '*pari passu* with the progress of science.' The virtue of the Federal Constitution seemed its flexibility, rather than any novel principle of federalism or republicanism. Its real immortality would consist in its capacity, by amendment, to 'keep pace with the advance of the age in science and experience.' [40]

The Jeffersonian political scientist worked under the shadow of a fear that by the time he had obtained any results they might no longer be applicable. A new generation, divinely privileged and obliged to make its own experiments and judge from its own experience, might already have come into being. While government was given an admirable flexibility it was at the same time given a disconcerting transience and instability. For actually men were being born and dying, not just every nineteen years, but every year and every day. If the Jeffersonian had insisted on pushing his republican principle to its logical conclusion, he would have kept his institutions in constant flux— which would, of course, have denied them the quality of institutions at all. Where then, would be the means to protect the weak from the strong, the sheep from the wolves? On the other hand, if he once qualified his argument, where should he stop? If institutions were to be borrowed from his father, why not from his grandfather, and then indeed why not also from Aristotle and the other ancients?

The Jeffersonian escaped from (or rather ignored) the strict logic of his position by hypostatizing 'the present generation' into a corporate entity, and marking it off by chronological boundaries as definite as the geographical limits of continents and nations. His line between the living and the dead generation seemed as integral with the Creator's plan as was the line between species of plants or animals. The natural corporation of contemporaries could thus serve in his thought as 'the State' or 'Community' or 'Institution' has served in the thought of many other political philosophers. He refused to see himself (as indeed his political theory might incline us to view him) adrift in the perpetual flux of time; and instead thought himself secure on an island. He was not too much disturbed if metaphysicians reported its boundaries to be uncertain or receding. While he found a security there which made him feel safe from the tyranny of past institutions, he had created a kind of Leviathan of his own. For the urgent needs of The Present Generation dominated his institutions, his thought and even his avenues to knowledge.

5. The Quest for Useful Knowledge

WHAT held philosophers together were the common needs and desires of men living in the same place and generation—in Paine's phrase 'the unceasing circulation of interest, which, passing through its million channels, invigorates the whole mass of civilised man.' The Jeffersonian found an unreality and transience in the most ancient traditions, and tried to anchor himself in the immediate present. If for us this has the look of paradox, for the Jeffersonian it was a simple fact. His American task seemed directly and externally assigned. When he spoke of 'useful' projects, he was sure that only a metaphysician would ask, 'Useful for what?' The Creator had already measured the utility of human enterprise; and by 'useful' the American philosopher meant whatever promoted the intended prosperity of man.

A consequence of this view was to amalgamate all experience and activity into a single undifferentiated mass where all objects were equally entitled to attention. The line was erased—or at least obscured—between enterprises which fulfilled man's moral purpose and devices for increasing his everyday comfort. The Jeffersonian integration of man into nature, his incorporation into the divine Work, left man as workman without a yardstick. It was inevitable that improvements in the minutiae of life should have been given a disproportionate significance. The largest questions of human destiny came to be examined in the same spirit and with the same tools as were the means for repairing the irritations of daily life. To view the works of philosophers through the eyes of the Creator—who, as Barton said, was impartially interested in 'the falling of a sparrow and the falling of an empire'—was theologically to justify the philosopher's refusing to evaluate the different projects of men.

The man who removed a physical inconvenience seemed a more genuine devotee of the Creator's plan than he who elaborated the vagaries of his own brain. The Jeffersonian circle had no small part in making the scientist and technician the 'philosopher' of American society, and 'lover of wisdom' a secondary connotation of the American word. For Shakespeare it seemed paradoxical that

> . . . there was never yet philosopher
> That could endure the toothache patiently.

For Jefferson the mark of a philosopher was his discovering a new way of pulling a tooth or curing the ache. In science this attitude led to the elevation of mechanics over mathematics, of invention over discovery, and of practice over theory. The American philosopher would have measured Sir Isaac Newton against Thomas Edison by asking which had added more to the comforts of life. His scheme of values could not have been better expressed than in the statement by Benjamin Smith Barton:

All the splendid discoveries of Newton are not of so much real utility to the world, as the discovery of the *Peruvian bark*, or of the powers of *opium* and *mercury*, in the cure of certain diseases. . . . If we could tell who first discovered the mighty strength of Mercury in strangling the hydra of pleasures and of generation: if we could even ascertain who was the native of Peru, that first experienced and revealed to his countrymen the powers of the Bark in curing intermittent fevers; would not the civilized nations of mankind, with one accord, concur in erecting durable monuments of granite and of brass to such benefactors of the species? [41]

The focus of the Jeffersonian's intellectual energies was, we must remember, 'The American Philosophical Society for Promoting *Useful* Knowledge,' and there can be little doubt that its activities represented his aspirations. We read in the Preface to the first volume of the Society's *Transactions*:

Knowledge is of little use, when confined to mere speculation: But when speculative truths are reduced to practice, when theories, grounded upon experiments, are applied to the common purposes of life; and when, by these, agriculture is improved, trade enlarged, the arts of living made more easy and comfortable, and, of course, the increase and happiness of mankind promoted; knowledge then becomes really useful. That this Society, therefore, may, in some degree, answer the ends of its institution, the members propose to confine their disquisitions, principally, to such subjects as tend to the improvement of their country, and advancement of its interest and prosperity.

Franklin himself had considered the founding of the Society evidence of America's progress beyond the 'mere necessaries' of life toward the cultivation of 'the finer arts' and the improvement of 'the common stock of knowledge.' Actually the Society's activities represented an expansion rather than a transformation of Franklin's commonplace and utilitarian interests. When we examine its *Transactions*, we cannot fail to be struck by Jeffersonian versatility and ingenuity, by the consuming and indiscriminate interest in all devices for smoothing the rough edges of environment. The volume prefaced by the passage just quoted was laden with articles on how to preserve wine, cure figs and distil persimmons; suggestions on the culture of the silkworm and the uses of sunflower seed; prescriptions against the fly weevil that destroyed wheat and the worm that attacked the pea; hints on curing sore throat; instructions on shipping seeds; and plans for a horizontal windmill. Except for those on astronomical subjects, virtually all the Society's papers were justified by a practical utility—and even astronomy was only an apparent exception, for it was studied mainly for its relevance to climate and navigation. The Philosophical Society became a forum of practical projects which claimed the dignity of philosophy because they increased the comfort of man. Here Franklin and Peale presented their plans for smokeless chimneys; and Jefferson proposed his design for the moldboard plough. It is impossible not to admire the prodigious resourcefulness of the American philosopher, who was as ready with a proposal to cure epilepsy or malaria, or to improve the navigation of Pennsylvania, as with a method for destroying wild garlic, or for preserving parsnips.

If *what* men needed was plain to common sense, was it not superfluous to worry *why*? Was it not pedantic to make a hierarchy among the items, or to restrain man's active hand while he sought a metaphysic to justify activity? It seemed practicable and necessary to provide men an easier life, but difficult to make them adroit philosophers. 'The greatest service which can be rendered any country,' Jefferson observed late in life, 'is, to add an useful plant to its culture; especially, a bread grain; next in value to bread is oil.' [42] Such preoccupation with material and commonplace human needs surely turned Jeffersonian energies to use. But so sparse a philosophy, failing to provide criteria of judgment, would not much help men of a later age whose choice was among less obvious and more numerous competing needs.

We cannot be surprised at the spirit in which the American philosopher approached the problem of education. In May, 1796, the Philosophical Society offered prizes for a number of projects: a simple method of computing longitude, an improvement of ship pumps, and of stoves or fireplaces, a method to prevent decay of peach trees, an experimental treatise on native American vegetables, and a satisfactory design for street lamps. Included in this list was an offer of reward for 'the best system of liberal education.' Such was the context in which the Jeffersonian viewed his educational task. What Jefferson sought was 'an useful American education'; it was his ambition (as he emphasized by his own italics) to make the University of Virginia an institution 'in which all the branches of science useful *to us*, and *at this day*, should be taught in their highest degree.' 'Modernity' was what entitled an institution to public support. To achieve that usefulness and modernity, Jefferson wrote Priestley, it was necessary to omit many branches of science formerly esteemed, and even some still studied in Europe— because they would remain useless to Americans for many years. Others which had never been studied in universities elsewhere should be introduced in America because of current needs. Jefferson strongly recommended the study of agriculture:

It is the first in utility, and ought to be the first in respect. The same artificial means which have been used to produce a competition in learning, may be equally successful in restoring agriculture to its primary dignity in the eyes of men. It is a science of the very first order. . . . In every College and University, a professorship of agriculture, and the class of its students, might be honored as the first . . . closing their academical education with this, as the crown of all other sciences. . . .[43]

In his early years, as a Visitor of William and Mary College, Jefferson had proposed changes in the professorships to make them more suitable to American conditions. The old subjects were: Greek and Latin; mathematics; moral philosophy; and divinity. The subjects which he recommended in their place were: law and police; anatomy and medicine; natural philosophy and mathematics; moral philosophy and the law of nature and of nations; fine arts; and modern languages. Jefferson urged that an endowment which had originally been given to support missionaries to the Indians should be employed instead to finance new expeditions to gather useful anthropological data. We gain a fuller notion of Jefferson's educational philosophy from the list of subjects 'useful and practicable for us' which he proposed two decades later in his own curriculum for the University of Virginia: 'Botany, chemistry, zoology, anatomy, surgery, medicine, natural philosophy, agriculture, mathematics, astronomy, geography, politics, commerce, history, ethics, law, arts, fine arts.' [44] The Jeffersonian approach to education encouraged a preoccupation with curriculum which has not yet disappeared from American educational thought.

Any subject in Jefferson's list which has the look of being 'useless' seems so only until we have heard his reasons. For example, he was friendly to the study of history, which he thought indispensable for a proper American education, because of the practical lessons which history could teach. How otherwise learn the designs and the methods of tyranny? Jefferson therefore proposed that history comprise the greater part of the curriculum of primary schools where the common people would receive their whole education. 'History, by apprizing them of the past, will enable them to judge of the future; it will avail them of the experience of other times and other nations; it will qualify them as judges of the actions and designs of men; it will enable them to know ambition under every disguise it may assume; and knowing it, to defeat its views.' [45] Since the human species had never changed, ancient history could be as useful as modern. Rush agreed with Jefferson on the importance of teaching history—because it provided valuable facts on 'the progress of liberty and tyranny.' Priestley, one of the earliest and most vigorous advocates of 'social studies' (and especially the study of modern history) left no ambiguity about the purpose of the subject. His argument, developed in his 'Essay on a course of Liberal Education, for Civil and Active Life' has an uncomfortably modern sound. It was here that he proposed 'new articles of academical instruction,'

. . . CIVIL HISTORY, and more especially, the important objects of CIVIL POLICY; such as the theory of laws, government, manufactures, commerce, naval force, &c. with whatever may be demonstrated from history to have contributed to the flourishing state of nations, to rendering a people happy and populous at home, and formidable abroad.

For all his vigorous advocacy of education, the Jeffersonian showed little interest in its effect on the educated person. Enrichment of one's inward life or enlarging of private consciousness were held of little account compared with utility against the obstacles of environment and against the ambition and avarice of one's fellow creatures. Such a preference is clearly revealed in the Jeffersonian attitude to the ancient classics. The Jeffersonians (and not least Jefferson himself) had been nourished on classical wisdom. It is hard to deny that they had been profoundly affected in thought and feeling—that their style had been subtly pervaded by classical idiom. In rhetoric and architecture, Jefferson warmly admired the Greeks and Romans, and embraced their example. At Nîmes in 1787 he gazed whole hours at the Maison Carrée, 'like a lover at his mistress.' The classics had provided no inconsiderable part of the political vocabulary of the age. Pamphlets were signed by 'Marcellus' and 'Titus Manlius'; letters abounded with appeals to the moral wisdom of Marcus Aurelius and Epictetus and Lucretius. We hear aspiration for 'truly Attic societies,' appeal to 'Roman principle,' and wistfulness for 'the purest times of Greece and Rome.' Jefferson was praised for his 'Roman love of country'; Burr was attacked as a 'Catilinarian character.' More and more in later years, Jefferson's letters quoted Greek and Latin phrases, and classical authors became his refuge from the acrimony of politics. Jefferson was not alone in his debt to the ancients. Rush, before he was twenty, had translated the aphorisms of Hippocrates. Barton's *Elements of Botany* quotes freely from Pliny, Virgil,

219

Ovid, and many others; his botanical articles abound with classical allusions. With the exception of Paine (and possibly Rittenhouse) the Jeffersonians had gone to school to the ancients.

We surely sense a lack of filial respect when the Jeffersonian uses classical idiom to deprecate the classics. But the dominant practical temper of his philosophy had blunted his sensibility to these sources of his own virtues. His crude question was how classical subject matter could be useful under local conditions. Rush posed this question in 1798 in an extensive essay entitled, 'Observations upon the study of the Latin and Greek Languages, as a branch of liberal education, with hints of a plan of liberal instruction, without them, accommodated to the present state of society, manners, and government in the United States.' [46] What use were the ancient classics, he asked, to a rude American society of mechanics, merchants, and farmers? The gist of Rush's argument was contained in the letter which he had received from the Reverend James Minor, principal of the Academy of Alexandria in Virginia, and which Rush quoted with approval:

I have read with satisfaction, in the Museum, your observations on studying the learned languages. There is little taste for them in this place. In our academy, where there are near ninety students, not above nineteen are poring over Latin and Greek. One of these nineteen was lately addressed by a student of Arithmetic in the following language—Pray, Sir, can you resolve me, by your Latin, this question, If one bushel of corn cost four shillings, what cost fifty bushels?—A demand of this kind from a youth, is to me a proof of the taste of Americans in the present day, who prefer the *useful* to the *ornamental*.

Rush's own more elegant way of disparaging the classics was to call them 'as useless in America, as the Spanish great-coat is in the island of Cuba, or the Dutch foot-stove, at the Cape of Good Hope.' Jefferson, though more moderate, and generally more friendly to the classics, did not disagree fundamentally with Rush's conclusion. While he admitted that in one sense the classics were 'a solid basis for most, and an ornament to all the sciences,' yet for eighteenth-century Americans, he considered Greek and Latin at best a 'sublime luxury.' Of all languages confronting an American student, Jefferson found Greek the least useful; we have seen what he thought of Plato and Aristotle. For an American education, Jefferson strongly preferred the modern languages which were the vocabulary of commerce and the avenue to the latest discoveries.

The study of the classics became a symbol for all activities which distracted men from urgent practical tasks. As Rush observed:

We occupy a new country. Our principal business should be to explore and apply its resources, all of which press us to enterprize and haste. Under these circumstances, to spend four or five years in learning two dead languages, is to turn our backs upon a gold mine, in order to amuse ourselves in catching butterflies.

Barton lamented that the classical tradition made the study of the physical universe 'yield its laurels to languages which are withered or dead, and to studies which are useless or ignoble.' He predicted in his *Fragments of the Natural History of Pennsylvania* that if only one-sixth of the time spent on Greek and Latin would be given to natural history, in less than twenty years the animal, vegetable, and mineral resources of the United States could be pretty well investigated.

The mysteries and ambiguities of classical studies made them (like theology and metaphysics) the potential weapon of designing men. Paine noted how priests had used obscure ancient documents to suppress the science which would have dethroned them, and how these same documents became their weapons against the people. Such misuses of classical learning were fashioned into an argument against all learning which was not universally intelligible and obviously useful.

Genuine knowledge must have been meant for a shield against tyranny, and not for one of its weapons. Surely the Creator would not have intended that men should govern themselves and be able to defend themselves against the designs of ambition, and still have made the knowledge necessary to

221

that end inaccessible to the great body of mankind. Whatever was theoretical, subtle, or cast in a recondite tongue, must then be human invention, designed by tyrants, priests and metaphysicians to serve unworthy personal ambitions. Not only was utility made the hallmark of genuine knowledge; any knowledge that was not obviously useful seemed liable to become socially dangerous. The Jeffersonians therefore tried to devise a curriculum specially adapted to American conditions which would be so practical that no man could turn it to a bad purpose.

Emphasis on the useful and the here-and-now seemed to equalize men before the objects of knowledge. For the questions to be discussed would then be put by the common environment; and all would have an equal chance to find the answers in current experience. The Creator must have intended superiority in knowledge to come not from a monopoly of a subject matter, but only from superior talents or from more intimate acquaintance with His creation. To recall men from the study of ancient languages and from all other useless subjects would, according to Rush, produce many broad advantages:

It will have a tendency to destroy the prejudices of the common people against schools and colleges. The common people do not despise scholars, because they know more, but because they know less than themselves. A mere scholar can call a horse, or a cow, by two or three different names, but he frequently knows nothing of the qualities, or uses of those valuable animals. . . . Men are generally most proud of those things that do not contribute to the happiness of themselves, or others. Useful knowledge generally humbles the mind, but learning, like fine clothes, feeds pride, and thereby hardens the human heart.[47]

All these and other reasons led the Jeffersonian toward vocationalism in education. A powerful, prosperous, republican community could result only if each class was qualified for its practical task. The Creator had been above all else Workman, the Builder and Orderer of the physical universe, and He must have intended education to serve His purpose. What better

222

assurance that knowledge would be useful than its direct relevance to earning a living? For a man, as for a nation, knowledge could be useful only if it suited his condition—not as it might be or ought to be, but as it actually was. Utopianism and visionary equalitarianism would only lead educators away from their proper work. The Jeffersonian therefore assigned the educator a largely conservative task, namely to adjust men to their present roles in society. To fail to shape education to the existing political and economic framework of society might imperil republicanism itself. Whenever men wandered off into the wilderness of metaphysics, priests and tyrants could easily mislead them. Any subject matter unrelated to the special condition of the student—instead of seeming a means for freeing him from the confinement of his present status—seemed a weapon for his oppression by the priestly custodians of 'useless' knowledge. In his eagerness to provide a useful American education the Jeffersonian overlooked the variety of human minds to which he otherwise attached so much importance; he actually prescribed educational stereotypes. Despite all that had been said about distributing educational opportunities in the proportions in which the Creator had distributed talents among men, the large outlines of the Jeffersonian educational system were designed to prepare each individual for the practical tasks assigned him by his present place in the social hierarchy. Consider, for example, Jefferson's stages of education:

1. ELEMENTARY SCHOOLS. It is highly interesting to our country, and it is the duty of its functionaries, to provide that every citizen in it should receive an education proportioned to the condition and pursuits of his life. The mass of our citizens may be divided into two classes—the laboring and the learned. The laboring will need the first grade of education to qualify them for their pursuits and duties; the learned will need it as a foundation for further acquirements. . . .

2. GENERAL SCHOOLS. At the discharging of the pupils from the elementary schools, the two classes separate—those destined for labor will engage in the business of agriculture, or enter into apprenticeships to such handicraft art as may be their choice; their

companions, destined to the pursuits of science, will proceed to the college. . . . The learned class may still be subdivided into two sections: 1, Those who are destined for learned professions, as means of livelihood; and, 2, The wealthy, who, possessing independent fortunes, may aspire to share in conducting the affairs of the nation, or to live with usefulness and respect in the private ranks of life. . . .

3. PROFESSIONAL SCHOOLS. At the close of this course the students separate; the wealthy retiring, with a sufficient stock of knowledge, to improve themselves to any degree to which their views may lead them, and the professional section to the professional schools.[48]

It is true that Jefferson proposed schemes for competitive scholarships to give a few of the ablest students the highest education. But this recognition of indigent genius, though admirable, was meant to be little more than an occasional means for mitigating injustice. Jeffersonian popular education on the whole was intended to be fitted closely to the existing social inequalities. Jefferson gave little thought to the education of women: their actual condition presumably required very little education. When he did consider the matter, he sought means merely to prepare women for their actual functions in the community, without regard to the equality of their capacities. Even Rush's argument for the improved education of women was based not on the extent of their natural talents, but on the fact that in a rude country men needed the daily help of their wives, who therefore should be given a broader practical training.

It is not surprising then that we read no substantial projects for the education of the Negro, and few for improving the Indian. Since the Indian had no clearly useful status in the Jeffersonian community, the role for which he was to be educated could not be known. Thus, where his Puritan predecessors had sent missionaries to the Indians—and in the early impecunious days of Harvard had built an 'Indian College' among its first and most expensive buildings—the Jeffersonian blessed the Indians with his anthropologists and traders. The Puritan belief

224

in the power of ideas, expressed in an emphasis on metaphysics and 'pure' science, prepared Harvard College to become a center of intellectual ferment, a breeding ground for potent and revolutionary ideas, for new and pregnant systems of philosophy; while the tradition of modernity and usefulness in which the University of Virginia was founded, tied it to the existing social structure of the community. Of course there have been other causes. But the Jeffersonian demand that education give men implements immediately and obviously useful, has surely helped establish the American tradition, which combines enthusiasm for education with an insistence that education be uncritical and conservative.

6. The American Destiny

THE history of human progress from the Jeffersonian point of view was thus 'the history of the condition of man.' Man's condition could and would be improved. But under American circumstances it was hard to distinguish improvement from expansion, progress from enlargement. The final extent of human expansion on this continent was indefinable, though of course not unlimited; and Jefferson hoped that here the happiness of the species might advance 'to an indefinite, although not to an infinite degree.' [49] The assignment which man found in America was less the attainment of any specific destination, than simple and effective activity. The continent offered a vague and nearly boundless arena for practical energies; and the fact that the task was without known (or perhaps knowable) limits, was one of its major attractions.

The Jeffersonian was not confined by any particular tradition: he had sought to reform the Christian tradition, he had

225

disavowed the humanist tradition, and he had set himself outside the English tradition. The past, through which other men had discovered human possibilities, was for him corrupt and dead. Yet there was surely little enough of Faust in the Jeffersonian character. For the Faustian takes his motive and his inspiration from an inward and a private voice: Faust (whether Marlowe's or Goethe's) risked a private doom for a personal ambition. But Jeffersonian expansiveness expressed no personal megalomania; from the nature of his universe, his destiny concerned the whole species and the entire continent. Even the concept of happiness was virtually emptied of its personal meaning: it was the 'happiness of the species' which concerned him. His indices of destiny therefore had to be outward and public.

The direction and boundaries of human achievement which he refused to let metaphysics, revelation, or history draw for him, he had sought to discover in the materials of natural history. For he too hoped to learn his destiny direct from his Creator. 'There is a natural aptness in man,' Paine observed, 'and more so in society, because it embraces a greater variety of abilities and resource, to accommodate itself to whatever situation it is in.' [50] Man's destiny was to fulfill this adaptation and not to allow accumulating institutions or traditions to obstruct it in any way. Institutions, from the Jeffersonian point of view, were not the skeleton but the instruments of society; they were therefore conceived, not as growing imperceptibly and by accretion, but as being consciously and purposefully shaped, to be repaired or discarded when they had lost their immediate utility. Not institutions, but nature itself was the receptacle and vehicle of values.

All the while the Jeffersonian was outlining the American destiny, he ingenuously insisted that he had not arrogated any mission to himself; rather, he saw his destiny declared by the character which God had given the American continent. Although he had summarily denied that variations in climate and geography could evidence natural inequalities within the human species, he nevertheless read in the peculiar physical conditions of America the Creator's designation of a special role. Nearly two centuries earlier, Edward Johnson had called the planting of New England an example of the 'Wonder-working Providence of Sions Saviour.' Jefferson now in his own terms ascribed to the American republic a no less providential destiny. Had such a vast and fertile continent not been destined for prosperity and for a special example for mankind, there would have been an unthinkable poverty in the Creator. Where the Puritan (in resignation to his environment) had found a proof of his election in the adversity which he suffered, the Jeffersonian boasted the unhampered prosperity of his enterprises. Lacking the more precise theology and the inward signs of the Calvinist, Jefferson discovered his election mainly in the promise of his physical universe and in the success of his attempt to master it. The approval of the Jeffersonian God could not have been expressed otherwise than in the health, wealth and prosperity of human undertakings. The Jeffersonian wore the shield of his Creator, not against the infidel or the legions of the Devil, but against political tyranny, physical adversity, and worldly disorder.

The lines of the immediate American battle were drawn in the environment itself which, if studied with care and discrimination, would reveal the special destiny of eighteenth-century Americans. And it seemed plain to the most superficial observer that America had been designed for an agricultural country. 'The United States possesses a vast territory fertile in many valuable productions,' the Reverend Nicholas Collin told the Philosophical Society in 1789. 'They will therefore, if truly wise, make agriculture the principal source of prosperity and wealth: to prefer other objects, however useful in a secondary view, would be perverting the order of nature, nay, opposing the will of nature's God.' [51] Jefferson symbolized the continental destiny by his design for an American order of architecture—a column fashioned like a bundle of cornstalks, and a capital in the shape of the leaves and flowers of tobacco. Frequently he observed that the agricultural capacities of our country constituted its distinguishing feature.

The extent of unexplored land especially fitted the continent for experiments in republican government. 'We can no longer say there is nothing new under the sun,' Jefferson wrote to Priestley (March 21, 1801). 'For this whole chapter in the history of man is new. The great extent of our republic is new. Its sparse habitation is new.' Malthusian pessimism would have no place in America, where the vastness of uncultivated land enabled every one who would labor, to marry young and to raise a large family.

Before the establishment of the American States, nothing was known to history but the man of the old world, crowded within limits either small or overcharged, and steeped in the vices which that situation generates. A government adapted to such men would be one thing; but a very different one, that for the man of these States. Here every one may have land to labor for himself, if he chooses; or, preferring the exercise of any other industry, may exact for it such compensation as not only to afford a comfortable subsistence, but wherewith to provide for a cessation from labor in old age. Every one, by his property, or by his satisfactory situation, is interested in the support of law and order. And such men may safely and advantageously reserve to themselves a wholesome control over their public affairs, and a degree of freedom, which, in the hands of the *canaille* of the cities of Europe, would be instantly perverted to the demolition and destruction of everything public and private.[52]

All this convinced the Jeffersonian that the full and fair trial of representative institutions had been reserved for man in America.

'The cause of America,' declared Paine in *Common Sense*, 'is in a great measure the cause of all mankind.' The New World would regenerate the Old. 'A just and solid republican government maintained here,' Jefferson wrote in 1801, 'will be a standing monument and example for the aim and imitation of the people of other countries.' The Jeffersonian could feel few misgivings at expressing complacency and hope in a world torn as his was by war and tyranny, for the success of his struggle would actually vindicate the human species and even

228

in a sense the Creator Himself. The American example would help disprove the heresy that man was incapable of self-government, or that God had made man in wrath. Jefferson clung to his conviction that sooner or later the whole world would benefit from the American assertion of the rights of man.[53]

The Creator's approval of the American experiment would be read in the prosperity of American enterprises. To strengthen America was to perpetuate institutions 'destined to be the primitive and precious model of what is to change the condition of man over the globe.' Every advantage of America was therefore an advantage for the species; and sentiments which served American interests were understandably praised as noble sentiments. The wide separation of this continent from Europe seemed to reveal the Creator's intention that, regardless of what happened to European man, America should prosper for the sake of the species. Jeffersonian isolationism expressed an essentially cosmopolitan spirit. The Jeffersonian was determined—even at the cost of separating himself from the rest of the globe, and even though he be charged with provincial selfishness—to preserve America as an uncontaminated laboratory.[54] When Rittenhouse prayed that nature make a voyage from America to Europe as impracticable as one to the moon, or when Jefferson wished for an ocean of fire, or that America should be as remote as China from the affairs of Europe, neither Rittenhouse nor Jefferson would have recognized any philistinism in his prayer. How otherwise than by keeping America peaceful and prosperous could the whole species be given that encouraging example which it sorely needed?

America was meant to be the asylum and the beacon for the oppressed of Europe. Nevertheless Jefferson thought that America could succeed in this only if she did not have too many European immigrants with their penchant for monarchy and their debilitating city-bred vices.[55] The perfection of the American model depended on the exploitation of peculiarly American advantages.

A providential ordering of human faculties and passions seemed to have made men always best qualified to investigate those matters closest at hand. By instilling in every man patriotism, or a special interest in his native land, the Maker had insured that the energies of the whole species would be most economically expended; and incidentally He had equipped Americans for their messianic task. 'Patriotic affections,' the Reverend Collin told the Philosophical Society, 'are . . . conducive to the general happiness of mankind, because we have the best means of investigating those objects, which are most interesting to us.' And Rush elaborated the use of patriotism in the animal economy:

The love of country is a deep seated principle of action in the human breast. Its stimulus is sometimes so excessive, as to induce disease in persons who recently migrate, and settle in foreign countries. It appears in various forms; but exists most frequently in the solicitude, labours, attachments, and hatred of party spirit. All these act forcibly in supporting animal life.[56]

Rush, Jefferson and Barton agreed that the unexplored wealth of America challenged simultaneously the practical, the patriotic and the philanthropic energies of the American philosopher.

A passion so beneficial to the species could hardly be one of which a cosmopolitan philosopher should be ashamed. In fact men in America were not likely to fulfill their mission for mankind unless they had their full measure of the patriotic stimulant. This was still another argument for the agrarian life which developed men's affection for their soil, and against the life of the merchant who knew no country except by the profits he drew from it. The Jeffersonian therefore desired a homogeneous population, he opposed immigration and travel which weakened native ties, and he favored a useful and uniform American education. Priestley ventured that the incentive which the Greeks and Romans had derived from their belligerent patriotism might be supplanted among modern peoples by concern for the nation's material interests.[57]

But the national interest also required an intellectual cosmopolitanism. The American philosopher included in his Society many of the major philosophers of Europe, for only by

230

freely interchanging useful knowledge with his foreign contemporaries could he invigorate the American experiment and hence serve the well-being of mankind. To improve the American condition would be the largest stride toward Barton's 'happiness that is inbosomed in the happiness of one's country, and the world.' Nothing could be more shortsighted than to allow the 'republic of science' to be affected by wars between geographical divisions of the earth.[58]

The national effort of the American philosopher was thus suffused with an aura of divine approbation, described in the well-known passage of Jefferson's First Inaugural Address. The United States, he said, was

kindly separated by nature and a wide ocean from the exterminating havoc of one quarter of the globe; too high-minded to endure the degradations of the others; possessing a chosen country, with room enough for our descendants to the hundredth and thousandth generation; entertaining a due sense of our equal right to the use of our own faculties, to the acquisitions of our industry, to honor and confidence from our fellow citizens, resulting not from birth but from our actions and their sense of them; enlightened by a benign religion, professed, indeed, and practiced in various forms, yet all of them including honesty, truth, temperance, gratitude, and the love of man; acknowledging and adoring an overruling Providence, which by all its dispensations proves that it delights in the happiness of man here and his greater happiness hereafter. . . .

Without an articulate system of values or a limiting tradition, the Jeffersonian was tempted to make expansion itself an end. Here was the latest and greatest episode in the dispersion of the human species over the continents, and in the fulfillment of environmental possibilities through the peculiarly adaptive animal of the Creation. Jefferson could not restrain himself from visions of such an 'empire for liberty' as had never been seen since the Creation. The Louisiana Purchase (appropriately the most important political act of Jefferson's administrations), was an authentic expression of the Jeffersonian spirit. The empire for liberty, Jefferson believed, would properly come into being only after the original colonies and the Western country had been enlarged to include Canada and Cuba. Near the end of his life Jefferson strongly urged the 'Monroe Doctrine' on his old friend President Monroe. In the context of Jeffersonian thought, that doctrine seems less a declaration of separateness from Europe than a manifesto of the expansive and exuberant spirit of American destiny—which hoped some day to add the southern continent to the Jeffersonian empire for liberty. 'America, North and South, has a set of interests distinct from those of Europe. . . . While the last is laboring to become the domicile of despotism, our endeavor should surely be, to make our hemisphere that of freedom.' 'What a colossus shall we be when the southern continent comes up to our mark!' exclaimed Jefferson. 'What a stand will it secure as a ralliance for the reason and freedom of the globe!' [59] But why stop at Hudson Bay and Cape Horn, when the human species covered the whole globe and all were equally entitled to such blessings? While the French Revolution seemed to prove the power of the American idea to cross the Atlantic, the fiasco of that Revolution, and other practical considerations, made Jefferson willing temporarily to confine his missionary activities to the New World.

When the American philosopher reflected on the destiny assigned him by his Creator, and his providential condition for fulfilling it, his enthusiasm overflowed the definitions of natural history. His professed belief, deeply rooted in his cosmology, that no piece of the universe was more important than another, that man's task everywhere had to emerge from his local condition, was overshadowed by the magnificence of the American destiny. He sometimes forgot all human weakness in aspirations which in sober moments he surely knew to be unattainable. Rush even conjectured that the Creator might have intended through the American Revolution to unfold on this continent unforeseen physical and moral potentialities of the human species. 'All the doors and windows of the temple of nature have been thrown open, by the convulsions of the late American revolution,' Rush wrote in 1789. 'This is the time, therefore, to press upon her altars.' Perhaps, he concluded, now at last men might discover cures for diseases hitherto thought incurable. 'Who knows but that, at the foot of the Allegany mountain there blooms a flower, that is an infallible cure for the epilepsy? Perhaps on the Monongahela, or the Potowmac, there may grow a root, that shall supply, by its tonic powers, the invigorating effects of the savage or military life in the cure of consumptions.' [60]

By indefinitely improving the condition of man in America, and thereby vindicating the human species, the Jeffersonian sought to satisfy his need for a divinely appointed mission. The immediacy with which he perceived his tasks; their concreteness, their obviousness and their appeal to his workmanlike talents and energies made any more elaborate definition seem distracting. If we cannot help feeling that he lacked some sense of destination or proportion in his enterprises, this is doubtless because the greater ambiguity of our environment requires subtler definitions.

While he confidently refused the aid of traditions and ancient institutions, the Jeffersonian could not fail to seek—in Jefferson's own phrase—some compass through 'the ocean of time' which opened on America. He was unwilling to chart his direction by looking backward to see how men had come for the past six thousand years. It was the ocean ahead that most concerned him. He was earnest and convinced that for him destiny should supplant tradition. He hoped simply by looking about him and by peering into the future to discover as much as his Creator had intended him to know about how and where he should go. Expansiveness and boundlessness seemed themselves a kind of destiny and definition. 'I like the dreams of the future,' confessed Jefferson, 'better than the history of the past.' His excellent situation for a life of expansion, activity and construction nourished a faith in his practical projects, which encouraged him to pursue them more and more vigorously. The satisfaction of functioning efficiently in the natural process often made metaphysics seem superfluous. Yet it could never wholly extinguish his hope for that fuller self-consciousness and that sharper definition of purpose which man's resemblance to his Creator always makes him desire. 'So we have gone on, and so we shall go on,' Jefferson predicted, 'puzzled and prospering beyond example in the history of man.' [61]

Conclusion

'It is not thy duty to complete the work, but neither
art thou free to desist from it.' Rabbinical Saying

1. The Promise of
Jeffersonian Thought

WHAT the Jeffersonians had to offer the world was not a new philosophic conception, not a novel political theory, nor a metaphysical system. What finally characterized their thought was less its specific theological or metaphysical doctrines than its attitude toward all theology and metaphysics. Philosophy was to be a by-product of right and fruitful activity: the fulfillment of man was not in theoretical formulation nor in abstract comprehension of the universe, but in the life he led and the society he built. The genius of Jeffersonian philosophy was intuitive and practical; reflection, speculation and contemplation were given second place. Its cosmology was supposed to spring directly from the sensitive observer's response to environment. The precepts of the good life were not the conclusion of laborious ratiocination but the immediate perception of the healthy moral faculty. Government was not the expression of a political theory, but the largely unreflective answer of healthy men to the threat of tyranny.

Despite its emphasis on activity this philosophy issued neither in Philistinism, nor in the blunt identification of power with right. For it expressed a spirit of prophecy—not only in the sense of inspired foresight, but in that of many of the great prophets of the Old Testament. These ancient Hebrew prophets, like Amos, Jeremiah and Isaiah, were similarly intuitive and practical. Without elaborate theology or metaphysics, the Hebrew prophet dealt with the concrete, the personal, and the here-and-now; he sought less to fathom the thoughts of God, than to find His commandments for men. He

237

was less interested in major premises than in conclusions. His aim was not the intellectual knowledge of God, but the practical imitation of Him: a new life, and not a new philosophy. For the Prophets, the Word of God was not remote and detached from man; it was in man, and its truth was to be manifest in man's behavior. For the commandment of God is 'not hidden from thee, neither is it far off.' (Deut. 30:11.) 'He hath shewed thee, O man, what is good.' (Mic. 6:8.) In the Prophet's universe there was no distinctively secular realm: everyday human activity possessed cosmic significance. He thought it less important to realize a sublime ethical ideal for its own sake than to find the plain connection between daily behavior and divine order. The Prophet was of all men the most active, and yet the most unremitting in his attention to the divine design. 'Prepare ye in the wilderness the way of the Lord, make straight in the desert a high way for our God. Every valley shall be exalted, and every mountain and hill shall be made low: and the crooked shall be made straight, and the rough places plain.' (Isa. 40:3 ff.)

It was precisely the prophetic character of Jeffersonian thought that saved it from the worst consequences of its particular doctrines. The fulfillment of man's material potentialities in America seemed distant, as the salvation of man's soul had been in Puritan theology; and yet the certainty of his achievement was no less than that which the Puritan had felt for the fate of the elect. His philosophy was cast in the future tense. Since the hope and the fact were not yet one, the Jeffersonians had a sense of living at the beginning of history. America was where the equal destiny of the human species might be realized and attested, where the adaptability and pioneering talents of man might be given superlative expression, where morality would have the reward of health and prosperity, and prosperity would prove the rightness of morality, where the political self-governing possibilities of the species would be demonstrated.

The disparity between these hopes and the actual facts of his day impressed on the Jeffersonian the reality and necessity of a God who would eventually bring them into accord. The Jeffersonian God objectified the tension between man's aspirations and his accomplishments so far on earth. The existence of a workmanlike, efficient God made credible the unity of the human species, proved the rightness of effective action, and gave the final assurance that the American destiny would be fulfilled. It was such a God whose orderly design made man's institutional tampering often superfluous and always dangerous.

The essential fact, then, about the pragmatic, activist and naturalistic temper of Jeffersonian thought was that it subsisted in an age which knew the incompleteness and imperfection of its practical accomplishment. Eighteenth-century America could provide the inspiration, but not the confirmation for a pragmatic philosophy. The Jeffersonians expected that the American posterity would provide tangible evidence that men had been created equal; that the prosperity of men in America would confirm the accord of health and morals; that the strength of American society would vindicate the Creator's social plan for the species. Still the distant futurity of the demonstration required a God to make the demonstration certain. The God invoked by the Jeffersonian was necessarily an intelligible being, to whom the ideas of virtue and order were not meaningless.

The Jeffersonian was not unaware that the condition in which he found himself had something to do with his philosophic needs. 'The scene which that country presents to the eye of a spectator,' we have heard Paine observe, 'has something in it which generates and encourages great ideas. Nature appears to him in magnitude. The mighty objects he beholds, act upon his mind by enlarging it, and he partakes of the greatness he contemplates.' No one knew better than the American philosopher that he was living a prologue to American history. 'Now is the seed-time of Continental union, faith and honour,' declared Paine in *Common Sense*. 'The least fracture now will be like a name engraved with the point of a pin on the tender rind of a young oak; the wound would enlarge with the tree, and posterity read it in full grown characters.'

The special philosophic mission of America for many years to come was to be the elaboration of the Jeffersonian spirit: the unhampered development of man's capacity for adaptation and adjustment, and the fruition of a society built on largely naturalistic foundations. It was the first great opportunity in modern times for men who had the accumulated culture, techniques and mistakes of Europe behind them, to show the prosperity and effectiveness of the species in a rich, a vast and an unspoiled environment. From this point of view, there is some justification in saying that the aspirations and spirit of the Jeffersonian group represented a peculiarly American contribution to the philosophical quest of Western man. And this was none the less the case even though Paine was not born in America and spent the major part of his life elsewhere, and Priestley did not emigrate to America until late in life. For the thought of both these men, as we have seen, was essentially harmonious with that of the other members of the Jeffersonian circle. The school would not have been characteristically American had it been entirely indigenous to America, had it not shown itself capable of incorporating the intellectual and physical contribution of late immigrants, wanderers, and men without a country.

The New World quality of Jeffersonian thought becomes still more apparent by comparison with other earlier and contemporary movements in American intellectual history. Puritanism —even allowing for its special New England characteristics— had not been in the same sense a peculiarly American development; nor has the rigid and intricate framework of Puritan thought shaped to any comparable extent the American intellectual character. The Federalist school—contemporary with the Jeffersonians—was not (except perhaps in those features which it shared with the Jeffersonians) especially qualified to express the American intellectual temper of the nineteenth century. The Federalists counted fewer distinguished natural historians in their number: and not only in this respect did their thought draw less on the specifically American sources of their day. Their affinity was to the aristocratic European tradition, with its faith in institutions. The thought of men like John Adams, John Marshall, Fisher Ames—and Hamilton himself—while in a sense pragmatic in temper, was supported by appeal to the past, to history and traditions. They were not stirred by the peculiar American hope that out of the naked processes of nature, and man's integration into those processes, a new and prosperous society would emerge.

The Jeffersonian philosophy was futuristic without being utopian or apocalyptic. Its vision of the future was foreshadowed not in any sacred document nor in any private revelation, but in the American continent itself, and the very shape of man. And it was thus in a special sense a philosophy and a mode of thought suited not for eternity but for man's potentialities at a particular stage in history and at a particular place on earth. The Jeffersonian philosophy was an incentive toward populating a continent and building a society; but it must have been hard even for the Jeffersonian not to surmise that once that work was achieved, much of the vitality of his philosophy might be lost.

The explicit and systematic formulation of the ultimate logical conclusions of Jeffersonian philosophy was to be reserved for an age when the practical promise of Jeffersonian philosophy had been fulfilled. By the later nineteenth century, men on the American continent had attained, if not exceeded, the wildest Jeffersonian dreams of populousness and environmental mastery. Even 'the mode of action called thinking' had begun to come under man's controlling hand. 'The quest for useful knowledge' had almost destroyed the line between the possible and the impossible; the 'empire for liberty' had begun to overflow the oceanic barriers. Man's material powers had attained a fulfillment unknown to history. With this fulfillment, the Jeffersonian philosophy reached something like its fruition. The naturalistic emphasis of the Jeffersonians under these circumstances became transfigured into the systematic and explicit pragmatism of the late nineteenth century. Many of the presuppositions, doctrines and attitudes of that latterday pragmatism were the extreme logical conclusion—in some cases perhaps the *reductio ad absurdum*—of the presuppositions, doctrines and attitudes of Jeffersonian thought.

This continuity has been obscured because 'liberals' who have arrogated the Jeffersonian tradition to themselves have been more concerned with programs and projects than with philosophies. They have therefore been ready to borrow the items on the Jeffersonian agenda without estimating their philosophic implications; and in a sense the Jeffersonians were willing to lend them on such terms. The paths of agriculture and natural history attracted the Jeffersonian because he had to follow these in his day if he was to increase the mastery of man over the American continent. Given the conditions of the year 1900, it is hardly likely that Jefferson would have urged his countrymen along the same path. 'Liberals,' struck by the obvious difference between the agrarianism and humanitarianism of the Jeffersonians and the ruthless competitive enterprise of late nineteenth-century industrial America, have overlooked the essential similarity of the major premises on which American civilization has been shaped from Jefferson's day till our own.

What Darwinism added to the Jeffersonian view of man was not the tendency to view him in a naturalistic context; the Jeffersonian estimate of man was already in that context. But while the Jeffersonians viewed man in the whole framework of nature, fitting into the inanimate creation, and struggling among myriad other species, the Darwinians (if not Darwin himself) became preoccupied with man's struggle against other creatures of his own species. This shift in emphasis was understandably congenial to late nineteenth-century America. The prosperity of the individual had already begun to depend less on his ability to master nature than on his ability to outwit or defeat his neighbor. Social Darwinism was a significant variant on the Jeffersonian naturalism, but was still only a variant. In most respects it was not so much a rebellion against the Jeffersonian view of nature as the stark presentation of its logical consequences for a later age. While Jefferson had believed that man's place in nature was to be discovered by how he was destined to fare in the natural process, the disciples of Herbert Spencer and William Graham Sumner one hundred years later believed that the destined place of any man in the moral hierarchy was to be discovered by how he had actually fared in the social process. Both looked to material effectiveness as the ultimate proof of equality.

The essential difference between the naturalism of the Age of Jefferson and the naturalism of the Age of Robber Barons was thus curiously enough less a difference in philosophies than a difference between stages in the development of the same philosophy. Jeffersonian naturalism was the stage of promise and prophecy; later naturalism, that of fulfillment and retrospect. This difference was by no means negligible. For to say that what made men prosperous was also what made them virtuous produced in Jeffersonian America a canon of virtues impressively different from those produced by applying the same test to the America of Andrew Carnegie, John D. Rockefeller and Henry Adams. Much of what we find admirable and worth perpetuating about Jeffersonianism must be discovered therefore not in the major premises and philosophic spirit of the naturalism and materialism which characterized it, but in the special character which the Jeffersonian age gave to those premises and that spirit.

2. The God of the Republic

EVERYTHING the Jeffersonian came to value in morals, in politics—and in thought itself—was affected by the dominant tone of his relation to nature. In the communal quest for mastery of the physical environment, collaboration and the free community of ideas were indispensable. The American Philosophical Society antedated the Continental Congress—and was the most eloquent witness that nature bound men together. Nature, moreover, was not to be overcome by rhetoric, chicanery or dishonesty of any kind; the winds were not to be predicted nor the poison of the rattlesnake combatted, except by actual knowledge. The Jeffersonian approach to the whole external universe, including society, was pervaded by a kind of integrity and intellectual morality. The desire to know nature was the strongest incentive to ingenuousness, and the most effective restraint against the deception of oneself or of one's neighbors. The Jeffersonian thus attained the 'scientific' frame of mind in the best sense of the word. Forthrightness, respect for fact, and a noncompetitive and collaborative attitude toward his neighbors were revealed not only in his science: the Jeffersonian somehow carried these attitudes into his theory of society.

His morality possessed virtues which a naturalistic morality in America one hundred years later would almost certainly lack. In the United States after the Civil War, but especially by the beginning of the present century, inanimate nature (no longer a part of the Creator's Scripture) had become almost exclusively a raw material of human enterprises. Insofar as thoughtful men in America drew sociological generalizations from the data of the new physics, it was to support the essentially antidemocratic and pessimistic conclusions of a Henry Adams. After Darwin and after the climax of American industrialism, the impressive fact about animate nature was competition among members of the same species. In Sumner's Age, the adjustment of the whole species to the environment seemed no longer the primary biological fact about man. The morality which William Graham Sumner extracted from man's relation to nature was therefore understandably different from that which the Jeffersonian had extracted—though, as we have observed, the one was no less naturalistic than the other. The context of nature was displaced by that of the market place. 'The best test of truth,' Justice Holmes could write by 1919, 'is the power of the thought to get itself accepted in the competition of the market.' He justified free expression in order to allow ideas to compete.

But Jefferson had justified toleration and the differences of ideas, primarily because a designing Creator had intended variety in minds as in the rest of the creation. It was this sense of creaturehood that finally gave the Jeffersonians their sense of community, and prevented an emphasis on 'rights' from becoming anarchy, or from making society seem a hopeless jungle. 'Who shall convince a believer in the theory of *rights* solely that he has to work for the common purpose and devote himself to the development of the social idea?' the Italian liberal Mazzini asked in his *Duties of Man* a half-century after Jefferson. 'Rights belong equally to every individual; the fact of living together in a community does not create a single one. Society has greater strength, not more rights, than the individual.' The Jeffersonian had the power to refuse this consequence of his doctrines because his sense of creaturehood had bound him to all other living beings. His belief in 'rights' was itself supported by faith in a benevolent God whose design had made the claims of individual men harmonious.

His sense of creaturehood—even his special brand of materialism—led him to a kind of humility, and this humility led him to a sympathy for the meek and the downtrodden. In the Jeffersonian search for the original teachings of Jesus, there was nothing pretentious, hypocritical or priggish. The Jeffersonian naturalism had remained compatible with an essentially Christian morality. To be sure, the spirit of his philosophy was materialist, antimetaphysical and activist. He came close to making Jesus a Son of Liberty, and a member of the American Philosophical Society. At the same time, the actual content of the Jeffersonian creed was impressively closer to that of Jesus than to that of Benjamin Franklin or Andrew Carnegie. Jeffersonians saw the precepts of the Sermon on the Mount confirmed by the data of natural history: the benevolence of God in the creation was their model for the benevolence of man. The instincts of the healthy moral sense confirmed Jesus' precept to act well and gently to one's neighbors. There still seemed no inconsistency between Christian morality and the practical work of man in America. The words of Jesus reassured

245

him, 'Ye are the light of the world. A city that is set on an hill cannot be hid. Neither do men light a candle, and put it under a bushel, but on a candlestick; and it giveth light unto all that are in the house. Let your light so shine before men, that they may see your good works, and glorify your Father which is in heaven.' (Matt. 5:14-16.) Jeffersonian Christianity was hardly a rich or spacious doctrine; it consisted of little more than the moral maxims of Christ. But by making Christianity simpler, the Jeffersonian also had made it more credible to himself and had given it a central place in his universe. Jeffersonian Christianity—unlike the Christianity of the later pragmatic age—was oversimplified and naïve rather than ingenious or attenuated. If it was to be confirmed not by revelation or an inner light but by natural history, it was because this was the authentic witness of the age.

The Jeffersonian could not imagine that the test which confirmed his faith might for another age confirm its doubts. The very temper of mind which made him found his morality in his fashion made him unwilling to face the issue which history would raise after him. He was so fortunately situated that, while he might explicitly deny the separate authority of revelation, it still seemed confirmed by the evidences of his natural science. When this happy coincidence should no longer exist, a naturalistic philosophy might no longer provide a foundation for a moral society.

The Jeffersonian had in a sense constructed his Omnificent God in his own image, for the conception of God as Supreme Maker embodied the Jeffersonian's highest aspiration for himself. The craftsmanship and physical mastery of the Creator were the superlative form of the virtue which the Jeffersonian most desired. But the excellence of his God as Workman also symbolized the Jeffersonian's sense of his own dependence and his own limitations. The bounty of his America he still attributed to a bountiful God, whose benevolence was not yet obscured by the ruthlessness of the social struggle. In a continent largely unexplored, and where explored largely agricultural, the main features of the landscape were still obviously

246

the work of the Creator: weather, animals, plants and minerals. By the early years of the present century, Americans had come to make their own environment. In the city the objects which surrounded man were plainly of his own making: on the farm, the railroad had become no less important than the weather in determining the farmer's reward for his labors. The Jeffersonian had drawn his power from the horse or the waterfall, fixtures of the natural landscape obviously placed there by a superior Workman. But a century after Jefferson, men drew their power from mobile and artificial sources like the steam engine and the internal combustion engine. The urban Leviathan—the railroad, the factory and the encompassing city life—seemed to suggest that man somehow could actually build his own social universe. He could even produce new species of plants and animals. Technology, which for the Jeffersonian had been a device for harnessing environment, itself had become the most striking and influential feature of human environment. The polarity of man and nature was disappearing.

Surely, then, it is no wonder that by the late nineteenth and early twentieth century alert observers like William James, George H. Mead and John Dewey were unimpressed by any tension between man and nature. The environment seemed no longer a rigid object external to the organism, to which the organism must adjust or die, but seemed itself continually being created and recreated by the organism. 'Our world is definitely mapped out for us by the responses which are going to take place,' Mead noted in *Mind, Self and Society*. 'The structure of the environment is a mapping out of organic responses to nature; any environment, whether social or individual, is a mapping out of the act to which it answers, an act seeking overt expression.' No longer would it be accurate to characterize man as Linnaeus and the Jeffersonians had—V*arians cultura, loco*, his culture varying with the place. It now seemed almost more accurate to say, V*arians locus, cultura*,—man's place varied with his culture. Man's culture seemed his one and only place in the universe. Nature no longer was a fixed point of reference. Everything seemed flux while the philosopher sought to make his definitions by reference to the varying needs of animate life. As Mead remarked, 'It is a difficult matter to state just what we mean by dividing up a certain situation between the organism and its environment. . . . Take the case of food. If an animal that can digest grass, such as an ox, comes into the world, then grass becomes food. That object did not exist before, that is, grass as food. The advent of the ox brings in a new object. In that sense, organisms are responsible for the appearance of whole sets of objects that did not exist before. . . . The organism, then, is in a sense responsible for its environment.'

What was this but another way of declaring that man's power and success as Workman had smothered his sense of creaturehood? He was hardly aware any longer that he himself was part of the Work. Having lost a sense of the antinomy of Man and God, men came to see still less clearly what is specifically human in man. One hundred years after Jefferson, man had arrogated to himself the energy, craftsmanship and power of his Creator. When the success of the Jeffersonian struggle for mastery was thus realized then surely the check which had saved the Jeffersonian from arrogance and dogma would have been removed. When man should conceive himself his own Creator, the full danger of what Mead called 'the will to power through the understanding of nature' would be laid bare.

Notes

Notes

Abbreviations

The following is not intended as a bibliography but is a list of abbreviations for several works frequently referred to in the notes. In all cases, full bibliographical information is also given at the first reference to a work.

Barton, *Elements of Botany*——Benjamin Smith Barton, *Elements of Botany: or Outlines of the Natural History of Vegetables* (2 vols.; Philadelphia: 1803).

Barton, *Fragments*——Benjamin Smith Barton, *Fragments of the Natural History of Pennsylvania* (24 pp., Part First; Philadelphia: 1799).

Barton, *Materia Medica*——Benjamin Smith Barton, *Collections for an Essay towards a Materia Medica of the United States* (Part I, Philadelphia: 1801; Part II, Philadelphia: 1804).

Barton, *New Views*——Benjamin Smith Barton, *New Views of the Origin of the Tribes and Nations of America* (2nd ed.; Philadelphia: 1798).

Barton, *Observations*——Benjamin Smith Barton, *Observations on some Parts of Natural History* (London: 1787).

William Barton, *Memoirs*——William Barton, *Memoirs of the Life of David Rittenhouse* (Philadelphia: 1813).

Early Proceedings——*Early Proceedings of the American Philosophical Society*—compiled by one of the Secretaries from the Manuscript Minutes of its meetings from 1744 to 1838 (Philadelphia: 1884).

Jefferson, *Works* (Ford ed.)——Thomas Jefferson, *The Works of Thomas Jefferson*, ed. Paul Leicester Ford (12 vols., Federal ed.; New York: 1904).

Jefferson, *Writings*——Thomas Jefferson, *The Writings of Thomas Jefferson*, ed. Albert Ellery Bergh (20 vols., 'Definitive' ed., sponsored by Thomas Jefferson Memorial Association; Washington, D. C.: 1907).

Paine, *Complete Writings*——Thomas Paine, *The Complete Writings of Thomas Paine*, ed. Philip S. Foner (2 vols.; New York: 1945).

Paine, *Writings*——Thomas Paine, *The Writings of Thomas Paine*, ed. Moncure Daniel Conway (4 vols.; New York: 1894).

Peale, *Catalogue*——Charles Willson Peale, *Scientific and Descriptive Catalogue of Peale's Museum* (Philadelphia: 1796).

Priestley, *History of Corruptions*——Joseph Priestley, *A History of the Corruptions of Christianity* (Reprinted from Rutt's ed., with notes; London: 1871).

Priestley, *Discourses*——Joseph Priestley, *Discourses on Various Subjects, including several on Particular Occasions* (Birmingham: 1787).

Priestley, *Lectures on History*——Joseph Priestley, *Lectures on History and General Policy* (2 vols.; Philadelphia: 1803).

Priestley, *Matter and Spirit*——Joseph Priestley, *Disquisitions Relating to Matter and Spirit* (London: 1777).

Rittenhouse, *Oration*——David Rittenhouse, *An Oration, Delivered February 24, 1775, before the American Philosophical Society* (Philadelphia: 1775).

Rush, *Diseases of the Mind*——Benjamin Rush, *Medical Inquiries and Observations upon the Diseases of the Mind* (Philadelphia: 1812).

Rush, *Essays*——Benjamin Rush, *Essays, Literary, Moral & Philosophical* (Philadelphia: 1798).

Rush, *Introductory Lectures*——Benjamin Rush, *Sixteen Introductory Lectures* (Philadelphia: 1811).

Rush, *Med. Inq.*——Benjamin Rush, *Medical Inquiries and Observations* (4 vols. in 2, 4th ed.; Philadelphia: 1815).

Smith, *Essay*——Samuel Stanhope Smith, *An Essay on the Causes of the Variety of Complexion and Figure in the Human Species to which are added Strictures on Lord Kaims's Discourse, on the Original Diversity of Mankind* (Philadelphia: 1787).

Taylor, *Arator*——John Taylor, *Arator; being a series of Agricultural Essays, practical and political: in sixty-one numbers* (3rd ed.; revised and enlarged; Baltimore: 1817).

ABBREVIATIONS

Trans. A. P. S.——*Transactions of the American Philosophical Society*, Vol. I (2d ed.; Philadelphia: 1789); Vol. II (Philadelphia: 1786); Vol. III (Philadelphia: 1793); Vol. IV (Philadelphia: 1799); Vol. V (Philadelphia: 1802); Vol. VI (Philadelphia: 1809).

Notes

INTRODUCTION

Full references for the relation of any individual to the American Philosophical Society are found in the elaborate index to Early Proceedings.

CHAPTER ONE

1. *Writings*, VI, 12:To Charles Thompson, Dec. 17, 1786. And see his plan for cataloguing the Library of the University of Virginia (circa 1820-1825); quoted in full in Saul K. Padover, *The Complete Jefferson* (New York: 1943), pp. 1091 f.

2. *Writings*, XVI, 171:To Dr. John P. Emmet, May 2, 1826. Cf. XI, 63; XII, 401.

3. *Writings* (Age of Reason), IV, 46. See also, 54, 60, 83, 128, 188, and 184 n.1. And see Jefferson, *Writings*, XV, 426:To John Adams, April 11, 1823. There was wide disagreement among the Jeffersonians (especially between Paine and Priestley) as to the possibility and extent of revelation; but all appear to have believed that the creation itself was the primary source of knowledge of God.

4. *Writings* (Age of Reason), IV, 67 f. See Rittenhouse, *Oration*, p. 20; and Priestley at *Trans.* A. P. S., VI, 120, 125. Cf. *ibid.*, I, 279.

5. *Oration*, p. 26; and see p. 11. See also Rittenhouse at *Trans.* A. P. S., II, 176; Paine, *Writings* (Age of Reason), IV, 67, 71.

6. *Writings* (Age of Reason), IV, 73. See Rittenhouse, *Oration*, p. 19.

7. *Introduction to a Course of Lectures on Natural History* (Philadelphia: 1800), p. 10. Delivered at the University of Pennsyl-

vania Nov. 16, 1799. 'There are however,' Peale explained in the *Scientific and Descriptive Catalogue of Peale's Museum* (Philadelphia: 1796), pp. vi f., 'some chasms in this connecting chain, of which the naturalist has happily availed himself in distinguishing the three kingdoms of which we have spoken. In each of these three great divisions there are also smaller intervals, which separate birds from quadrupeds, these from amphibious animals, *amphibiae* from fishes, fishes from serpents, serpents from insects, insects from worms. Each of these also presents divisions and subdivisions, which in their turn are still further divided and subdivided.'

For the antiquity and European history of this idea, see Arthur O. Lovejoy, *The Great Chain of Being* (Cambridge, Mass.: 1936).

The American philosophers significantly used the less metaphysical 'chain of *beings*' more commonly than 'chain of being.'

8. *Trans. A. P. S.*, IV, 212.

9. 'Memoir on the Discovery of certain Bones . . . ,' read before the Philosophical Society, Mar. 10, 1797, *Trans. A. P. S.*, IV, 255 f. This hypothetical animal soon came to be known as 'Jefferson's Giant Sloth' or *Megatherium Jeffersonii*; see John D. Godman, *American Natural History* (3 vols.; Philadelphia: 1826-28), II, 196 ff.

This generalization about the unwillingness of the Jeffersonians to believe in the extinction of animals should be qualified with respect to Barton's *later* thought. Benjamin Smith Barton published in 1814 (the year before his death) a little volume entitled *Archaeologiae Americanae Telluris Collectanea et Specimina* (Pt. I; Philadelphia: 1814) which stated in the clearest possible terms the belief that some species might have become extinct. But in 1800, for example ('Concerning a Vegetable found under Ground,' *Trans. A. P. S.*, V, 160 f.), he had been so convinced that such extinction was impossible that he had suggested that many apparently extinct plants might actually have been designed to continue their existence underground. When he observed 'a singular blossom . . . not in full bloom, nearly of the colour of the lilac,' found six feet underground, and similar to plants seen above ground near by, he saw a new clue to the mystery of fossils: 'We have abundant proofs, that many species of animals are capable of subsisting, for a long time, in the *bowels* of the earth, though the *surface* of the earth appears to be, and no doubt is, the natural place of

255

residence of these very animals. Why, then, should we doubt, that the same species of vegetables are capable of accommodating themselves to these two situations? . . . Perhaps many of those impressions of vegetables upon slate, free-stone, coal, and other stony matters, which are so abundantly diffused through the earth, are the impressions of vegetables *which have passed through all the stages of their existence in the bowels of the earth.*' This expressed, perhaps, the extreme of the American philosopher's unwillingness to believe that any link in the chain of beings could disappear. Nevertheless in the 1814 volume Barton collected instances of 'extinct animals and vegetables of North-America together with facts and conjectures relative to the ancient condition of the lands and waters of the continent.' This admission of such a possibility stands virtually alone in Barton's own writings (cf. an isolated comment in his *Fragments of the Natural History of Pennsylvania* [Part First; Philadelphia: 1799], p. 24); and I have found a hint of such a possibility in only one other place in the published writings of the Jeffersonians (Rush, *Introductory Lectures*, p. 311). Moreover, Barton explained in his Dedication that 'the sublime science' —which studied 'the numerous animal and vegetable existences, once common and extensively diffused over the earth, which are now no longer seen'—was a creation of Barton's own age. In stating his unorthodox view in 1814, Barton was still careful to explain that such extinction of particular species would not disorder the large plan of nature. This he declared (*Archaeologiae* . . . , pp. 32 f.) in his Letter to Jefferson on the Mammoth: 'There is something awful in the consideration of this subject: and yet this very subject is admirably calculated to display to us the wisdom, as well as power, of Him who formed all things. The harmony of nature is not, in the smallest degree, disturbed by the total destruction of what many have deemed *necessary* integral parts of a common whole. Nor is this business of the extinction of species *at an end.*' All this was, of course, quite another matter from suggesting that new species might emerge, or that one species might ever change into another. But see below, notes 13 and 23; and Chapter Four, note 4.

10. See the Announcement at the beginning of *Trans. A. P. S.*, Vols. IV and V. The word 'fossil,' commonly used in the period to describe such remains, still had its primary meaning from Latin *fossilis*, which means anything 'dug up'—and still lacked

its recently acquired connotation of the surviving remains of a now extinct creature.

'I cannot . . . help believing,' Jefferson wrote to Col. Stuart, Nov. 10, 1796, 'that this animal [the great-claw], as well as the mammoth, are still existing. The annihilation of any species of existence, is so unexampled in any parts of the economy of nature which we see, that we have a right to conclude, as to the parts we do not see, that the probabilities against such annihilation are stronger than those for it.' *Writings*, IX, 350. Where Jefferson speaks of 'animals' becoming 'extinct' (e.g., *Writings*, II, 234) he refers to individuals and not to species. But see George Turner's 'Memoir on Extraneous Fossils, denominated Mammoth Bones . . . ,' July 21, 1797, *Trans. A. P. S.*, IV, 516. Even while disputing Jefferson's conclusion on the mammoth, Turner could not discuss the matter otherwise than in terms of the conception of a chain of beings.

For Jefferson's interest in fossils, see his *Writings*, IV, 201 f.:To Steptoe, Nov. 26, 1782. See also Jefferson, *Works*, ed. Paul Leicester Ford (Federal ed., 12 vols.; New York: 1904), IV, 239:To Madison, Feb. 20, 1784, on certain pretended South American fossils. A vivid example is in his letter to Dr. Caspar Wistar (Mar. 20, 1808), later his successor as president of the Philosophical Society, whom he invited to come to the White House to examine the 'precious collection, consisting of upwards of three hundred bones, few of them of the large kinds which are already possessed,' which he desired Wistar to try to fit together. *Writings*, XII, 15 f. Jefferson was willing to use his own funds to complete the skeleton of a mammoth. *Ibid.*, XI, 158:Feb. 25, 1807. See also the summary account of Jefferson's assistance to Peale's enterprise of excavating the mammoth skeletons at Newburgh, New York; one of these skeletons is still exhibited in the American Museum of Natural History in New York City. H. S. Cotton, 'Peale's Museum,' *Popular Science Monthly*, LXXV (1909), 227 f., and W. M. Smallwood, *Natural History and the American Mind* (New York: 1941), p. 138.

11. '*Species tot numeramus, quot diversae formae in principio sunt creatae.*' Linnaeus, *Philosophia Botanica* (Berlin: 1780), para. 157 at page 99.
   '*Species tot sunt, quot diversas formas ab initio produxit Infinitum Ens; quae formae, secundum generationis inditas leges, produxere plures, at sibi semper similes. Ergo species tot sunt, quot diversae formae s. structurae hodienum occurrunt.*'

Quoted by Linnaeus from his earlier *Classes Plantarum* (5) in his *Philosophia Botanica,* para. 157 at page 99. See also *ibid.,* para. 162 at page 101; and Genesis, chapter 1, verses 11-12.

12. *Trans. A. P. S.,* VI, 120: Nov. 18, 1803.

13. *Writings* (Notes on Virginia), II, 61. And see Rush, *Introductory Lectures,* p. 151.

It is notable that Barton did on one occasion admit the possibility of new *vegetables* being created by the process of hybridization. But even in this instance, he did not say that actual 'species' might be newly created. Barton wrote to the Swedish biologist Thunberg, April 29, 1792: 'I think, it was the genius of Linnaeus which first suggested the idea that, with respect to vegetables, the business of creation is not *stationary:* or, in other words, that new plants are constantly creating from the admixture, or union, of two distinct species, either of the same, or of a different genus. This idea of your illustrious countryman has received very powerful confirmation from the discoveries which have been made, of late years, in various parts of the globe. In America, I have observed a considerable number of these new, or *hybrid,* vegetables. Our woods, our fields, and our meadows, are full of them.' *Trans. A. P. S.,* III, 346. Note that Barton's observations are here carefully confined to vegetables. For the development of his ideas on extinction of species, see above, note 9. See Conway Zirkle, *The Beginnings of Plant Hybridization* (Philadelphia: 1935). Cf. Linnaeus, *Philosophia Botanica,* paras. 157-162.

One of the few suggestions found in the writings of the Philosophical Society that in primitive times there may have been some animals different from those now to be seen, is the ingenious conjecture of Rev. Nicholas Collin (also clearly based on a concept of the unity and uniformity in the design of nature): 'The analogy so visible in the order of Divine Providence makes it very probable that a rude earth and barbarous men had congenial animals; and that some of these became extinct in the course of moral and physical improvement. Works of ancient naturalists, and popular traditions confirm this; a true philosopher will not deem the whole fabulous, because a part is extravagant. That the *hydra* in the *Lerna*-marsh had seven heads is less probable; but that monsters with more than one have existed is very credible to those who know the double headed serpents of America.' *Trans. A. P. S.*, IV, 506: June 1, 1798.

14. *Writings*, XVII, 234: June, 1787. Jefferson wrote Rittenhouse on another occasion that he found it 'so unlike the processes of nature, to produce the same effect in two different ways,' that calcareous stones in the shape of shells were not likely to have been produced spontaneously. *Writings*, VI, 302:Sept. 18, 1787. Jefferson took considerable trouble while in France to examine the evidence at Tours on which De la Sauvagiere had based his theory in his 'Sur la végétation spontanée des coquilles du Chateau des Places.' *Ibid.*, XVII, 233. See also *ibid.*, V, 256 and II, 39.

Jefferson similarly argued that the economy of nature made it likely that there was only a single cause of yellow fever. *Works* (Ford ed.), X, 96:To John Page, Aug. 16, 1804.

15. 'And indeed, all external miracles, all that appear to have ever been provided in the history of the various dispensations of God to man, have been insignificant.' *Discourses*, p. 221 (1779).

See Jefferson, *Writings*, XIII, 192:Dec. 27, 1812; Paine, *Writings* (Age of Reason), IV, 194, 79; Rush, *Essays, Literary, Moral & Philosophical* (Philadelphia: 1798), p. 28.

16. *Discourses*, p. 303 (1764). For a post-Darwinian expression of a similar idea, see Lawrence J. Henderson, *The Fitness of the Environment* (New York: 1927).

17. *Complete Writings* (Foner ed.), II, 1048:June 25, 1801. Du Pont de Nemours, 'Sur la Théorie des Vents,' *Trans. A. P. S.*, VI, 35. Rittenhouse, *Oration*, p. 20.

Cf. Jefferson's observation that the heats of Northern climates were probably stronger than those of Southern climates even though they were shorter—perhaps because vegetation required it so. *Works* (Ford ed.), VI, 265: To Martha Jefferson Randolph, May 31, 1791. The American philosopher's preoccupation with animate nature is not wholly explained by the abundance of the animal and vegetable inhabitants of the virgin countryside. While relations among inanimate physical objects could be described in the formal symmetry of physical 'laws' which showed 'design' in a limited sense, *life* always presented a purpose to be fulfilled, a need to be satisfied. For life always makes demands of its environment, and those very demands, originating in the shape given to nature by the Creator, seemed to provide a value and a purpose implicit in the observed fact. 'Design' in the sense of a purpose in nature was therefore most readily discerned when a living creature was on the scene. Therefore it was animate nature (in the study of which that age made its greatest contribution) that provided the Jeffersonian the most convenient examples of design in the creation. Barton's *Elements of Botany* supplies numerous examples: buds (I, 241); seeds (I, 249); and see also I, 101.

The American philosopher was ready to use the part of the design which he could see, to help him fill in facts which still remained obscure. E.g., Jefferson argued from the great size (and probable ferocity) of the 'great-claw' that it could never have existed in large numbers: 'If lions and tygers multiplied as rabbits do, or eagles as pigeons, all other animal nature would have been long ago destroyed, and themselves would have ultimately extinguished after eating out their pasture. It is probable then that the great-claw has at all times been the rarest of animals. Hence so little is known, and so little remains of him.' 'Memoir on the Discovery of certain Bones . . . ,' *Trans. A. P. S.*, IV, 256:Mar. 10, 1797. From similar premises, George Turner made detailed conjectures about the mammoth (from the fact that its bones were found among others which were often broken): 'Nature had allotted to the Mammoth the beasts of the forest for his food. . . . May it not be inferred, too, that as the largest and swiftest quadrupeds were appointed for his food, he necessarily was endowed with great strength and activity? . . . The Author of existence is wise and just in all his works. He never confers an appetite without the power to gratify it.' *Trans. A. P. S.*, IV, 517 f.: July 21, 1797.

18. 'Experiments and observations, on the atmosphere of marshes,' read Dec. 21, 1798, *Trans. A. P. S.*, IV, 429. Seybert (1773-1825) was for many years secretary and held several other offices in the Society; he was commissioned to arrange the Society's collection of minerals. For an account of his remarkable career, see the *Dictionary of American Biography*.

19. *Arator; being a series of Agricultural Essays, practical and political* (3rd ed., revised and enlarged; Baltimore: 1817), pp. 52, 60, 152. And see Jefferson, *Writings*, X, 13:March 23, 1798. See also his letter to Taylor where Jefferson agrees 'that the atmosphere is the great storehouse of matter for recruiting our

lands.' *Writings*, XVIII, 192 f.:Dec. 29, 1794. Cf. Everett E. Edwards, *Jefferson and Agriculture* (Agricultural History Series No. 7; U.S. Department of Agriculture: 1943).

20. *Trans. A. P. S.*, IV, 74 ff. (also separately published, Philadelphia: 1796), presented in abbreviated form to Philosophical Society, April 4, 1794. Cf. Bartram, *Travels*, ed. Mark Van Doren (New York: 1940), p. 222; Peter Kalm, *Travels into North America . . .*, trans. Foster (3 vols., Warrington: Vol. I, 1770; Vols. II & III, 1771), I, 61 f.

The simplest course for those who fell in with the traditional view had been to admit the power of fascination, but to present some qualifying facts to show how even this power fitted into the large economy of nature. Linnaeus, for example, piously noted that 'the merciful God' had appointed the hog to persecute the rattlesnake; he observed further that since the Creator had given the rattlesnake a slow creeping motion, and had placed rattles on its tail in order to warn other animals of its approach, the creature might have become extinct (which the Creator never could have wished) had He not 'favoured it with a certain power of fascinating squirrels from high trees, and birds from the air into its throat, in the same manner as flies are precipitated into the jaws of the lazy toad.' Quoted by Barton, *loc. cit.*, from Linnaeus, *Reflections on the Study of Nature*, trans. Smith (Dublin: 1786), pp. 33 f. Franklin, perhaps ironically, had noted that 'the rattle-snake gives warning before he attempts his mischief,' Carl Van Doren, *Benjamin Franklin* (New York: 1938), p. 202. Bartram, more seriously, described the rattles as a 'warning alarm,' *Travels*, p. 221. Barton made much of his having discarded all such prejudiced and fanciful explanations.

Even after Barton had expounded his elaborate theory, members of the Philosophical Society were urged by M. de Beauvois not to disbelieve the power of fascination until there was fuller evidence, gathered under more favorable circumstances. M. de Beauvois thought one should not casually discard belief in the existence of a faculty which fitted so readily into the apparent scheme of nature: 'If then the effects in question [fascination] really exist, we may be allowed to believe that serpents, destined by nature (our common mother, always consistent with herself; always equally beneficent and just,) to subsist on animals which have the advantage of superior flight and speed, ought to be endowed with proper arms and a power by whose aid they may surprize and secure their prey.' *Trans. A. P. S.*, IV,

364: read Feb., 1797. The mere fact that the rattlesnake lacked other 'weapons' thus seemed to Beauvois a strong argument for the existence of the controverted power.

21. Rush, 'Inquiry into the Cause of Animal Life,' *Medical Inquiries and Observations* (4 vols. in 2, 4th ed.; Philadelphia: 1815), I, 44. Italics added. See also Priestley, *Discourses*, p. 304. (1764).

22. Samuel L. Mitchell, at *Trans. A. P. S.*, V, 139-147.

23. *Introductory Lectures*, p. 311; and pp. 296, 298, and lecture xiii, *passim*. And see Jefferson, *Writings*, IX, 360:To Madison, Jan. 1, 1797, on man's place in the scheme. Rush's discussion in lecture xiii is, however, in many respects discordant with the prevailing tone of Jeffersonian thought: e.g., in his use of theological and eschatological distinctions for connecting man and the lower animals, pp. 296, 309 ff.; and the hint (though only in a phrase) that if man did not look after the domestic animals, their species might become 'extinct,' p. 311. Of course, the use of this word did not imply the practical possibility of their extinction, since man's function in nature was partly to prevent the contingency. Cf. above, note 9.

24. 'Account of the State of Body and Mind in Old Age,' *Med. Inq.*, I, 245. See also, Jefferson, *Writings*, XV, 96 f.:Jan. 11, 1817, where Jefferson agreed that the tendency of men to tire of life's routine seemed to serve a benevolent purpose. And see Jefferson, *ibid.*, XV, 189: May 11, 1819. Even the grief which accompanied human ills seemed to have a use in the natural economy: Jefferson, *Writings*, XIV, 467:To Adams, April 8, 1816; XV, 8, 12, 15, 67:Adams to Jefferson; XV, 73:Jefferson to Adams. Both Adams and Jefferson seemed to assume that the question was not whether grief served a function in the economy of nature, but simply for what function it was designed.

Since the Creator had made the facts of the after-life inaccessible to man, He must not have required that man understand death in order to live fruitfully. 'The laws of nature have withheld from us the means of physical knowledge of the country of spirits,' Jefferson observed, 'and revelation has, for reasons unknown to us, chosen to leave us in the dark as we were. When I was young I was fond of the speculations which seemed to promise some insight into that hidden country, but observing at length that they left me in the same ignorance in which they had found me, I have for very many years ceased to read or to think concerning them, and have reposed my head on that pillow of ignorance which a benevolent Creator has made so soft for us, knowing how much we should be forced to use it. I have thought it better, by nourishing the good passions and controlling the bad, to merit an inheritance in a state of being of which I can know so little, and to trust for the future to Him who has been so good for the past.' *Writings*, X, 299:To Rev. Isaac Story, Dec. 5, 1801. Paine also seemed to believe in immortality, but again on his own terms (*Writings*, Age of Reason, IV, 178 f.), drawn from his study of natural history. The American philosopher did, however find that *belief* in an after-life was essential to morality and fruitful action. If one believed 'that there be a future state, the hope of a happy existence in that increases the appetite to deserve it.' Jefferson, *Writings*, VI, 260:To Peter Carr, Aug. 10, 1787. On the usefulness of Jesus' doctrine of immortality, see *ibid.*, X, 374 f.:To Priestley, April 9, 1803; and X, 385:To Rush, April 21, 1803.

Even when Jefferson professed wishful belief in an after-life, as on the death of his daughter (*Writings*, XI, 31:June 25, 1804); or when, an old man, he wrote to Lafayette (XIV, 254:Feb. 14, 1815), or to John Adams (XV, 174:Nov. 13, 1818) he spoke the language of metaphor. See below, Chapter Three, section 5, and note 49.

25. *Med. Inq.*, I, 263. See also Nathan G. Goodman, *Benjamin Rush* (Philadelphia: 1934), p. 208, from 'Proofs of the Origin of Yellow Fever in Philadelphia and Kingston.' I have not been able to see the original of this essay. And see *Med. Inq.*, IV, 138 f.: 'Heaven has surrendered every part of the globe to man, in a state capable of being inhabited, and enjoyed. . . . To every natural evil, the Author of Nature has kindly prepared an antidote. Pestilential fevers furnish no exception to this remark.' And see Jefferson, *Writings*, X, 173:To Rush, Oct. 23, 1800.

26. Rev. Nicholas Collin, rector of the Swedish Churches in Pennsylvania, who catalogued the library of the Society, and whose versatile accomplishments included a prize design for an elevator, essays on the theory of probability, plans for a botanical garden, and investigations of the methods of lead glazing, told the Society (*Trans. A. P. S.*, Vol. III, p. xxvii:April 3, 1789): 'The bountiful Creator discovers his marvels in proportion to our wants . . . every country has native remedies against its

natural defects; is it not then probable that as the *Polygala Senega* [a North American plant] was given us against the rattle-snakes, so may we have faithful prognostics of the dangerous caprices of our climate? Let us therefore study nature, and nature's Ruler shall reward our labour.'

See also Barton's 'Account of the most effectual means of preventing the deleterious consequences of the bite of the *Crotalus Horridus*, or *Rattle-Snake*,' *Trans. A. P. S.*, III, 112 f.: Aug. 19, 1791. Barton came to the conclusion 'that, in the fullness of her benevolence, nature, ever attentive to our welfare, has enriched her series of animals, of vegetables, and of minerals, with beings, with objects, and with means, which man, in every stage of his improvement, is instructed to employ for preventing, for alleviating, or for curing at least some of those infirmities the whole of which constitute, as it were, a part of his essence, or nature.'

27. *Med. Inq.*, I, 83. Rush explained that to have expected the Creator to furnish every land with medicines for its local ills would have given too high a place to man's peculiar needs. 'We are taught to believe that every herb that grows in our woods is possessed of some medicinal virtue, and that Heaven would be wanting in benignity, if our country did not produce remedies for all the different diseases of its inhabitants. It would be arrogating too much, to suppose that man was the only creature in our world for whom vegetables grow. The beasts, birds, and insects, derive their sustenance either directly or indirectly from them; while many of them were probably intended, from their variety in figure, foliage, and colour, only to serve as ornaments for our globe. It would seem strange that the Author of nature should furnish every spot of ground with medicines adapted to the diseases of its inhabitants, and at the same time deny it the more necessary articles of food and clothing.' *Ibid.*, I, 82. Rush suggested that the Fire of London may have been designed by Heaven to remove the causes of diseases, *ibid.*, IV, 135.

CHAPTER TWO

1. *Writings* (Rights of Man, Part II), II, 402 (1792).

2. Julian P. Boyd, *The Declaration of Independence: The Evolution of the Text* (Princeton: 1945), p. 19. Italics added. Boyd

suggests that the change in phrase was made in the Committee of Five, *ibid.*, p. 29.

3. *Writings* (Notes on Virginia), II, 200 f. Paine, *Writings* (Rights of Man, Part I), II, 303 f.; I, 75. Rush, *Essays*, pp. 8 f.

In Rush's 'Defence of the Use of the Bible as a School Book,' he writes that 'this divine book, above all others, favours that equality among mankind, that respect for just laws, and all those sober and frugal virtues, which constitute the soul of republicanism.' *Ibid.*, pp. 112 f. Even Paine was willing to appeal to the Bible on the point of human equality, *Writings* (Rights of Man, Part I), II, 305.

4. *New Views of the Origin of the Tribes and Nations of America* (2nd ed.; Philadelphia: 1798), pp. cii ff. The *Oxford English Dictionary* points out, *s.v.* 'species,' that around 1711 'the species' began to be used as a synonym for the human race.

5. *Systema Naturae*, I, 28.

6. *Writings*, XIII, 395:Oct. 28, 1813. We can gain some notion of the state of Jeffersonian knowledge of embryology and heredity from such an article as that by Dr. John Morgan (Rush's predecessor as Professor of the Theory and Practice of Medicine) entitled, 'Some Account of a motley coloured, or pye Negro Girl and Mulatto Boy,' which accompanied an exhibit of these creatures before the Philosophical Society in May, 1784. 'Mons. le Vallois relates that the mother of Adelaide [the motley coloured Negro Girl],' Dr. Morgan explained, 'whilst pregnant with her, was delighted in laying out all night in the open air, and contemplating the stars and planets, and that the great grandmother of Jean Pierre (a white lady) during the time of her being with child of her daughter, his grandmother by the father's side, was frightened on having some milk spilled upon her.' *Trans. A. P. S.*, II, 395. Although, as the doctor explained, some doubted that these facts caused the motley color of Jean Pierre's skin, many thought otherwise. Jefferson himself, partly perhaps because of the relevance of the Negro's color to his place in the human species, recounted in detail the phenomenon of albinism which he considered an 'anomaly of nature.' But he was hesitant to give an explanation, being uncertain what might be 'the cause of the disease in the skin, or in its coloring matter, which produces this

change.' In support of his suggestion that albinism might be a disease of the skin, he recounted the case of a Negro who had become partly albino after birth. *Writings* (Notes on Virginia), II, 101 ff.

7. *The Natural History of Carolina, Florida, and the Bahama Islands* . . . (2 vols.; London: 1771), Vol. I, Preface, p. xxxv. And see Jefferson, *Writings*, VII, 328:To Dr. Willard of Harvard, Mar. 24, 1789, and *ibid.*, X, 190. For an example of the more naïve hypotheses of the earlier writers who argued against the separate creation of man, see Edward Brerewood's *Enquiry touching the diversity of Languages and Religions* . . . (London: 1674), pp. 117 ff.

8. *New Views*, pp. ci ff. See also Barton, *Fragments of the Natural History of Pennsylvania* (Part First, Philadelphia: 1799), p. 14. The jumping rodent which interested Barton was one of the genus Dipus, or the Jerboas. See *Trans. A. P. S.*, IV, 118.

9. *New Views*, p. cviii. Here he refers particularly to Buffon. William Dunbar, 'Description of the river Mississippi . . . ,' *Trans. A. P. S.*, VI, 169: April 6, 1804.

10. Quoted by Barton in *New Views*, p. vii note, from Voltaire's *Philosophy of History* (London: 1766), p. 46. Barton, attempting to take the sting out of Voltaire's whimsy, remarked: 'By the way, it may be doubted whether flies, any more than bees, are natives of America.' See also Barton's discussion of the origin of the population of America in *Trans. A. P. S.*, IV, 187, note. John Adams, *Life and Works*, ed. C. F. Adams (10 vols.; Boston: 1856), X, 17 f.

11. *Observations on some Parts of Natural History* (London: 1787), pp. 65 f. Similarities in methods of constructing fortifications suggested that the Danes, for example, had come to America at a very early period. 'From these circumstances I am induced to think,' he concluded, 'that the DANES have contributed to the peopling of *America*; and that the TOLTECAS, or whatever nation it may have been, that constructed the eminences and fortifications in that continent, were their descendants. I will not attempt to assign the aera at which the DANES migrated to the NEW WORLD.' *Ibid.* And see Jefferson, *Writings*, XIII, 248: To John Adams, May 27, 1813; and pp. 156 ff. Catesby had written that the general opinion was that the

earliest peopling of America was from Northern Asia. *Carolina*, Vol. I, Preface, p. vii.

12. *Trans.* A. P. S., VI, 155: Oct. 21, 1803. Cf. William Thornton's essay, 'Cadmus,' Magellanic Prize Essay for 1793, especially at *Trans.* A. P. S., III, 295 f., where he explains the origin of language in man's efforts to imitate and decoy animals.

13. 'Hints on the Etymology of certain English Words . . . ,' *Trans.* A. P. S., VI, 151 f.:Oct. 21, 1803.

14. *New Views*, p. lxxv. The thesis of this cautious work was 'that the nations of America and those of Asia have a common origin.' Collin, *Trans.* A. P. S., IV, 478:read June 1, 1798. Dunbar, *ibid.*, VI, 1 ff.

15. Jefferson, *Writings*, XII, 312 f.:To B. S. Barton, Sept. 21, 1809. XI, 79 ff.:To Dr. John Sibley, May 27, 1805. VII, 267: From Paris, Jan. 12, 1789.

Jefferson actually called his projected work an inquiry 'as to the probability of a common origin between the people of color of the two continents' (America and Asia). *Writings*, XI, 102: To Levett Harris, April 18, 1806. And see *Writings* (Notes on Virginia), II, 128, 139 ff.

16. *Writings* (Notes on Virginia), II, p. 87.

17. *Introductory Lectures*, pp. 116 f.

18. *Ibid.* And see his 'Inquiry into the Natural History of Medicine among the Indians . . . ,' *Med. Inq.*, I, 72 f., 85 f., and *passim*. 'Inquiry into the Cause of Animal Life,' *ibid.*, I, 36 f. The proverbial Indian weakness for alcohol, if one accepted Rush's argument in his 'Inquiry into the Effects of Ardent Spirits upon the Human Body and Mind,' was simply another example of 'the different employments, situations, and conditions of the body and mind, which predispose to the love of those liquors.' *Ibid.*, I, 164. While, in his 'Account of the Vices peculiar to the Indians of North America' (*Essays*, 257-262), Rush enumerated their characteristic moral weaknesses, he nowhere suggested that these were to be explained from other than environmental or institutional causes. Barton, *Observations*, Note (M), p. 73.

19. *Writings*, V, 5 f.:To Gen. Chastellux, June 7, 1785. Specially relevant in the *Notes on Virginia* are: *Writings*, II, 82 note 2; 96 note 1, 87, 89; and Appendix, pp. 304 ff.

20. *Trans. A. P. S.*, IV, 181 ff., at 213 f. And see Jonathan Heart, *ibid.*, III, 221.

21. *New Views*, pp. v f.

22. *Trans. A. P. S.*, IV, 289 ff.:Read to Society, July 14, 1792. For the relevant discussions of albinism by Jefferson and Dr. John Morgan, see above, note 6.

23. *Writings* (Notes on Virginia), II, 192 f. Jefferson opposed miscegenation; *ibid.*, I, 72 f. But Rush observed: 'It is possible, the strength of the intellects may be improved in their original conformation, as much as the strength of the body, by certain mixtures of persons of different nations, habits, and constitutions, in marriage. The mulatto has been remarked, in all countries, to exceed, in sagacity, his white and black parent. The same remark has been made of the offspring of the European, and North American Indian.' *Introductory Lectures*, p. 117.

24. *Writings* (Notes on Virginia), II, 200 f.

25. *Writings*, V, 6:From Paris, June 7, 1785.

26. *Writings* (Notes on Virginia), II, 199, 94. See also Jefferson, *Works* (Ford ed.), V, 447:To Dr. Edward Bancroft, Jan. 26, 1789, where Jefferson explained the tendency of free Negroes toward thievery to be the effect of slavery on the moral sense.

27. *Writings*, XII, 255:To M. Henri Grégoire, Feb. 25, 1809. XII, 322:To Joel Barlow, Oct. 8, 1809. VIII, 241:To Benjamin Banneker, Aug. 30, 1791. *Works* (Ford ed.), VI, 311: To Marquis de Condorcet, Aug. 30, 1791.

28. *Writings*, XII, 255:To M. Henri Grégoire, Feb. 25, 1809.

29. *Spirit of Laws*, trans. Thomas Nugent (2 vols.; New York: 1899), from Bk. XIV, found at I, 221 ff.

30. *Writings* (Notes on Virginia), II, 62 f. In this work Jefferson supplied detailed tables to substantiate his refutation of Buffon; unfortunately several popular editions of the work have omitted these significant tables.

31. Abbé Raynal, *The Revolution of America*, trans. from French (London: 1781), pp. 179 f. See also Raynal's *L'Histoire philosophique et politique des établissements et du commerce des Européens dans les deux Indes* (Maestricht, 1774), p. 92. Quoted by Jefferson in *Writings*, II, 94. Part of Buffon's attack on the Indian is quoted by Jefferson at *ibid.*, II, 80 f.

32. *Writings*, XVIII, 170 f., from Jefferson's 'Anecdotes of Benjamin Franklin,' written at the request of Robert Walsh, and inclosed in letter to Walsh dated Dec. 4, 1818. Barton, like Jefferson himself, attempted a more serious reply; he tried 'to vindicate, from the aspersions of certain popular and eloquent writers [Buffon, De Pauw, Raynal and Robertson] the intellectual character of the Americans.' *Trans. A. P. S.*, IV, 187.

33. *Writings* (Notes on Virginia), II, 61. And see 64 f., 76 f., 93. But there was no lack of eager and credulous philosophers who discovered elixirs in the climate, the atmosphere or the water. See William Barton, 'Observations on the probabilities of the Duration of Human Life, and the progress of Population, in the United States of America,' *Trans. A. P. S.*, III, 25 ff.:Mar. 18, 1791. William Dunbar in his 'Description of the river Mississippi,' described the peculiar 'salubrity' of its waters: 'It seems to be admitted (perhaps without due investigation) that it possesses properties favorable to the multiplication of the human species, by promoting fecundity; it is probably more certain that the use of its waters contributes to banish several disorders common in other countries: the gout would be unknown were it not introduced by strangers; and instances of the stone and gravel are extremely rare. The Creoles who drink this water are a comely race . . . ' *Trans. A. P. S.*, VI, 177 f.: April 6, 1804. But the more respectable (and more cautious) philosophers, among whom all the Jeffersonians should be counted, would not only deny such thaumaturgic qualities, but would even freely admit that in many respects the American environment might be inferior. 'It is a folly,' observed Benjamin Smith Barton in his *Memoir concerning . . . Goitre* (Philadelphia: 1800; p. 80), 'to attempt to prove that the climate of America is *peculiarly* healthy . . . A list of the indigenous diseases of America . . . would not be found much, if at all, less extensive than the list of these infirmities in other parts of the world.'

Closely related was the interesting question whether there was a greater or less number of harmful animals and insects

present on this continent than elsewhere. Still more fundamental to any inquiry into the Creator's design was how many
of the noxious creatures were *native* to the American continent.
E.g., Barton on the Hessian fly (*Fragments*, p. 23); on the
rat, mouse, moth, flea, bedbug, and honeybee (*Trans. A. P. S.*,
III, 242). Cf. *Materia Medica*, I, pp. 5 f. And see Jefferson on
the honeybee in the *Notes on Virginia*.

CHAPTER THREE

1. *Med. Inq.*, I, 8. 'Life,' Rush said, 'is the *effect* of certain
   stimuli acting upon the sensibility and excitability which are
   extended, in different degrees, over every external and internal
   part of the body. These stimuli are as necessary to its existence,
   as air is to flame. Animal life is truly . . . "a forced state".
   . . . [As Dr. Cullen said] "The human body is an automaton,
   or self-moving machine; but is kept alive and in motion, by the
   constant action of stimuli upon it." ' *Ibid.*, p. 7. 'Air' was
   simply the first of these stimuli.

2. *Disquisitions relating to Matter and Spirit* (London: 1777),
   pp. 114 f.

3. 'Inquiry into the Cause of Animal Life,' *Med. Inq.*, I, 52.
   Priestley, *Discourses*, pp. 305 f. (1764). Jefferson, *Writings*,
   XV, 274:To John Adams, Aug. 15, 1820.

4. *Writings*, XV, 274:To John Adams, Aug. 15, 1820.

5. *Writings*, XV, 241:To John Adams, Mar. 14, 1820. 'So on
   dissolution of the material organ by death, its action of thought
   may cease also . . . nobody supposes that the magnetism or
   elasticity retire to hold a substantive and distinct existence.
   These were qualities only of particular conformations of matter;
   change the conformation, and its qualities change also.' *Ibid.*,
   240.

6. *Matter and Spirit*, p. 18. See also pp. 17 f., 108 f., 145, and
   passim. Rittenhouse, *Oration*, pp. 14 f.

7. *Writings*, XVI, 91:Jan. 8, 1825. And see *Works* (Ford ed.),
   XII, 400:To Francis Adrian Van Der Kemp, Jan. 11, 1825.
   The title of Flourens' work was *Recherches expérimentales sur*

les propriétés et les fonctions du système nerveux dans les animaux vertébrés. For his view of Cabanis, see Jefferson, *Writings*, XIII, 177 ff.:To Thomas Cooper, July 10, 1812; X, 404:To Cabanis, July 12, 1803.

8. *Writings* (Notes on Virginia), II, 61. Rush, 'Inquiry into the Cause of Animal Life,' *Med. Inq.*, I, 54, 43 f. Priestley, *Matter and Spirit*, pp. 127 f.

9. *Writings*, XIII, 279 f.:June 27, 1813. 'The same political parties which now agitate the United States, have existed through all time.' *Ibid.* 'Men by their constitutions are naturally divided into two parties.' *Writings*, XVI, 73 f.:Aug. 10, 1824; and *ibid.*, IX, 377:Feb. 9, 1797. Variety of opinion compared or related to variety of physical features: *Writings*, XIII, 116:To Rush, Dec. 5, 1811. *Ibid.*, X, 85:To Gerry, Jan. 29, 1799. X, 436:To Randolph, Dec. 1, 1803. XIII, 67:July 25, 1811. See also Jefferson, *Works* (Ford ed.), XII, 348, April 3, 1824; *Writings*, XII, 315, Sept. 27, 1809; XV, 324, Feb. 27, 1821.

   Rush, *Introductory Lectures*, p. 102. And see generally, lecture iv, 'On the influence of physical causes, in promoting the strength and activity of the intellectual faculties of man.'

10. 'Inquiry into the Cause of Animal Life,' *Med. Inq.*, I, 50. And see *Introductory Lectures*, p. 241.

11. *Writings*, X, 85:Jan. 26, 1799. VI, 261:To Carr, Aug. 10, 1787. Cf. Madison's 'Memorial and Remonstrance against Religious Assessment,' to General Assembly of Virginia in 1785; at Madison, *Writings*, ed. Gaillard Hunt (9 vols.; New York: 1900), II, 184 f. See also Jefferson, *Writings* (Notes on Virginia), II, 221.

12. *Writings* (Rights of Man, Part II), II, 515 f.:Feb. 17, 1792.

13. *Writings*, XII, 199 f.: To T. J. Randolph, Nov. 24, 1808. *Ibid.* (Notes on Virginia), II, 221.

14. *Writings*, XIII, 333 f.:To Isaac McPherson, Aug. 13, 1813.

15. *Writings*, XIV, 283:Mar. 13, 1815; see also XV, 394 f.: Sept. 5, 1822. Rush, *Introductory Lectures*, pp. 116, 150. Priestley, *The Doctrine of Phlogiston Established, and that of the Com-*

position of Water Refuted (Northumberland, Pennsylvania: 1800), p. x.

16. *Discourses*, pp. 175 f. (1785). *Ibid.*, p. 200. (1779). Specifically on the uses of mental variety in purifying Christianity, see Priestley, *A History of the Corruptions of Christianity*, reprinted from Rutt's edition, with notes (London: 1871), p. 310 (1782).

17. *Introductory Lectures*, p. 290. And see pp. 103, 168, 291 f. 'This science [natural history] is strongly recommended to our notice and attention, by its having been the first study of the father of mankind, in the garden of Eden. It furnishes the raw materials of knowledge upon all subjects.' *Ibid.*, p. 103. 'By the fermentation they [facts] excite in the mind, they prepare it for embracing with facility the principles of general science.' *Ibid.* 'Observation, reading, and experiments, in the order in which I have mentioned them, resemble the juice of the grape on the vine, and in the press; while reasoning may be compared to the fermenting process which changes it into wine. It belongs exclusively to this sublime operation of the mind to strain the knowledge, derived from other sources, from its feculent parts, and to convert it into pure and durable science.' *Ibid.*, pp. 291 f. And see Goodman, *Benjamin Rush*, pp. 144 f. For other strictures on the notion that knowledge might come from introspection, see Barton, *Observations*, p. 29; Priestley, *Lectures on History and General Policy . . .* (2 vols.; Philadelphia: 1803) I, 57 ff.

18. Jefferson, *Writings*, XV, 492:Nov. 4, 1823.

19. *Doctrine of Phlogiston* (Northumberland, Pennsylvania: 1800), p. xii.

20. *Memoir concerning . . . Goitre*, p. 80. Jefferson warned the philosopher against belief in 'some . . . ingenious dream, which lets him into all nature's secrets at short hand.' *Writings*, XI, 245:To Dr. Caspar Wistar, June 21, 1807.

21. Rush, *Introductory Lectures*, p. 6.

22. *Med. Inq.*, II, 206. *Ibid.*, I, 78 f., 183 f. *Introductory Lectures*, pp. 150 ff.

23. Jefferson, *Writings*, XI, 244. XIV, 200 f.:To Thomas Cooper, Oct. 7, 1814. *Ibid.*, XIII, 133: Feb. 14, 1812. VI, 321: Sept. 20, 1787. And see his letter to Dr. Wistar, XI, 244 f.: June 21, 1807.

24. *Writings*, XI, 245 f.:To Dr. Wistar, June 21, 1807. XIII, 224: To Rush, Mar. 6, 1813.

25. Jefferson's draft prospectus for Tracy's *Political Economy*, April 6, 1816, found at Jefferson, *Writings*, XIV, 463 f. And see *Writings* (Anas), I, 63; II, 190; XV, 272 f.: Aug. 15, 1820. See also XVI, 134: Nov. 9, 1825.

26. *Writings*, XIV, 97 f.: To Dr. John Manners, Feb. 22, 1814. See also *ibid.*, X, 192: To William Dunbar, Jan. 12, 1801; XI, 244 f.:To Dr. Wistar, June 21, 1807. And cf. Priestley, *History of Electricity* (1st ed.), p. 418, quoted by Sir Philip Hartog in 'The Newer Views of Priestley and Lavoisier,' *Annals of Science*, Vol. 5, No. 1 (Aug. 1941), pp. 1-56, at p. 13. *Barton, Elements of Botany*, I, 3 f.: II, 4.

27. *Elements of Botany*, II, 61. Linnaeus himself had remarked: '*Methodus naturalis adhuc detecta non est . . . sed sunt Methodi in quibus aliquae classes naturales reliquis immixtae cernuntur, & sunt etiam methodi in quibus nulla Classis naturalis conservatur. . . .*' *Classes Plantarum* (Leyden: 1738), Preface, para. 4. See also Barton, *Elements of Botany*, 1, 144 and II, 25. But Barton was still hopeful. He wrote in 1792, 'I cannot help wishing that the day may arrive . . . when the sexual arrangement shall give way to a more natural method, one in which the order, or assemblage, of nature will be pursued more rigorously than it has been by Linnaeus.' *Trans. A. P. S.*, III, 340.

Perhaps it was a distrust of all systems of classification (rather than a belief in the fluidity of species) which Barton was expressing when, in 1794, he protested against the 'common' notion that it was impossible that 'animals of the same species should any where differ.' *Trans. A. P. S.*, IV, 101. Also, although he said many animals in America were of distinct species from those in Europe or Asia, he often showed a reluctance to mark off the boundaries of species (e.g., *Trans. A. P. S.*, IV, 118, 123). The 'natural' botanist might thus share the astronomer's belief that 'every enlargement of our faculties, every new happiness conferred upon us, every step we advance towards the perfection of the divinity, will very probably render us more and more sensible of his inexhaustible stores of communicable bliss, and of his inaccessible perfections.' Rittenhouse, *Oration*, p. 27.

See Jefferson, *Writings*, XIV, 99 ff.:To Dr. Manners, Feb. 22, 1814.

28. *Writings*, XV, 25:To Francis W. Gilmer, June 7, 1816.

29. Jefferson, *Writings*, XII, 315:To James Fishback, Sept. 27, 1809.

'It is really curious that on a question so fundamental [the foundation of morality], such a variety of opinions should have prevailed among men, and those, too, of the most exemplary virtue and first order of understanding. It shows how necessary was the care of the Creator in making the moral principle so much a part of our constitution as that no errors of reasoning or of speculation might lead us astray from its observance in practice.' *Ibid.*, XIV, 139:To Thomas Law, June 13, 1814. 'Morals were too essential to the happiness of man, to be risked on the uncertain combinations of the head. She [Nature] laid their foundation, therefore, in sentiment, not in science. That she gave to all, as necessary to all; this to a few only, as sufficing with a few.' *Ibid.*, V, 443:To Mrs. Cosway, Oct. 12, 1786. 'The evidence . . . of our right to life, liberty, the use of our faculties, the pursuit of happiness,' Jefferson insisted (in discussing the natural right of expatriation), 'is not left to the feeble and sophistical investigations of reason, but is impressed on the sense of every man.' *Ibid.*, XV, 124: To Dr. John Manners, June 12, 1817. See also VI, 257 f.: To Peter Carr, Aug. 10, 1787; and XV, 76:To John Adams, Oct. 14, 1816.

Rush, 'Inquiry into the Influence of Physical Causes upon the Moral Faculty,' *Med. Inq.*, I, 104.

30. *Writings*, VI, 257 f.:From Paris, Aug. 10, 1787. See also *ibid.*, XIV, 142:To Thomas Law, June 13, 1814; and XV, 76 f: Oct. 14, 1816.

31. The American philosopher had not distinguished sharply between the exercise of 'reason' and other forms of behavior. One correspondent of the Philosophical Society, for example, noted that a species of wasp would repair a few cells of its nest when these were broken by the experimenter, and he was ready to

find here an instance of 'reasoning' in insects (B. H. Latrobe, *Trans. A. P. S.*, VI, 78:Jan. 21, 1803). Jefferson himself believed that the faculty of thought was a universal characteristic of animals. *Writings*, XVI, 19:Mar. 24, 1824. But from time to time, the Jeffersonians seemed to express an uneasiness at not having distinguished more sharply between the mental process of man and that of the lower animals. Rush seemed to suggest that man was to be distinguished from the lower animals by the fact that in him 'reason' was the *dominant* faculty. See his description of insanity at *Introductory Lectures*, p. 208.

32. 'Inquiry into the Influence of Physical Causes upon the Moral Faculty,' *Med. Inq.*, I, 103. 'The Creator would indeed have been a bungling artist, had he intended man for a social animal, without planting in him social dispositions. It is true they are not planted in every man, because there is no rule without exceptions; but it is false reasoning which converts exceptions into the general rule.' Jefferson, *Writings*, XIV, 142:To Thomas Law, June 13, 1814.

For Rush's amplification of the influence of environmental and other circumstances in perverting the moral faculty, see also his *Medical Inquiries and Observations upon the Diseases of the Mind* (Philadelphia:1812), hereafter cited as *Diseases of the Mind*. Esp. chap. x, 'Of Derangement in the Will'; chap. xvii, 'Of Derangement of the Passions . . .'; chap. xviii, 'Of the Morbid State of the Sexual Appetite'; and chap. xix, 'Of the Derangement of the Moral Faculties.' Also, pp. 351, 353.

33. *Introductory Lectures*, pp. 415, 444.

34. Rush noted 'the sameness of the laws which govern the body and the moral faculties of man. I shall venture to point out the sameness of those laws in a few instances, by mentioning the predisposition and proximate causes, the symptoms, and the remedies of corporeal and moral diseases. . . . Is debility the predisposing cause of disease in the body? so it is of vice in the mind.' *Diseases of the Mind*, p. 360. Throughout the familiar sayings of 'Poor Richard' and other of Franklin's writings there runs a similar notion; but Franklin did not give the idea the scientific elaboration which we find later in Rush. 'Be studious in your Profession,' Franklin had advised, 'and you will be learned. Be industrious and frugal, and you will be rich. Be sober and temperate, and you will be healthy. Be in general virtuous, and you will be happy.' *Writings*, ed. A. H. Smyth

(10 vols.; New York:1907), V, 159. Such connection between physical and moral well-being was, of course, not novel. It had been presupposed in the early Christian liturgy (though with a quite different emphasis), in which the sacrament for example was treated as having a medicinal effect. See Dom Theodore Wesseling, *Liturgy and Life* (New York:1938), p. 76.

35. Jefferson, *Writings*, VI, 258 f.:Aug. 10, 1787. He advised Peter Carr (Aug. 19, 1785), 'Encourage all your virtuous dispositions, and exercise them whenever an opportunity arises; being assured that they will gain strength by exercise, as a limb of the body does, and that exercise will make them habitual.' *Ibid.*, V, 83. As early as 1771, Jefferson had observed the providential fact that the Creator had not confined the exercise of the moral faculty to the incidents of real life; men had been 'wisely framed to be as warmly interested for a fictitious as for a real personage.' *Ibid.*, IV, 237-239:To Robert Skipwith.

36. Jefferson, *Writings*, V, 93 f.:To Jay, Aug. 23, 1785. *Ibid.*, XV, 168 f.:May 17, 1818. X, 431:Nov. 14, 1803. Rush's essay on ardent spirits is found at *Med. Inq.*, I, 151-176. Tobacco, in addition to its own peculiar derangements of the body, predisposed men to the use of ardent spirits. Rush believed that 'diseases, like vices, with a few exceptions, are necessarily undisciplined and irregular.' 'Outlines of the Phenomena of Fever,' *Med. Inq.*, III, 21.

37. *Arator*, p. 180. And see Jefferson at *Writings*, XI, 3:To J. B. Say, Feb. 1, 1804.

38. *History of Corruptions*, p. 94 (1782). Rush, *Introductory Lectures*, p. 87. *Med. Inq.*, III, 14. *Diseases of the Mind*, pp. 360 f.

39. 'Inquiry into the Cause of Animal Life,' *Med. Inq.*, I, 14, 17. And see also, *Introductory Lectures*, p. 310. Cf. lecture xiii, 'On the duty and advantages of studying the diseases of domestic animals, and the remedies proper to remove them,' esp. pp. 295 f.

40. On the emergence of new diseases and vices, see Rush, *Med. Inq.*, I, 73, 77, 79; *Introductory Lectures*, p. 151.

41. *Writings*, XV, 384:To Dr. Benjamin Waterhouse, June 26, 1822. *Ibid.*, XVI, 101:To Gen. Alexander Smyth, Jan. 17, 1825. Paine, *Writings* (Age of Reason), IV, 83, 188.

42. *Writings*, XIV, 197 f.:To Miles King, Sept. 26, 1814.

43. *History of Corruptions*, p. 93; and see pp. 91 f. The dogmas of original sin, atonement, redemption and election were said to be the mere fabrications of priests—attempts to abstract the qualities of man from the process of nature; they were all, according to Priestley, unknown in the primitive church (p. 97). 'This [free will] is a simple and a pleasing view of God and his moral government, and the consideration of it cannot but have the best effect on the temper of our minds and conduct in life.' p. 92.

44. 'Inquiry into the Cause of Animal Life,' *Med. Inq.*, I, 43. See also his 'Inquiry into the Effects of Ardent Spirits upon the Human Body and Mind,' *ibid.*, 167, 172.

45. *Writings* (Age of Reason), IV, 188, 65. 'Truth is simple upon all subjects, but upon those which are essential to the general happiness of mankind, it is obvious to the meanest capacities.' Rush, *Introductory Lectures*, p. 154. See also, *Med. Inq.*, I, 104 ff., and 'Outlines of the Phenomena of Fever,' *ibid.*, III, 17 f.

46. Jefferson, *Writings*, XIII, 377 f.:Sept. 18, 1813. *Ibid.*, XV, 99: To John Adams, Jan. 11, 1817. On the need of these common precepts for the plan of nature, see *ibid.*, XII, 315:To James Fishback, Sept. 27, 1809. But Jefferson sometimes suggested that even the dogmatic disagreements among men were only apparent: 'I very much suspect that if thinking men would have the courage to think for themselves, and to speak what they think, it would be found they do not differ in religious opinions as much as is supposed.' *Ibid.*, XIII, 349 f.:To John Adams, Aug. 22, 1813. See Paine, *Writings* (Age of Reason), IV, 83 f.

   Dr. S. S. Smith had pointed out some consequences of the erroneous belief in multiple human species: 'The science of morals would be absurd; the law of nature and nations would be annihilated; no general principles of human conduct, of religion, or of policy could be framed; for, human nature, originally infinitely various, and, by the changes of the world, infinitely mixed, could not be comprehended in any system.' *Essay on Causes of Variety* . . . (Philadelphia: 1787), pp. 109 f.

47. *Writings*, I, 170:1820. See also Jefferson's system of library classification (ca. 1820-1825): 'Metaphysics have been incorporated with Ethics, and little extension given to them.' Pad-

over, *Complete Jefferson*, p. 1092. See also *Writings*, XV, 60:
Aug. 6, 1816; and XIV, 197 f., Sept. 26, 1814. And see (on
Unitarianism) XV, 410:To James Smith, Dec. 8, 1822. See
Priestley, *Discourses*, pp. 165 f. (1785); and Paine, *Writings*
(Rights of Man, Part II), II, 515; and IV (Age of Reason),
186, 20.

48. *Writings*, XIV, 385:Jan. 9, 1816. *Ibid.*, X, 380:To Rush, April
11, 1803. Jefferson considered his collection of Jesus' teachings
a document in further proof that he was 'a *real* Christian.' Late in
life he came to believe that Unitarianism was the revival of
primitive Christianity and he even ventured that the living generation would see Unitarianism become the general religion of
the United States. *Ibid.*, XV, 408 f.:Dec. 8, 1822.

49. *Writings*, XIII, 377 f.:Sept. 18, 1813. *Ibid.*, X, 381 f.:To Rush,
April 21, 1803. See also, X, 384; and XV, 430:To John Adams,
April 11, 1823. And, on the nature of Jesus' reforms further,
X, 374 f.:To Priestley, April 9, 1803. Paine agreed: 'Jesus
Christ founded no new system. He called men to the practice of
moral virtues, and the belief of one God. The great trait in his
character is philanthropy.' *Writings* (Age of Reason), IV, 39 f.,
and see 28. For the Jeffersonian attitude toward immortality,
see above, Chapter One, note 24. Jefferson considered 'the doctrine of a future state' primarily as a belief which encouraged a
moral life; he thought its truth was not demonstrable (nor even
perhaps discussable) and seemed hardly interested in whether
it was 'true,' since a belief in it was so undeniably 'useful.'

50. Jefferson, *Writings*, X, 383:To Rush, April 21, 1803. Paine,
Writings (Age of Reason), IV, 28, 39 f.

51. Jefferson, *Writings*, XIII, 389 f.:To John Adams, Oct. 13, 1813.
Jefferson is here referring to his earlier compilation (not the
one reprinted in facsimile in the Bergh edition in Vol. XX).
It is the later more extended version of this anthology that is
found at the end of *Writings*, Vol. XX. Cyrus Adler there provides an introduction explaining the process of its compilation
(ca. 1819) and giving the story of the earlier anthology which
Jefferson had made while in the White House. Both were
literally scissors-and-paste jobs in which Jefferson arranged
chronologically those episodes in the life of Jesus and those
utterances attributed to him which Jefferson considered
genuine.

52. *Writings*, X, 228:To Priestley, Mar. 21, 1801. *Ibid.*, XIV, 200 f.:To Thomas Cooper, Oct. 7, 1814; and XIV, 232 f.:To Charles Clay, Jan. 29, 1815. On the relation of theology to the self-interest of priests, see these letters to John Adams: *ibid.*, XIII. 389 f.:Oct. 13, 1813; and XIV, 149, July 5, 1814. For a sample of Jefferson's comment on Priestley's *History of Corruptions*, see *ibid.*, XIII, 352:To John Adams, Aug. 22, 1813.

53. *History of Corruptions*, p. 157, and Part V, 'The History of Opinions concerning the State of the Dead,' *passim*. For the perverse and profitable uses of the doctrines of immaterialism, see also Priestley, *Matter and Spirit*, pp. 50, 74 f., 208. Jefferson, *Writings*, XV, 274:To John Adams, Aug. 15, 1820. And XVI, 18 f.:To Judge A. B. Woodward, Mar. 24, 1824, 'Jesus Himself, the Founder of our religion, was unquestionably a Materialist as to man.' (But note a rare observation *contra*, XV, 244:To William Short, April 13, 1820.)

54. *Writings*, XIV, 149:To John Adams, July 5, 1814. See also *ibid.*, XIII, 390:To John Adams, Oct. 13, 1813. And cf. Adams to Jefferson, Adams, *Life and Works*, X, 103:July 16, 1814. For some of Jefferson's strictures on Plato, see: *Writings*, XIV, 148 f.; XV, 219:Oct. 31, 1819; XV, 258:To William Short, Aug. 4, 1820; XV, 385:June 26, 1822. And see Priestley, *History of Corruptions*, pp. 9, 31, 108 f., 113, 217, and *passim*.

55. *Writings*, XII, 315:To James Fishback, Sept. 27, 1809.

56. *Med. Inq.*, I, 96. In 'infernal spirits' the moral faculty itself had been lost. Rush illustrated this by one of Satan's speeches (*Paradise Lost*, Bk. IV):

> Farewell Remorse; all good to me is lost.
> *Evil*, be thou my good.

'In them the will has probably lost the power of choosing, as well as the capacity of enjoying, moral good.' *Ibid.*, I, 99 f. and note. Although these 'infernal creatures' lacked the moral faculty, they still had a conscience, or an ability to judge in particular situations the consequences of their perverse morality. 'It is true, we read of their trembling in a belief of the existence of a God, and of their anticipating future punishment, by asking whether they were to be tormented before their time: but this is the effect of conscience, and hence arises another argument in favour of this judicial power of the mind being

279

distinct from the moral faculty.' The common defect of man was just the opposite of that of 'fallen spirits': men seldom lost the moral faculty, but they did lose their power of judging consequences. Thus it was their 'conscience' that was most commonly defective. 'Perhaps the essence of moral depravity in man consists in a total, but temporary, suspension of the power of conscience. Persons in this situation are emphatically said in the scriptures to "be past feeling," and to have their consciences seared with a "hot iron"; they are likewise said to be "twice dead," that is, the same torpor, or moral insensibility, has seized both the moral faculty and the conscience.' *Ibid.*, p. 100.

57. *Writings*, XIV, 143:To Thomas Law, June 13, 1814.

58. *Writings*, XI, 3:To J. B. Say, Feb. 1, 1804. See also, III, 375 f.:Second Inaugural Address, 1805; and XI, 394 f.:On the Indian Policy of the Committee of Friends, Nov. 16, 1807.

CHAPTER FOUR

1. On the physiological foundations of political parties, see above, Chapter Three, note 9. On the inevitability of political disagreement see Jefferson, *Writings*, IX, 388 f.:To Thomas Pinckney, May 29, 1797; XVIII, 207-209:To John Taylor, June 4, 1798. 'In every country where man is free to think and speak, differences of opinion will arise from differences of perception, and the imperfection of reason.' X, 235:Mar. 23, 1801. 'I had always expected that when the republicans should have put down all things under their feet, they would schismatize among themselves.' **XI, 265:To Thomas Cooper**, July 9, 1807. See also X, 320:May 3, 1802.

2. Paine, *Writings* (Rights of Man, Part II), II, 408 f.

3. Jefferson, *Writings*, IX, 359:To Madison, Jan. 1, 1797. See also VI, 58:Jan. 16, 1787. Peale, *Discourse Introductory to a Course of Lectures on the Science of Nature; with Original Music, composed for, and sung on, the occasion*, delivered in the Hall of the University of Pennsylvania, Nov. 8, 1800 (Philadelphia: 1800), pp. 9 f.

4. 'Natural History of Medicine among the Indians,' *Med. Inq.*, I, 66 ff. Jefferson, *Writings*, IX, 359 f.:To Madison, Jan. 1, 1797;

and XVIII, 283 f.:Aug. 20, 1814. Although from an anthropocentric point of view man's destructive temperament gave no 'honour to our boasted reason' (Peale, *Discourse on Science of Nature*, pp. 9 f.), there was no denying that from the point of view of the Creator, man's very vice performed a necessary function. 'This pugnacious humor,' observed Jefferson, '. . . seems to be the law of his [man's] nature, one of the obstacles to too great multiplication provided in the mechanism of the universe.' *Writings*, XV, 372: June 1, 1822. (Cf. above Chapter One, note 9.) As some of the above passages and others would indicate, the American philosopher even before Malthus had found use for war, misery and vice in the economy of nature. Jefferson greatly admired the 'masterly work' of Malthus; but he thought his doctrines required considerable modification before being applied to America. E.g., *Writings*, X, 447 f.:To Priestley, Jan. 29, 1804; and XI, 1:To J. B. Say, Feb. 1, 1804.

5. *Writings* (Rights of Man, Part II), II, 411 f. Jefferson wrote from Paris (Sept. 30, 1785): 'I find the general fate of humanity here most deplorable. The truth of Voltaire's observation, offers itself perpetually, that every man here must be either the hammer or the anvil. It is a true picture of that country to which they say we shall pass hereafter, and where we are to see God and his angels in splendor, and crowds of the damned trampled under their feet.' *Writings*, V, 152 f. Some examples of Jefferson's characteristic metaphors for the predatory nature of the traditional European governments: *Writings*, II, 128 f.; VI, 251 f.:Aug. 6, 1787; VI, 279:Aug. 14, 1787; VI, 373:Nov. 13, 1787; XVII, 291 f.:1788; X, 422:To Rush, Oct. 4, 1803. His letters abound with them.

6. *Writings*, VI, 58:To Edward Carrington, Jan. 16, 1787.

7. Jefferson, *Writings* (Notes on Virginia), II, 207.

8. *Writings* (Notes on Virginia), II, 164 f. On the dangers of the Society of the Cincinnati, *ibid.*, IV, 217 f.:To Washington, April 16, 1784. 'Bad men will sometimes get in, and with such an immense patronage, may make great progress in corrupting the public mind and principles. This is a subject with which wisdom and patriotism should be occupied.' *Ibid.*, X, 237:Mar. 23, 1801. A failure to face these stark facts of human nature had been one of the mistakes of the Jacobins in the French Revolution. 'Yet these were men, and we and our

descendants will be no more. The present is a case where, if ever, we are to guard ourselves; not against ourselves as we are, but as we may be; for who can now imagine what we may become under circumstances not now imaginable?' *Ibid.*, XV, 360:To Jedidiah Morse on the dangers of forming a strong private association to improve the Indians, Mar. 6, 1822.

9. *Writings*, XIII, 396 f.:To John Adams, Oct. 28, 1813. And see *ibid.*, VI, 151:To Hartley, July 2, 1787; VIII, 18:To Duchesse d'Auville, April 2, 1790; XIV, 421:To Joseph C. Cabell, Feb. 2, 1816. Jefferson would not believe that man was a 'beast of burden made to be rode by him who has genius enough to get a bridle into his mouth.' XII, 351:To Joel Barlow, Jan. 24, 1810.

10. *Med. Inq.*, I, 127-134.

11. On the succession of human passions: Rush, *Med. Inq.*, I, 27. Jefferson, *Writings*, V, 152 f., Sept. 30, 1785.

   On financial speculation as a symptom and cause of mental disorder see Rush, 'Inquiry into the Cause of Animal Life.' *Med. Inq.*, I, 41. Jefferson, *Writings*, XIV, 381:To Col. Charles Yancey, Jan. 6, 1816. 'The tide of public prosperity almost unparalleled in any country is arrested in its course, and suppressed by the rage of getting rich in a day. No mortal can tell where this will stop; for the spirit of gaming, when once it has seized a subject, is incurable. The tailor who has made thousands in one day, though he has lost them the next, can never again be content with the slow and moderate earnings of his needle.' *Ibid.*, VIII, 233:To Edward Rutledge, Aug. 25, 1791. And see also *ibid.*, VIII, 344:To Washington, May 23, 1792.

12. *Med. Inq.*, I, 40. See also his *Introductory Lectures* where (p. 109) he notes 'the effects of liberty in producing the greatest quantity of animal life'; and adds that 'it promotes the same increase of the quantity of mind.' On the failure of artificial expedients to increase population under despotic governments, *Med. Inq.*, I, 89.

13. Jefferson, *Writings*, XI, 55:To Lithson, Jan. 4, 1805, explicitly disavowing certain interpretations of Query XIX of the *Notes on Virginia*. Generally, on the farmer's life: *ibid.*, XI, 2 f.:To J. B. Say, Feb. 1, 1804. On the future extent and increase of American population: *ibid.*, V, 259:Jan. 25, 1786; VI, 186:

July 23, 1787; X, 287:To William Short, Oct. 3, 1801; III, 330: First Annual Message to Congress, Dec. 8, 1801; XIII, 365: To John W. Eppes, Sept. 11, 1813; XIV, 271:Mar. 4, 1815; XIV, 285:Mar. 16, 1815. See Rush, *Med. Inq.* I, 89.

14. *Writings* (Rights of Man, Part I), II, 385; and see 303, 305 f.

15. *Writings* (Query XIV, *ad fin.*), II, 207 f. There is a curious similarity between Jefferson's argument here and Blackstone's way of justifying the *restriction* of the suffrage, both being based on the corruptibility of men. 'The true reason of requiring any qualification, with regard to property, in voters,' Blackstone argued, 'is to exclude such persons as are in so mean a situation that they are esteemed to have no will of their own. If these persons had votes, they would be tempted to dispose of them under some undue influence or other. This would give a great, an artful, or a wealthy man, a larger share in elections than is consistent with general liberty.' *Commentaries on the Laws of England*, I, 171. See Daniel J. Boorstin, *The Mysterious Science of the Law* (Cambridge, Mass.: 1941), p. 160. Jefferson was only slightly less of a pessimist than Blackstone: he believed men placed a somewhat higher price on their virtue. On the quantitative virtue of the people, and their capacity to resist tyranny, see Jefferson, *Writings*, XII, 282:May 19, 1809; XV, 23:May 28, 1816; and XV, 214:Sept. 6, 1819.

16. The 'good sense' and 'steady character' (e.g., *Writings*, X, 255: Mar. 29, 1801) of the common man were frequently remarked by Jefferson, and the tradition of Jacksonian democracy has made these familiar. But for the American philosopher these qualities of the people held no promise of utopia. Jefferson warned against the excesses of the people, e.g., at *Writings*, XVI, 346:Mar. 2, 1809; and I, 122. 'An *elective despotism* was not the government we fought for.' II (Notes on Virginia), 163. After the Revolution, Jefferson feared that the people 'will forget themselves, but in the sole faculty of making money, and will never think of uniting to effect a due respect for their rights,' II, 225. The times when rulers were honest and people united were infrequent enough, and should be seized for giving some legal fixity to men's rights. (But see, *contra*, section 4 below, on the importance of limiting the duration of laws.) For Jefferson's ideas on the proper form and extent of popular participation in government see *Writings*, VII, 231:Mar. 18, 1789; also, XIV, 130:April 28, 1814. See also

VII, 422 f.: July 19, 1789 where Jefferson added that whenever judges were suspected of partiality, the people might judge even questions of law. He believed of course in the existence of a natural aristocracy grounded in virtue and talents —'the most precious gift of nature, for the instruction, the trusts, and government of society.' *Ibid.*, XIII, 396 f.:To John Adams, Oct. 28, 1813.

17. *Writings*, X, 232 f.:To Nathaniel Niles, Mar. 22, 1801. See also IX, 299 f.:To M. D'Ivernois, Feb. 6, 1795; XI, 390:To Gov. Robert Williams of Mississippi Territory, Nov. 1, 1807; XIV, 120:Mar. 17, 1814. 'I still believe that the Western extension of our confederacy will ensure its duration, by overruling local factions, which might shake a smaller association.' XV, 330:To Gen. Henry Dearborn, Aug. 17, 1821. Cf. Madison: 'The inconveniences of popular States contrary to the prevailing Theory, are in proportion not to the extent, but to the narrowness of their limits. . . . As a limited monarchy tempers the evils of an absolute one; so an extensive Republic meliorates the administration of a small Republic.' *Writings* (ed. Hunt), II, 368:April, 1787. See also *The Federalist*, Number X, to the same effect.

18. *New Views of the Constitution of the United States* (Washington: 1823), p. 240; also 242 and sec. 16 *passim*. See also his *Construction Construed and Constitutions Vindicated* (Richmond: 1820), esp. sec. 5.

19. Paine, *Writings* (Rights of Man, Part II, chap. iv), II, 443, 439.

20. Boyd, *The Declaration of Independence: The Evolution of the Text*, p. 19.

21. 'I tremble for my country when I reflect that God is just; that his justice cannot sleep forever.' *Writings* (Notes on Virginia), II, 227. After describing the virtues of the class Hexandria (which includes the rice-plant), Barton observed, 'But how greatly is it to be regretted, that this vegetable, in the most free and happy country upon earth, should be cultivated, almost exclusively, by the hands of slaves! Shall we never learn to be just to our fellow-creatures? Shall we blindly pursue the imaginary advantages of the moment, and neglect the still but solemn voice of God, until—"Vengeance in the lurid air, Lifts her red arm expos'd and bare."' *Elements of Botany*,

II, 29 (Part III). See Rittenhouse, *Oration*, p. 19. For the item which Jefferson wrote into his draft of the Declaration of Independence, but which was later removed out of deference to southern sentiment, see *Writings*, I, 34. In his draft constitution for Virginia, Jefferson provided that slavery should come to an end on Dec. 31, 1800. *Ibid.*, II (Notes on Virginia), 288. When the Missouri question began to be agitated, and perhaps even before, Jefferson began to have fears of the manner in which the slavery issue might be settled, and forebodings even of civil war. See, for example, his observations in 1820-1821: *Writings*, XV, 238, 249, 301, 311, 315. Despite his opposition to the institution of slavery, Jefferson insisted on the dangers of arguing on 'abstract principle,' XV, 249 f.:April 22, 1820. Rush was outspoken in his antislavery sentiments: besides being a founder of one of the earliest antislavery societies in the colonies, he wrote effectively against the institution (e.g., 'Address to the Inhabitants of the British Settlements in America, upon Slave-keeping,' 1773). Peale, as we have noted, freed the slaves which he had brought to Pennsylvania from Maryland, and voted in the Pennsylvania assembly (1779, 1780) for the abolition of slavery. Paine also wrote against slavery (e.g., *Writings*, I, 4 ff.; II, 29 ff.).

22. *Writings*, XIII, 10:To John Lynch, Jan. 21, 1811. *Ibid.*, X, 294:To Monroe, Nov. 24, 1801. On the matter of the *Notes on Virginia* see *ibid.*, V, 14: To Monroe, June 17, 1785; and II, 192.

23. *Writings* (Notes on Virginia), II, 229. For Jefferson's observations on the new independence possible in America: *Writings*, XIV, 183: To Thomas Cooper, Sept. 10, 1814. Many years earlier he had remarked: 'A manufacturer going from Europe will turn to labor of other kinds if he finds more to be got by it, and he finds some employment so profitable, that he can soon lay up money enough to buy fifty acres of land, to the culture of which he is irresistibly tempted by the independence in which that places him, and the desire of having a wife and family around him.' *Ibid.*, VII, 48:From Paris, June 19, 1788. See also XIII, 401:To John Adams, Oct. 28, 1813. For Crèvecoeur's connection with the Philosophical Society, see *Early Proceedings*, pp. 168, 173.

24. *Writings*, V, 258:From Paris, Jan. 25, 1786. He observed that the British, by destroying the credit of the new Confed-

eracy had done us a service, by having 'checked our disposition to luxury.' *Ibid.*, V, 182. See VI, 229:From Paris, Aug. 4, 1787; also, VII, 339:May 8, 1789. When in Paris in 1786, Jefferson received a letter from Franklin informing him that 'the consumption of goods was never greater, as appears by the dress, furniture, and manner of living, of all ranks of the people' (*Ibid.*, V, 349); he was not happy to know of what we might call a rise in the 'standard of living.' 'All my letters,' Jefferson complained, 'are filled with details of our extravagance. From these accounts, I look back to the time of the war as a time of happiness and enjoyment, when amidst the privation of many things not essential to happiness, we could not run into debt, because nobody would trust us.' *Writings*, VI, 188:From Paris, to Skipwith, July 28, 1787. While the war was on, the American 'under all the privations it obliged him to submit to . . . slept sounder, and awaked happier than he can do now.' *Ibid.*, p. 192. When Jefferson returned to Paris from a visit to England, he noted disapprovingly 'the splendor of their shops, which is all that is worth looking at in London.' *Writings*, VI, 145:June 30, 1787. He observed that the luxury of the British upper classes had left their passions uncontrolled. See also *ibid.*, V, 305, 325; and VIII, *passim*. According to Jefferson, 'formality, etiquette, ostentation and luxury' were always found together, *ibid.*, VI, 335. Further, on the antagonism between luxury and liberty, *ibid.*, XV, 39:July 12, 1816; V, 128:To Baron Geismer, Sept. 6, 1785; XIV, 183:To Thomas Cooper, Sept. 10, 1814. See also, V, 187. To the same effect, Rittenhouse, *Oration*, p. 20; and Paine, *Writings* (Rights of Man, Part II), II, 448.

25. Jefferson, *Writings*, VI, 261:To Peter Carr, Aug. 10, 1787. From Paris (Oct. 15, 1785): 'If he goes to England, he learns drinking, horse racing, and boxing. These are the peculiarities of English education. The following circumstances are common to education in that, and the other countries of Europe. He acquires a fondness for European luxury and dissipation, and a contempt for the simplicity of his own country; he is fascinated with the privileges of the European aristocrats, and sees, with abhorrence, the lovely equality which the poor enjoy with the rich, in his own country; he contracts a partiality for aristocracy or monarchy . . . ; he is led, by the strongest of all the human passions, into a spirit for female intrigue. . . . It appears to me, then, that an American, coming to Europe for education, loses in his knowledge, in his morals, in his

health, in his habits, and in his happiness.' V, 186 f.: To J. Bannister, Jr. See also, V, 82. And, for his further advice to travelers, XVII, 290. Cf. below, note 57.

26. *Writings*, X, 411:To John Breckenridge, Aug. 12, 1803. Henry Adams, in his *History of the United States during the First Administration of Thomas Jefferson* (2 vols., New York: 1931), Vol. II, esp. chaps. iv and v, has told this story with an admirable fairness which makes plain the instability of the Jeffersonian limitations on power. For Jefferson on the judiciary, see *Writings* ('Autobiography'), I, 121.

27. *Writings* (Rights of Man, Part II, chap. iii), II, 421 (Paine's italics). See also, Taylor, *Construction Construed*, p. 51, where he used this notion to support his argument that the division of powers was itself as much an ingredient in government as 'monarchy, aristocracy, and democracy.'

28. *Writings*, VI, 380 f.:To William Carmichael, Dec. 11, 1787. See also, VI, 386 f.:To Madison, Dec. 20, 1787.

29. *Writings*, VI, 65:To Madison, from Paris, Jan. 30, 1787. 'The tree of liberty must be refreshed from time to time, with the blood of patriots and tyrants. It is its natural manure.' *Ibid.*, VI, 373:Nov. 13, 1787. Jefferson (*ibid.*, VI, 391:To Madison, from Paris, Dec. 20, 1787) remarking that Shays' rebellion in Massachusetts had given too much alarm abroad, calculated that one rebellion in 13 states in the course of 11 years, was but one for each State in a century and a half: 'No country should be so long without one.'

30. *Complete Writings* (ed. Foner; Rights of Man, Part II, chap. iv), I, 376. The Conway edition (*Writings*, II, 428 f.) differs from most others in reading 'a world' instead of 'the world'; but the context of Paine's preceding paragraph seems to require 'the world.'

31. *Writings*, XV, 470:Thomas Earle, Sept. 24, 1823. On the separateness of generations: *ibid.*, XIII, 270:To John W. Eppes, June 24, 1813.

32. *Writings* (Rights of Man, Part I), II, 278. Jefferson, *Writings*, XV, 470; and *ibid.*, XV, 43, 46:July 12, 1816.

33. *Writings* (Rights of Man, Part I), II, 304 f.

34. *Writings*, VII, 455:To Madison, from Paris, Sept. 6, 1789. Was it not true, Jefferson asked, that there was 'between generation and generation, as between nation and nation, no other law than that of nature? And is it the less dishonest to do what is wrong, because not expressly prohibited by written law?' XIII, 360:To John W. Eppes, Sept. 11, 1813. Paine, *Writings* (Rights of Man, Part I), II, 278.

35. *Writings*, VII, 454-463:To Madison, from Paris, Sept. 6, 1789. The details of his calculation (with later improvements) are given at *ibid.*, XIII,, 269 ff.:To John W. Eppes, June 24, 1813. See also XIII, 360:To Eppes, Sept. 11, 1813; XV, 42 ff.:To Samuel Kercheval, July 12, 1816; XV, 470 f.:To Thomas Earle, Sept. 24, 1823.

36. Jefferson, *Writings*, XIII, 272 f. See also *ibid.*, XIII, 357; and VII, 460.

37. Jefferson, *Writings*, VII, 463:To Dr. Gem, Sept. 6, 1789. *Ibid.*, XV, 471:To Thomas Earle, Sept. 24, 1823. VII, 460. Paine, *Writings* (Rights of Man, Part II, chap. iv), II, 440 f. For the common-law rule generally, see C. K. Allen, *Law in the Making* (2nd ed.; Oxford: 1930), pp. 91, 283; and C. H. McIlwain, *The High Court of Parliament and its Supremacy* (New Haven: 1910); and for Blackstone's view, *Commentaries on the Laws of England*, I, 74, 472. And see Boorstin, *Mysterious Science of the Law*, p. 157.

38. *Writings*, VII, 459. Paine, *Writings* (Rights of Man, Part II, chap. iv, 'Of Constitutions'), II, 436. But cf. Jefferson's discussion of the Virginia constitution of 1776 in *Writings*, II, 165 ff.

39. *Writings*, X, 256:To Dr. Walter Jones, Mar. 31, 1801. And see *ibid.*, VI, 65:To Madison, from Paris, Jan. 30, 1787.

40. Jefferson, *Writings*, XVI, 15:Feb. 14, 1824. See also *ibid.*, X, 419:Sept. 7, 1803; and XIII, 254:To John Adams, June 15, 1813. For Jefferson's application of similar criteria to the French Constitution, see *ibid.*, VIII, 110:To de Moustier, Dec. 3, 1790; and XII, 283:May 27, 1809. And see XV, 484:Oct. 31, 1823. On Aristotle: XV, 65:Aug. 26, 1816. See also Priestley, *Lectures on History and General Policy* (2 vols.; Philadelphia: 1803), pp. 57 f.; and Paine, *Writings* (Rights of Man, Part II, chap i), II, 406 ff.

41. *Materia Medica,* Part First, p. 40.

42. *Writings,* I, 259, in note appended to 'Autobiography.'

43. *Writings,* X, 429:Nov. 14, 1803. And, generally, on modernity and usefulness in American education see *Writings,* V. 186: From Paris, Oct. 15, 1785; X, 140 f.:Jan. 18, 1800; XIV, 173: To Thomas Cooper, Aug. 25, 1814.

44. *Writings,* X, 141:To Priestley, Jan. 18, 1800. For his earlier program for William and Mary, *ibid.* (Notes on Virginia), II, 209. See also the list of subjects in the new University of Virginia, set forth in his draft Education Bill, item 34, quoted at XVII, 436 f. (1817); and I, 74. On Jefferson's related objections to European education, see above note 25.

45. *Writings* (Notes on Virginia), II, 207. From sec. 1, chap. lxxix, of the *Report of the Revisors* (1779) which is quoted in Padover, *Complete Jefferson,* p. 1048. See also *Writings,* XVI, 124-129:Oct. 25, 1825.

46. *Essays,* pp. 21-56. 'You ask my opinion on the extent to which classical learning should be carried in our country,' Jefferson wrote to a scholar of Greek. 'The utilities we derive from the remains of the Greek and Latin languages are, first, as models of pure taste in writing. . . . Second. Among the values of classical learning, I estimate the luxury of reading the Greek and Roman authors in all the beauties of their originals. . . . Third . . . in the stores of real science deposited and transmitted us in these languages, to wit: in history, ethics, arithmetic, geometry, astronomy, natural history, etc. But to whom are these things useful? Certainly not to all men. There are conditions of life to which they must be forever estranged, and there are epochs of life too, after which the endeavor to attain them would be a great misemployment of time.' *Writings,* XV, 208 f.:Aug. 24, 1819. In natural history, the Jeffersonian debt to the ancients was great, and not always unrecognized (*ibid.,* p. 210); his very concept of the subject had been shaped by ancient writers. See Charles A. Browne, *Thomas Jefferson and the Scientific Trends of His Time,* reprinted from *Chronica Botanica,* Vol. VIII (Nov., 1943), at p. 5. Cf. Franklin's 'Observations relative to the Intentions of the original Founders of the Academy in Pennsylvania,' *Works* (Sparks ed.), II, 158 f., where in a characteristic extended

metaphor he calls the Latin and Greek languages 'the *chapeau bras* of modern literature.'

47. *Essays*, p. 43. Rush believed that the inferior status of women was due in large part to their ignorance of classical learning; his proposal for improving their status was not to give them a classical education, but, to see that male citizens were given none. *Ibid.*, p. 44. American conditions required that women, like men, be given a more extensive and more practical education here than in Europe. *Ibid.*, p. 75. See also, Rush's essay, 'Of the Mode of Education Proper in a Republic,' *Essays*, pp. 6-20; and his earlier 'Plan for Establishing Public Schools in Pennsylvania, and for Conducting Education Agreeably to a Republican Form of Government.' Goodman, *Rush*, p. 308. The Prize offered by the Philosophical Society (*Trans. A. P. S.*, IV, p. iv) was not for *any* good system of education, but for one adapted to the genius of American government and designed to promote the general welfare.

48. *Writings*, XIX, 213 f.:To Peter Carr, Sept. 7, 1814. He had also observed the relation of a man's 'condition in life' to whether he should study the classics, *ibid.*, XV, 209:Aug. 24, 1819. Cf. Franklin's *Proposals Relating to the Education of Youth in Pennsylvania* (1743), quoted at Van Doren, *Franklin*, p. 190: 'It is therefore proposed that they learn those things that are likely to be most useful and most ornamental, regard being had to the several professions for which they are intended.' Franklin remained concerned that an education should enable a man 'to bustle and make his Way.' *Writings* (Smyth ed.), VIII, 305: Sept. 13, 1781. Jefferson on several occasions proposed schemes by which 'the best geniuses will be raked from the rubbish annually.' *Writings* (Notes on Virginia), II, 203. See also *ibid.*, XIII, 396:To John Adams. Oct. 28, 1813. On the education of women, see Jefferson's advice to Martha Jefferson (*Writings*, IV, 446: Nov. 28, 1783), which was very much on the side of elegance; and also *ibid.*, XV, 165:To Nathaniel Burwell, Mar. 14, 1818. And see Rush, *Essays*, p. 75.

49. *Writings*, XV, 400:Oct. 21, 1822; and XIII, 133:Feb. 14, 1812. See also XII, 351:To Joel Barlow, Jan. 24, 1810; XIII, 255:June 15, 1813; XIV, 491:April 24, 1816. And cf. XI, 106:To the Emperor of Russia, April 19, 1806.

50. *Writings* (Rights of Man, Part II, chap. i), II, 407.

51. *Trans.* A. P. S., Vol. III, pp. vii f.

52. Jefferson, *Writings*, XIII, 401 f.:To John Adams, Oct. 28, 1813. And see *ibid.*, XV, 28:June 20, 1816; and XV, 65 f.: Aug. 26, 1816. For Jefferson's comments on Malthus, see above note 4. But John Taylor of Caroline saw dangers in the American condition: in England oppression and the lack of uncultivated hinterland forced the farmer who wanted to improve his condition to do so by increasing his skill and industry; in America such an incentive was lacking simply because the oppressed farmer or laborer could flee into the wilderness. *Arator* (1817), p. 38.

53. *Writings*, X, 217:Mar. 6, 1801. *Ibid.*, XIII, 58:May 5, 1811; XIII, 130:To Benjamin Galloway, Feb. 2, 1812; XIV, 237: Jan. 31, 1815; XVI, 26:April 4, 1824. On the influence of American example on the French: VII, 227, 253; XIII, 402. And cf. above note 9.

54. 'I . . . bless the Almighty Being, who, in gathering together the waters under the heavens into one place, divided the dry land of your hemisphere from the dry lands of ours, and said, at least be there peace. I hope that peace and amity with all nations will long be the character of our land, and that its prosperity under the Charter will react on the mind of Europe, and profit her by the example.' Jefferson, *Writings*, X, 400: To Earl of Buchan, July 10, 1803. See also *ibid.*, X, 287: Oct. 3, 1801; XI, 196:April 22, 1807; XVIII, 287:1815. He advised in 1820 that America should have a system separate from that of Europe. XV, 286. His advice to President Monroe was clearly in line with such ideas; it might be necessary to keep the *whole hemisphere* uncontaminated by European institutions if the United States was to remain healthy (XV, 436: June 11, 1823; and XV, 478:Oct 24, 1823).

55. Jefferson was torn between belief in the need for asylum, and fear that a provision of unlimited asylum might destroy the special opportunity of America to provide in the long run a refuge and example for mankind. For his fears that unrestricted immigration might corrupt the principles of American society, see *Writings* (Notes on Virginia), II, 120; and V, 21 on dangers of 'contagion.' But Jefferson asked in his First Annual

Message (1801): 'Shall we refuse the unhappy fugitives from distress that hospitality which the savages of the wilderness extended to our fathers arriving in this land? Shall oppressed humanity find no asylum on this globe?' He here connected this with his argument against the naturalization policy of the Federalists: 'Might not the general character and capabilities of a citizen be safely communicated to every one manifesting a *bona fide* purpose of embarking his life and fortunes permanently with us?' III, 338. 'The last hope of human liberty in this world rests on us. We ought, for so dear a state, to sacrifice every attachment and every enmity.' XIII, 29:Mar. 28, 1811. In 1817 he wrote of his desire 'to consecrate a sanctuary for those whom the misrule of Europe may compel to seek happiness in other climes. This refuge once known will produce reaction on the happiness even of those who remain there . . . a single good government becomes thus a blessing to the whole earth, its welcome to the oppressed restraining within certain limits the measure of their oppressions.' XV, 141. Cf. IX, 385; and V, 183. Rittenhouse, *Oration*, p. 20.

56. 'Inquiry into the Cause of Animal Life,' *Med. Inq.*, I, 42. For benefits to the species from patriotism, see also *Essays*, p. 11; and Rev. Nicholas Collin at *Trans. A. P. S.* III, Intro., p. iii. For the challenge of the American continent: Rush, *Essays*, p. 39; Barton, *Materia Medica*, Part I, p. 41; and Jefferson, *Notes on Virginia, passim*.

57. 'Essay on Education,' *Lectures on History*, p. xxxv. 'I conceive the education of our youth in this country to be peculiarly necessary in Pennsylvania,' Rush urged (*Essays*, p. 7), 'while our citizens are composed of the natives of so many different kingdoms in Europe. Our schools of learning, by producing one general and uniform system of education, will render the mass of the people more homogeneous, and thereby fit them more easily for uniform and peaceable government.' The fact that foreign travel tended to weaken the patriotic tie was one of Jefferson's principal objections to it. See above, note 25, and especially *Writings*, V, 186: From Paris, Oct. 15, 1785. Jefferson urged that no person be continued on a foreign mission beyond eight years; he should return periodically to be Americanized, to have his patriotic affection reinforced. X, 284 f.: Oct. 3, 1801. 'Cast your eye over America: who are the men of most learning, of most eloquence, most beloved by their countrymen and most trusted and promoted by them? They are

those who have been educated among them, and whose manners, morals, and habits, are perfectly homogeneous with those of the country.' V, 188. For much of Jefferson's life he used the phrase 'my country' to refer to Virginia (e.g., *Writings*, VIII, 409:Sept. 9, 1792; and XV, 364:April 9, 1822). Jefferson had in fact left the *Continental* Congress for the *Virginia* Assembly. As the slavery controversy came to a head, his sectional feelings revived in a fear that Southern youth would be corrupted by being sent north to 'Harvard, Princeton, New York and Philadelphia' (*ibid.*, XVIII, 313:Feb. 14, 1821). But on at least one occasion (*ibid.*, XII, 182) Jefferson used 'Americanism' as equivalent to patriotism. See also *ibid.*, XVII, 116:1786; XII, 272; XIV, 119; XII, 439.

58. Barton, *Materia Medica*, Part I, p. 41; Jefferson, *Writings*, XIII, 87:Sept. 11, 1811. And see Preamble to Act of Pennsylvania Assembly of March 15, 1780, quoted in *Trans. A. P. S.*, Vol. II, pp. xi f.

59. *Writings*, XV, 59:To John Adams, Aug. 1, 1816. In his 'Monroe Doctrine' letter (*ibid.*, XV, 477, 479:To Monroe, Oct. 24, 1823), Jefferson remarked that he had 'ever looked on Cuba as the most interesting addition which could ever be made to our system of states.' And earlier the same year, also to Monroe, concerning Cuba that 'her addition to our confederacy is exactly what is wanting to round our power as a nation to the point of its utmost interest.' XV, 454:June 23, 1823. While Cuba's voluntary incorporation into the United States was most to be desired, the independence of Cuba was 'our second interest,' XV, 479. Jefferson had an eye on the future of South America even earlier (XIV, 21:Dec. 6, 1813); but he came to fear the development and consolidation of the southern republics into a commercial rival (XIV, 432:Feb. 4, 1816). As early as 1785, he had feared the French design of colonizing the west coast of North America under the guise of a geographical expedition, V, 63:To Jay, from Paris, Aug. 14, 1785.

When in 1809 Jefferson suggested to Madison that Napoleon might be willing to allow the United States to have Cuba, he urged, 'We should then have only to include the north in our Confederacy . . . and we should have such an empire for liberty as she has never surveyed since the creation; and I am persuaded no constitution was ever before so well calculated as ours for extensive empire and self-government.' *Writings*,

XII, 277:April 27, 1809. During the period of the War of 1812 he hoped for the 'conquest of Canada' (XIII, 173:June 29, 1812; also, p. 161 on advantages of possession of Canada), and looked forward to 'the final expulsion of England from the American continent.' XIII, 180:Aug. 4, 1812.

The Lewis and Clark expedition and the Louisiana Purchase both suggest the scope of Jefferson's vision of Westward expansion. For Jefferson, the Western territories were 'that vast and fertile country which their [the inhabitants']sons are destined to fill with arts, with science, with freedom and happiness.' *Writings*, XVIII, 160:1813. Although a half-century might be required to fill the country on the Atlantic side of the Mississippi (X, 423:Nov. 1, 1803), it surely would be filled. From one point of view, the West was itself a new America. In a letter to John Jacob Astor in 1813, comparing Astor's ventures to those of Columbus and Raleigh, Jefferson foresaw a 'great, free and independent empire on that side of our continent, and that liberty and self-government spreading from that as well as this side, will ensure their complete establishment over the whole,' XIII, 432:Nov. 9, 1813. On the relation of expansion to 'national existence,' cf. Madison's letter to Lafayette, Mar. 20, 1785, *Writings* (ed. G. Hunt), II, 121. And cf. note 55 above.

60. 'Observations on the Duties of a Physician,' *Med. Inq.*, I, 264; and see 'An Account of the Influence of the Military and Political events of the American Revolution upon the Human Body,' *ibid.*, p. 134.

61. *Writings*, XIII, 123:To John Adams, Jan. 21, 1812. And see XV, 59:Aug. 1, 1816.

Index

Index